A PARTHENON IN PEFKI

MORE ADVENTURES OF AN ANGLO-GREEK
MARRIAGE

THE PARTHENON SERIES
BOOK 2

PETER BARBER

Illustrated by
CHARLY ALEX FULLER

ᴀᴘ

CONTENTS

A NOTE FROM THE MAYOR

When this book was complete, we made an appointment to meet the mayor. As we were writing about his beloved village, we felt it was important to ask for his blessing. We met over breakfast for a chat. He looked at the cover, then stared at us incredulously.

"How do you know about the Parthenon in Pefki? We have only just discovered it. The excavations are going on now." He waved his hand toward the nearby hills. "Over there," he said.

This was news to me. When I started this book about our adventures in our Greek village, nobody realised there was a real Parthenon near our house.

Another Parthenon in Pefki.

But then you can never have too many Parthenons.

Over to our mayor for his introduction:

It is with great pleasure that I hold in my hands the book of a good friend and worthy author, Peter Barber, *A Parthenon in Pefki*. This is the second book of the trilogy *Parthenon books* based on Greek life and mainly on the experiences of Peter and his wife, Alexandra. The book focuses on the life of the couple in the seaside fishing village of Pefki in the Municipality of Istiea – Edipsos, in Northern Evia. Their love for the village was followed by their decision to build a house where the sea meets the sky and nature flourishes.

Through the author's bright, humorous and at the same time realistic writing, a genuine truth emerges: Greece hides in every corner a "Parthenon", the largest and globally recognizable symbol of the country's culture and long history. It is the confirmation of the words of the French writer Victor Hugo, *"The world is the expanding Greece and Greece is the shrinking world."* Pefki has its own "Parthenon", through the history of the ancient Artemision, the Greek nature and culture, but also the hospitality and the special characteristics of its inhabitants.

I firmly believe that the readers will enjoy reading a book written by a "Greek-made" British who remains amazed by this magical place.

The Mayor of Istiea – Edipsos
Ioannis G. Kontzias

This book is dedicated to my other brother Menelaos, known by his friends and family as Meno.
I will always be grateful for his love and humour during my adapting to Greek culture and family life.

The beauty of Greece and the wonder of you.
I was alone in the darkness, dreaming of pastures new.
I then found the beauty of Greece and with it you.
Greece took my soul while you stole my heart.
Little did I know a new life would start.
Beginning a new life, I could never have known,
Never again would I feel alone.
A wonderful Greek wife with a heart of fire,
Who would change my life, filling my world with desire.
You showed me the wonder of the world hidden from view.
How could I know life would begin anew,
With the ultimate love, that would keep me true.
I now live with the beauty of Greece and the wonder of you.

THINK OF WAYS YOU WANT TO DIE

I had never driven a boat in a storm before and didn't want to start now. We needed to get back across the Straits of Artemision before the serious weather came. We abandoned our remaining lunch, jumped onto our small vessel, and headed out away from the harbour.

At first, the waves were just uncomfortable. As we rounded the point of land, we were driving directly into the open sea.

Water crashed over the bow, soaking Alex, who was sitting at the front of the boat. I switched on the bilge pump and noticed a powerful stream of water shooting out of a hole in the side. We continued to battle the increasingly high waves, both of us soaking wet and cold. Alex shouted above the wind.

'What the hell are you doing? Turn back,' she yelled.

I was standing at the centre console, steering, so with my elevated view I could see much more than Alex, who was huddled on the floor, gripping the handrails with white fingers, waves gushing over her with every dip of the boat. I looked behind us. The sea seemed bigger and angrier there. We had already travelled a long way from our starting point and were in the middle of the sea. If anything, Pefki was nearer. I thought about turning to follow the waves rather than plough through them, but they were all heading in the same direction, smashing with a roar and a mass of foam onto the jagged coastline.

We were in trouble.

The normally calm blue Aegean Sea had erupted into a maelstrom, and we were in the middle.

The Persian navy knew these straits well. In August 480 BC, a series of naval engagements took place over three days during the second Persian invasion of Greece. But the weather was about to do more damage to the Persians than the Greeks could ever do. They were caught in a gale and lost hundreds of their ships.

This was worrying. If a Greek summer storm had wiped out almost the entire Persian navy, what chance did we have on our little four-metre boat?

I tried to adopt a confident expression and forced a smile to reassure Alex that I was not at all worried. I pretended to look as if I was enjoying myself, just out for a pleasure cruise. This infuriated Alex even more. She would not let me forget this. Whatever the sea gods could throw at me was nowhere near as scary as Alex in a rage. I was in big trouble either way. Even if we survived this tempest, my survival would be short-lived as I had Alex to deal with, who was a much bigger threat than a simple sea storm.

We had been married for a few years now. Alex had welcomed me into her family and introduced me to Greek culture. It was an eye-opening experience. Alex was the most beautiful woman I had ever met, her being a firm ten on the beauty scale and me lucky to achieve a four, and then only with the light behind me and my hair combed. I was in awe of this Greek goddess.

Alex was born in the land of philosophy and proves her heritage every day. She is a true Greek philosopher, open and honest with everyone she meets. She often gets herself into trouble. Some people mistakenly assume her to be rude. This is not the case; rather, she has never learned the art of diplomacy. Most people find her openness attractive and refreshing, but others have no idea how to take her vibrant personality. Greeks express themselves in different ways. 'I'm not shouting, I'm Greek' is a common expression.

In Greece, friends often disagree, have incredibly loud and ferocious arguments, throw things across tables. Then suddenly the bomb is defused and they are instantly friends again. I come from a different culture. In England, the system is more complicated. It's rare for a stranger to discuss anything deeper than the weather, while keeping a respectable distance in case you invade their space. A conversation with friends is generally polite and rarely involves throwing things at each other. We tend to be a little more guarded and feel too uncomfortable to probe too deeply. We keep our conversations more superficial; in Greece, no subject is taboo.

When Alex asks you how you are, she really wants to know. She has a way of seeing a problem where there seems to be none. She will invade your space and slowly pick away at your shell until the truth is exposed. Most of us try to show a calm surface to others; we are unwilling to open up and reveal our true feelings. But Alex can see below our calm village pond exterior. She will see the old bicycle frames and discarded supermarket trolleys hidden below the surface. She will then help you drain your pond and refill with clear fresh water. This is the Greek way. But it is something we are not used to.

I lost my old bike frames years ago, thanks to Alex. Still working on the discarded supermarket trollies, though.

Greeks are naturally welcoming and good, generous people. But Alex is Greeker than most Greeks. Her kindness is still amazes me every day. If we have a visitor to our home who admires a lamp, or a piece of china, or a painting hanging on the wall, when they leave it's been put into a bag as a gift. If she is cooking and the guest comments on the delicious aroma coming from the kitchen, if they refuse the offer to join us for lunch the entire meal is packaged and given away, leaving us with sandwiches.

She is kind to others, incredibly logical and a deep thinker. She has the playfulness of a child but with the mind of a laser beam. But when she gets angry, even the gods take cover. Alex's temper is legendary. She will ignore the small things in life, never complain about my feet on the table, or my little habits like snoring so loud the windows vibrate or wandering around the house in my underwear scratching my bits. No, she focuses her anger on the important things in life. She will not tolerate injustice, she gets angry at pointless bureaucracy, she will not tolerate fools or idle thinking. But above all else, Alex hates stupidity. And me insisting on crossing the bubbling sea in the height of the worst storm for many years was not the smartest decision I have ever made.

By now the waves had reached epic proportions. One

second, we were in a valley looking up at mountainous waves topped with white foam; the next, we were on top, looking down into the abyss. The engine was struggling on each incline, trying to motor up the watery walls, so I pushed the throttle a little further forward to increase speed. This resulted in even more water splashing into the boat and soaking my seething wife. The next wave washed over us as we climbed the next mountain. From the top of the wave, though the spray, I caught a glimpse of the tree-lined beach, and a little further, the relatively calm water of the safe harbour. Were we going to be safe at last? I began to feel hopeful. I called to my wet, angry wife.

'Look behind you. We're nearly there.' I needed to give her some hope. I think she had accepted we were on the verge of a shipwreck, but instead of reaching for life jackets, she was stroking the big metal anchor, ready to attack me with it as a last act of vengeance before we plunged to the seabed.

She refused to look up and remained stubbornly staring at her weapon. She was planning my demise in the most painful way possible. The fast-approaching harbour looked welcoming, but Alex looked even more threatening. I shouted again.

'Please, look behind you. We are nearly home.' She turned her head, saw the harbour walls, and scowled at me.

'You're still dead,' she confirmed.

I loved living in Greece. Born in the town of Watford in Hertfordshire, I lived my life as others of my generation did: working to make a living, holidays once a year to somewhere sunny for a fortnight's break or sitting on a windy day on an English beach while looking at the sky, hoping it wouldn't rain, before going back to work and discussing the weather with colleagues while wishing I were somewhere else. As a young child, I was obsessed with the stories of ancient Greece. I would sit in the local cinema watching technicolour films of Hercules, Medusa turning men into stone, and my all-time favourite, *Jason and the Argonauts*. I would sit for hours and watch these films over and over, imagining being there next to the impossibly blue sea and walking through ancient temples fighting with harpies and looking for Greek princesses who needed rescuing.

Then it happened. Alex arrived like a hurricane out of a cloudy sky, and with her, she brought sunshine. All my British upbringing and convention and everything I knew was blown into confusion. I had married a Greek and my life changed. Gone was the grey sky of London. No more holidays on cold, windy beaches. I now lived in paradise. I had found my very own Greek princess, and it was not her who was rescued. It was me.

Alex, my beautiful and fiery Greek wife, introduced me to the real Greece. From the first day I arrived, she made me feel part of her incredibly loving family and introduced me to the people of this beautiful and historic culture. Over the years, I have peeled back the onion that is Greece, only to find another undiscovered layer that can only be experienced from inside a Greek family – traditions, customs and beauty that are unseen by fleeting visitors. This wonderful land has accepted me with open arms, and there is so much to explore.

We've been together for twenty years and she still surprises me daily. Early in our relationship, she had tested my resolve by trying to kill me on a mountain road when she lifted the hand-brake on a dangerous bend above the clouds as a joke. Her complete lack of formality combined with an almost childlike love of fun makes her the perfect companion. Her charm is infectious. We visit a new taverna; she becomes a lifelong friend with the owner. We visit officious-looking government departments, meeting with aggressive and miserable bureaucrats; after a few minutes in her company, they are smiling and obliging. She has a remarkable charm, elegance, and honesty, which shows in her smile. But beware. If anyone dares to upset her, then the fireworks begin.

We had recently finished building our new apartment block in Glyfada, near Athens. We made a deal with an architect to demolish our wonderful old family home and replace it with a five-storey apartment block on the same land. Instead of payment, we agreed to allow the architect to keep two apartments and a retail shop. We would have three apartments and a shop as our share. It seemed a good deal at first, as we had the most valuable part: the penthouse. But as the construction began, we realised we were swimming with a large shark in a small pond – and it was his pond.

Alex spent the next two years locked in a war. Daily fights, heated arguments, and threats of violence and death kept him as honest as possible. Without this, we would probably have lost most of our property. But it all worked out fine in the end. We had what we wanted, only he had more.

So, with the building complete, our home was finished and everything was the way we liked it. We had rented out our newly constructed shop, and being in an upmarket area, we were receiving a great rent.

Although the Athens suburb of Glyfada is a pleasant environment, July and August, being the hottest months, can be stifling. Temperatures regularly rise to above forty degrees and rarely drop below thirty-five degrees centigrade, even at night. In August, most Athenians will leave the city in favour of the cooler islands. I took a break to do the same.

Our problem was that we had two dogs. Jack, a golden Labrador, was the doggie equivalent of a naughty toddler who found everything edible and spent most of his time eating furniture. Bella was a more mature golden retriever and spent most of her time growling at Jack. They had only recently left the cooler climate of England and were slow to adapt to the warmer weather. Most days, their walk would include a swim in the sea, a quick vomit on the beach (Jack never got rid of his habit of drinking seawater) and the rest of the day sleeping on the balcony in the shade. So taking them on holiday would be a challenge. Greek hotels do not welcome dogs. An afternoon's web surfing looking for dog-friendly hotels revealed only a couple of options, the first being in Crete, which was a long ferry ride. The other was in a small village in northern Evia called Pefki, only a three-hour drive. We had been to this village before on our quest for marble floors during our building project. We had only passed through and didn't really get to see much of the village. The picture and description of the hotel looked nice, so we made our reservation and started to plan the trip.

The day came. I walked them around the village but avoided the beach. I didn't want the smell of wet dogs during the long car journey. We loaded up the dogs into the car and set off on our holiday. We left hot, stuffy Athens behind us as we headed north up the motorway, crossed the suspension bridge at Chalkida, and climbed towards the mountain peaks. We passed through olive groves and cultivated fields of pumpkins and watermelons ripening in the sun before taking the steep road north. As the road took us higher into vast forests of pine, I held my hand out of the window and felt the refreshing chill of the air. The dogs also felt the difference in temperature from the hot, overpowering heat at sea level and poked their heads out of the open windows. The sound of flapping ears in the wind and the constant high-pitched hum of the cicadas screaming from the endless forest drowned out the sound of the motor as we reached the peak of the mountain.

There was a lay-by where we could stop and look down into the valley. As we left the car, the scent of pine trees mixed with the clean smell of damp earth wafted around us in an invisible cloud. We were used to the fragrance of mountain herbs, oregano, wild sage and thyme. But this was different. We were too high into the mountains for these wild Greek herbs. The only things capable of making a home here were the green, densely packed pines of Evia. Where there would normally be grass verges and wild flowers mixed with fragrant herbs, there were only poles spread along the road to show the depth of snow which fell here every winter. Between some poles were ornate shrines with a flame flickering inside to remind us this was a dangerous road. They were there to remember the less fortunate motorists who had strayed off the tarmac into the abyss, adding their souls to the legacy of the mountain.

I carefully stopped the car to appreciate the view. From our vantage point, we looked back and saw Chalkida far below us, with the golden shimmer of sun on the Aegean Sea. We were too high to make out the buildings, which appeared as a light sprinkling of sand on a green blanket. Ahead of us were more mountain peaks rising above valleys full of countless pines which extended forever into the distance.

We continued our drive along the winding road, past broken crash barriers accompanied by more shrines to unfortunate drivers, over the peak of the mountain and through the endless pine forests. As we descended, the snow poles vanished. Soon we passed multicoloured beehives spread randomly on meadows, and clear mountain springs gurgled through holes in rocks forming rivers across our path. Eventually we arrived at the central Evia village of Prokopi. This is the home of St John, the Russian. He rests in an ornate golden case

topped with glass. His face is half-covered with a mask; the rest
of his body wears a light-blue gown with gold embroidery
portraying lilac flowers. They uncovered his feet to show that
he was still whole and preserved after all the years since his
death far away in Russia. He rests peacefully in the centre of
the church built especially for him at the centre of the village.
This is a place of pilgrimage. Believers come to this place of
worship from all over the world in the hope of an answer to
their prayers, or to give thanks for a miracle. On the streets
around the perimeter of the church are shops selling religious
icons, honey, nuts and assorted souvenirs. Cafes and tavernas
with their tables spreading onto the pathway, all with fragrant
smoke discharging from long, tin chimneys of countless barbecues, are ready to feed traditional Greek fare to the pilgrims
and visitors.

We left Prokopi behind us and followed the road through
the valley along the banks of a sparkling river, dappled
sunshine throwing rays onto the water through overhanging
willows, and started our drive up through the endless forest of
pine towards our destination.

The first thing you see when entering Pefki is the majestic
Pefka trees, the gateway to the village. Under the green arch,
the road leads a few metres around a bend. There ahead is the
sparkling blue Aegean Sea and the village harbour complete
with multicoloured fishing boats of all sizes, awaiting their crew
for the night's fishing trip. A few small pleasure craft secured to
buoys bob about in the centre of the bay. Beyond the stone
harbour wall, across the expanse of sea, are the high mountains
of the mainland; green trees merge into the water in stark
contrast to the grey barren peaks too high to support vegetation.
Looking to the right, in the distance is the island of Skiathos, its
blurred green landscape shimmering under the perfect azure

sky, and just visible a little further away is the island of Skopelos.

The road continued past the harbour lined with traditional fish tavernas. Waiters were busy crossing the road, balancing trays of food and glass carafes of wine to fulfil lunch orders to hungry diners relaxing on the paved terraces above the small sandy beach and crystal-clear water. Further into the village, the road was lined with palm trees. There were no buildings to obscure the view of the sea, and tables, chairs, sunbeds and parasols were spread in tidy blocks along the beach.

Leaving the village behind, we drove along the road parallel with the shingle beach. Although it was midsummer and the height of the tourist season, the beach was almost deserted. Being one of the longest beaches in Greece, you can pick a spot and swim in complete privacy in the inviting, clear water, gazing out at the distant islands.

A right turn away from the sea, we found our hotel which would be our home for the next week.

We soon settled into a routine as we enjoyed the beach and village.. We found a section of beach well away from other sunbathers and swimmers and let the dogs run and swim freely. Lunch would be at a taverna near the harbour, or one of the small establishments dotted along the coast, all with their typical blue tin tables sitting outside under trees or canopies.

Quickly we realised how much we loved this village. Although tourist season was well underway, it still felt peaceful. The people we met were charming and genuine, the views over the Straits of Artemision were spectacular ... We were falling in love with this place.

So. on the fourth day. we accidentally bought a piece of it.

2

HERE WE GO AGAIN

W ell, I say we bought a piece of this beautiful village. More truthfully, we agreed to buy land, but with no money in our pockets – and my bank manager was still angry with me for splashing out on pink marble floors for our new home in Glyfada.

We were relaxing in a picturesque taverna overlooking the harbour. I was sipping an ice-cold glass of wine, with a nice

Greek salad covered with glistening olive oil and a sprinkle of oregano in front of me, incredible views of mountains in the distance across the shimmering sea, and the dogs happily snoozing under the blue tin table.

Alex left me at the table and crossed the road to pick up some dog food from the small supermarket opposite. A few moments later, she came running back towards me.

'Leave the meal, bring the dogs and follow that car,' she yelled.

By now, I was used to Alex's impetuous behaviour. It was one of the many things I loved about her. I asked the waiter to hold the food, and woke our snoozing dogs, loaded them into the back seat of the car, sat alongside Alex, and followed the small silver Toyota away from the harbour.

We drove parallel with the beach, past the palms and green Pefka trees, then made a right turn towards our hotel, leaving the sea behind us.

'Where are we going in such a hurry?' I asked. 'Why are we going back to the hotel?'

Alex was tight-lipped as we drove the short distance to our unknown destination, only speaking to tell me to wait and see. Just before the turn into our hotel, the Toyota parked by the side of the road. We stopped behind. A large lady squeezed out of her car and introduced herself as Anna before taking a key and unlocking a rusty metal-link fenced gate.

There before us was a field. Tall bamboo sprouted in patches towards the rear of the land, and apart from some long grass and a profusion of prickly brambles, there was nothing else. I tugged at Alex's sleeve to get her attention.

'Why are we here?' I whispered.

'To look at this land. It's for sale. Isn't it lovely?'

While Alex chatted with the agent, I wandered around the land. I stepped over brambles and pushed a path through some tall bamboo, trying to get an idea of the overall size. It was impossible to assess. As I pushed deeper into the brambles, the bamboo thickened and had formed an impenetrable wall. I could go no further. I stepped back into the clearing and looked around. Above us was the foothill to the mountain. It was a dark shade of green at the base and covered with olive groves. Higher up the mountain, the olive groves disappeared and were replaced with pine forests leading to the peak. A few picturesque houses were dotted randomly on the hill looking down towards us. A minor road led up the hill and disappeared behind the olive groves. Opposite, behind our parked cars, was a stone-built house with a matching stone wall topped with iron railings. A small sign swung on a hinge. It read 'George and Helen's holiday nest'.

The neighbouring land to one side was a small forest containing platanus, the sturdy hardwood tree which is protected in Greece. This would assure us that no house would never be built there. In mythology, Platanus was a beautiful girl, and as great in stature as her enormous brothers and sister. When Zeus slew the Aloadae with a lightning bolt for trying to wage war against the heavens, Platanus was so sorrowful that her shape changed to that of a tree bearing her name, keeping the great size and beauty she had in her previous life.

Past the platanus was the main road bypassing the village. The plot bordering the other side was overgrown, a mixture of sandy soil and weeds. An old rusty tractor sat to one side, along with a machine that appeared to be used for cutting wood, with a pile of logs stacked beside it. Next was a large, detached house with wrought-iron railings around the balconies to the front and back. From here I could look towards the sea and see the mountains of Volos with their sandy-coloured peaks, and the iconic cut rock of the mountain, which is still a marble quarry mined by generations of Greek families.

It was a beautiful location, far enough from the main road so the local traffic wouldn't disturb us, and in the other direction, only five hundred metres to the beach. It was perfect. But we had no way of seeing the rest of our proposed purchase. It was an impenetrable jungle, so we just had to imagine.

Alex was born in Athens and was a city girl. But she had often talked about her dream of owning a summer house on a Greek island. In the time since we had been married, Alex had opened my eyes to the beauty of Greece. We had already visited so many islands, all with their own individual charm and character. Some, like Mykonos, were party islands; others, like Santorini, were visited for the stunning beauty. But most of the Greek islands were just like this. A mixture of wonderful scenery, sunshine, and warm, welcoming people. This village had everything we wanted. It was a haven of peace and tranquillity. Perhaps this was our chance to make Alex's dream come true?

As Alex continued to walk around the plot with the agent, my mind focused on the practicalities of this proposed venture. The first problem was quite clear at once. We didn't have any money.

We had only just finished the two-year building project in Glyfada. Most of the process involved daily squabbles with the architect, who most weeks would come up with increasingly cunning ways to fleece us of large portions of our property. Although we had thwarted most of his avaricious plans, it was a tiring period. But we had what we wanted, and even though he had more, we were happy with the result. We had a nice new penthouse apartment in a beautiful suburb of Athens, and a nice new shop recently let for a good monthly rent. Alex's parents had their own fine apartment in the building. So overall it had been a great success.

In theory, it shouldn't have cost us anything. In Greece, if you own a house in a valuable area, it is common to make a deal with a developer. He will take your home and land, knock down the building, and construct a new apartment block. The developer will make his profit by retaining a portion of the new building. But as the building project went on, we realised the developer was more interested in cutting costs than good finishing. So, we had to step in to ensure our new home would be the way we liked it, and that cost money. We used every penny we had to lay marble floors rather than ceramic tiles. We had to pay for unexpected items like water and electricity meters. Instead of emulsion-painted walls, we made a deal with a young art student to help with the revised decorating plan. Then, the ultimate folly, we built a Parthenon on our roof.

The past few months had been a flurry of activity, buying new furniture and getting our home the way we liked it. I was still commuting to work in England. Every Thursday evening, I would catch the EasyJet flight from Luton, arrive in Athens by 3 a.m., crawl into bed and snuggle up to a sleeping Alex, ready for the weekend. The flight back early Monday morning got me to Luton at 8.30 a.m., ready for a week of eighteen-hour days until the whole procedure started again. This was tiring. I could never sleep on a plane, but the long commute and even longer workdays were necessary if we were eventually going to make our home here. With low-cost carriers, flying was quite cheap. A ticket from Luton to Athens was around the same price as a train journey from London to Liverpool. But we had finished our dream apartment and could relax a little.

But now, here we were. Standing in a field, thinking about doing it all again.

I watched Alex as she happily pushed through brambles to pick a red wildflower from between a patch of weeds. She held it up in the air to show me with a smile on her face. I could see her eyes twinkling as she was imagining the possibilities. How could I possibly disappoint her?

We thanked the agent and made an appointment to come to her office that afternoon to discuss it further. She locked the gate and drove away, leaving us staring at the land.

'Let's go back to the taverna,' I suggested. 'We can discuss it there.'

For the first few moments, neither of us spoke. I was trying to formulate a plan to get hold of a few thousand euros. Alex was busy designing the house that would sit on the land we had just promised to buy. Her confidence in me was infectious. I poured another glass of local wine and, slowly, the warm embrace of the cold nectar combined with a view of the distant mountains across the shimmering Aegean Sea gave me a tremendous feeling of optimism. Contentment flowed through my soul, assuring me that all would be well.

'Shall we do it?' I asked Alex.

Alex took my hand and looked into my eyes. She was aware of our financial situation and the struggle to come if we went ahead with this project.

'Are you sure you are ready for this?' she asked.

Alex had changed my life already. She had given me a new life in this beautiful country. She had welcomed me into the open arms of her family and I truly felt I belonged here. I would do anything for her. My dream had come true. It was time to chase hers.

'Look, we are both still relatively young. We are both healthy. It won't be easy, but think of the adventures we are going to have. Let's do it.'

In that beautiful taverna overlooking the Aegean Sea sparkling in the late afternoon sunshine, I lifted my glass of wine. The light shone through the amber liquid and cast sunbeams onto the white paper tablecloth. Alex lifted her glass, and with a clink, we sealed the deal.

Now we had decided, the first problem was our lack of funds, and how to explain that to the real estate agent.

Anna's office comprised a small, untidy desk in the large kitchen of her home. It was positioned by the window so that natural light could illuminate her working area. There was a mouth-watering smell of roasting meat and wine sauce combined with the fragrance of fresh home-made bread. The far side of the large kitchen was darker, and as we walked around the desk to take our seats, I could just make out a slight form huddled in the shadows, sitting beside the oven. She was dressed in black and holding a piece of lace in one hand and a darning needle in the other. It was Yiayia. She was an elderly lady of around ninety years old. She smiled and waved her piece of lace as she rose from her chair and ambled across the room to greet us.

'Kalosta pedia,' (Welcome, children) she said while holding out her hand.

Alex took her hand and placed her other hand on top in the traditional greeting and spoke to her in plural. 'Giassas ti Kanete?' (How are you all?) I did the same.

Alex has a deep love of older people and an ingrained respect. After we greeted the old grandmother, she returned to her chair near the oven while we took our seats opposite Anna as she fumbled with papers and passed one to us for a signature. I hesitated, and Alex took over to save my embarrassment.

'Look, we really want the land, but at the moment, we don't have any money,' she announced. 'Not even enough for the deposit.'

Anna's smile faded as she realised we had wasted her time, just another couple of tourists with unrealistic dreams. She stood up to show the meeting was at an end. Alex put her hand on my knee to signal me not to stand, so we both remained seated. Anna sat back down and studied us curiously.

Alex spoke again.

'We do not have any money now, but we really want the land. We will give you five hundred euros now if you agree to hold it for three months. If we don't return with the balance within this time, you can keep it.'

Anna was looking annoyed. She again stood up from her desk to show us it was time to leave. Grandmother's reedy voice came from a dark corner of the room.

'Einai kaloi anthoppoi,' (They are good people) she told her daughter.

Greek Yiayias rule. They are wise, beautiful people who are respected and venerated by the entire family. It would be unthinkable to make a family or business decision without the blessing of a grandmother. She rules with a pantófla (slipper) of iron, and she will always have the last word. Young men of the family will cower in fear if they have inadvertently upset Yiayia. The famous Greek slipper is her weapon of choice and all fear it. They passed its correct use down through the generations from mother to daughter and it is the Greek equivalent of a sawn-off shotgun. No one messes with Yiayia.

Greeks respect their elders. They recognise the wisdom offered from the older family members. It is unthinkable to go against the advice of Grandmother, who has lived a hard life and learned enough from her experiences to guide her family along the right road.

Wisdom comes from suffering. It's a fact of life. We learn nothing from the sunny days. Wisdom is always forged in the fire of adversity. Education will only begin in a storm. Greeks have suffered throughout their long history: frequently occupied by invasive nations, repressed, starved and abused. Brave Greeks faced the Persian invasion with strength and honour.

The Ottoman Empire put Greece under the yolk of slavery for four hundred years. The Italians and Germans invaded and subjected the Greeks to starvation and atrocities. Then the civil war set brother against brother and neighbour against neighbour. But the spirit of this small, ancient country remained intact and defiant.

So, when Anna's grandmother gave us a helping hand, Anna had little choice other than to agree to our offer.

Although I was outwardly happy with the result, part of me was secretly hoping that Anna would refuse. The glow of the wine had worn off, and I was beginning to question whether we had made the right move in committing ourselves to the purchase. It would likely mean years of panicking and dealing with the brutal bureaucracy. Not least, I had no idea how we were going to pay for it. I was still secretly worried that we were undertaking a project that might commit us to poverty for years to come. But looking into Alex's eyes and seeing the true happiness of my beautiful wife, I had to try.

I shook Anna's hand as Alex stood up and put her arms around the frail old lady and gently kissed her cheek. Grandmother's eyes sparkled as she looked at Alex and spoke.

'You only live this life once, my daughter. You have a good man by your side. Build your house.'

Alex's own grandmother, Bia, was born into an Anatolian Greek family in a small village on the outskirts of Constantinople, one of millions of Greeks who were born, lived and died in what they believed to be their country.

Under Ottoman rule, the villages comprised a variety of religions and ethnic culture that mixed happily together.

Although Bia's family were looked upon as Greeks because of their religion, they mostly spoke the language of the Ottomans, Greek being spoken by only a few.

The village had one church and one mosque. The church had a small cemetery, with an ossuary nearby to store the bones of long dead Christians. They buried the Muslim dead in their own cemetery in a wooded area near the village. Irrespective of their religion, they were all Ottomans.

Bia's father, Costas, was the doctor of the village, so the family was better off than most. He cared for Christians and Muslims equally. The local midwife was a Muslim and would assist in the delivery of both Christian and Muslim newborn with equal compassion.

This is the way they lived for generations, and Bia's early childhood was a happy one. To Bia, her friends were her friends, her neighbours were her neighbours. The subject of religion was not important to her or others. She knew that some of her friends didn't come to the church, as she didn't visit the mosque. But this made no difference to everyday life. Until one day, someone far away decided she was Greek.

With the outbreak of the First World War, the Ottoman Empire sided with the Germans. All Ottoman males aged between twenty-one and forty-five were conscripted. The Muslims were drafted into the army but they sent the Christians to labour battalions (Amele Taburlari). The lives of ordinary people became complicated, raising issues of identity: who was 'Turkish' and who was 'Greek'. As far as Bia's family was concerned, they were born in this village and were all Ottomans. They had never been to Greece and had only ever known this village.

Soon, news filtered back to the village about the fate of the Christians, who were being forced to work around the clock with little food or water. Most were dying under appalling conditions. Bia's brothers, Georgios and Pandelis, had so far evaded the forced conscription and, like other young Christians, made plans to run away.

They arrived at the port with money in their pockets, intending to buy boat tickets. But because they were on the run from the authorities, they had hidden their identification papers, and without these they could not travel. So, the money was used to bribe a ship captain who, for the right price, would assist them.

Because the military closely guarded all ships and nobody could board without scrupulous checks, they agreed that the ship's crew would seal them in salted fish barrels. They would then be carried to the ship and added to the cargo.

With her brothers gone, it left Bia in the village with her mother and father and a growing fear. They had all heard about 'Greeks' being rounded up and moved to who knows where. Stories of forced marches were being whispered and fear among the people was growing.

Then one day the militia arrived in Bia's village. Going from house to house, they rounded up Christian families. She could hear cries from houses as they turned people out into the streets to gather under the eyes of watchful guards. Bia's family were not taken as her father, being a doctor, would be useful for the army when the imminent war began. He was told to stand by and make himself ready for the call to attend the battlefield.

Bia watched as they marched her friends out of the village in a long, straggling line, all carrying the one bag of possessions they were allowed, containing their most valuable items. She would always remember the cries of her friends and the looks of fear on so many faces as they disappeared from sight.

Now Bia's family was in imminent danger. Shortly, her father would be taken to war, leaving Bia and her mother to fend for themselves. Hostility grew in the village. Anti-Greek propaganda had started its evil influence. People who until a few days ago were friends and neighbours directed hostility towards them. It was time to leave.

They waited until night when all was quiet and slipped unseen out of the village.

They came across the first body at midnight. It was Xanthos the carpenter. Xanthos was in his early sixties and always carried a limp because of his time in the army fighting with the Ottomans in the Italo-Turkish War. He had been proud to fight for his country and was rewarded with a medal for his bravery and a small pension. But he was no longer a war hero. He was a Greek.

After the victory of the Turkish nationalists, led by Mustafa Kemal Ataturk, the European powers met to negotiate a new order. The result was the Lausanne Agreement of 1923, which formalised the expulsions of Greek Christians from Turkey.

Greece, with a population of just over 5,000,000 people, had to absorb 1,221,489 new citizens from Turkey. By the end of 1922, Bia and her family, along with most ethnic Greeks, had fled Turkey because of the genocide against them.

No one asked the opinion of these people, though their identities as Greeks and Turks, Christians and Muslims were far less clear-cut than the Lausanne arrangement implied. Orthodox Christian and Muslim communities had lived side by side for centuries before the pernicious rise of nationalism.

It was not easy to categorise such differing religious backgrounds. The language they spoke was equally blurred. Refugees arriving for the first time in Greece were strangers in their supposed homelands, often unable to communicate and facing hostility from their new neighbours.

The Greek genocide was the systematic killing of the indigenous Christian Ottoman Greek population of Anatolia, which was carried out during the First World War and its aftermath (1914–1922), based on their religion and ethnicity and perpetrated by the government of the Ottoman Empire. The genocide included massacres, forced deportations, death marches and executions. Several hundred thousand Anatolian Greeks died during this period. Most of the refugees and survivors fled to Greece, adding over a quarter to the prior population.

Bia's brothers, Georgios and Pandelis, survived the journey and arrived in Greece as stowaways in fish barrels to begin a new life. Eventually, Pandelis became a priest, and his brother Georgios went to sea and became a captain of his own ship.

After evading the death squad, Bia and her family arrived in Piraeus. Bia's father set up a medical practice, and Bia, Alex's grandmother, married a sea captain, Jannis, Alex's grandfather, who was destined to become a war hero during the German occupation of Athens. Bia gave birth to two children: Vasilis and Debbie, Alex's mother.

The people of Greece have huge respect for their elders. They all know the history and suffering they have endured. They respect the wisdom offered.

So, with Anna's Yiayia on our side, the deal was done. Anna never really had a choice once her grandmother had sided with us. She gave us a receipt for the money, and we left.

I was determined to follow through on my promise and buy this land. I didn't know how I would raise the money, but I had a few ideas.

3

I NEED TO ROB A BANK

W e had already spent our holiday money on the deposit for the land. So, we cut short our break and headed back to Glyfada. I was keen to get back to the UK and start my own Herculean task of finding the cash for our new folly. This would be my own Greek odyssey, but I had made a promise to Alex and would do my best.

Back in Glyfada, we told Alex's mother, Debbie, about our plans. She was horrified. As the Yiayia of our family, we needed her approval; otherwise, we would not be buying land.

'Why do you want to get yourselves into another struggle?' she asked. 'We are only now recovering from building here, and you want to put pressure on yourselves again?'

Alex pleaded with Debbie that we were still young and wanted to keep building for our future. Yes, we would suffer, but is anything worthwhile easy? she asked.

Debbie sat back and considered this. She had been through the war years; she had seen suffering and starvation. She had fought all her life to stand still and had fended off terrible troubles which were not her making. Just as she felt the future would be comfortable, we had hit her with this proposal. All of her life, Debbie had been a fighter. Her real name was Despina, but she was known to everyone affectionally as Debbie. She was a large, wonderful lady with a smile that never left her face. She was wise, kind, and had the gift of lighting up any room she entered.

Debbie was born in Castella, a seaside suburb of Athens, the eldest of two children. Her brother Vasilis was two years younger. Debbie's father, like his father before him, was a sea captain. Her mother, Bia, was a loving mother who cared for the family and was loved by her many friends and neighbours in the village. As children, Debbie and her brother would swim amongst the wooden fishing boats in the small natural harbour. When they were hungry, they would pick some fruit from the choice of peach and pomegranate trees which grew wild around the village. It was a carefree existence until the age of twelve, when the Germans arrived and her life changed. Greeks were starving and food scarce. Debbie, for the first time in her life, experienced hunger.

The Nazis imposed a nightly curfew. No doors or windows

were to be left open. They would keep their curtains closed. Even a chink of light shining through the window would call for immediate arrest and detention. The occupying force permitted no lights other than a small candle to ease the pitch darkness at night. Debbie remembers trying to sleep through the sounds from the street from starving and homeless people's cries of 'Eímaste peinasménoi' (We are hungry) throughout every night. Most mornings, thin, starved bodies would lay lifeless in the streets after the hunger had finally taken its toll.

One night, the family got a message that Jannis, Debbie's father, had been arrested and taken away to Gestapo headquarters for questioning. Everyone knew what this meant. It was likely Debbie would lose her father. Her fears were realised when a letter was received notifying Bia that Jannis had been sentenced to death by the Nazis for being a member of the fierce Greek resistance and for aiding the British with their war effort. After his arrest and elaborate escape, he was forced to flee abroad and leave his young family to fend for themselves.

Bia did all she could during these dark years to cope and feed the family, but hunger was everywhere and even when money arrived, smuggled into Greece from Jannis in exile, there was very little to buy. Debbie remembered one episode where there was a fight in the square over a donkey's head, the only edible item presented for sale in the market. During the first winter of German occupation, cats and dogs disappeared from the city, while they sold donkeys as 'beef'.

After four years of occupation, the war ended, and Jannis returned and set about reuniting the family.

The Nazi occupation wiped out the Greek economy and brought terrible hardships to the Greeks. Over forty thousand civilians died in Athens alone from starvation. Tens of thousands more died from reprisals by Nazis and collaborators.

After the war, Debbie's family embarked on a programme

to help the village recover. Then Greece was to suffer yet another conflict. This time it was civil war. By the time the communists were defeated, and many more people died, Greece at last had peace.

At this early age, Debbie had two passions. One was her music, the other her faith. Her father arranged music lessons for her at the local academy and her natural talent for the piano shone through. By the age of nineteen she was playing in front of appreciative audiences at the university and was well on her way to earning her teaching degree. But for Debbie, this was not enough. She had felt the calling and announced to her parents that she wanted to enter the convent and become a nun.

Her mother fully understood, as like Debbie, she was a devoted Christian and faith played an important part in her life. Her father, however, thought otherwise.

Jannis hated the idea of his only daughter being isolated in a convent at such an early age. Her life was before her, and Jannis wanted to live to see grandchildren. So, he did all he could to discourage Debbie and Bia, suggesting that she should continue her music studies and a husband should be found so Debbie could live a normal life.

Debbie reluctantly accepted her father's wishes and agreed not to take holy orders, but had no intention of finding a husband. She threw herself into her music studies. Over the next two years, she passed her teaching degree and took a job at Athens University as a music teacher.

It was summer break. Bia suggested a trip to visit some relatives in Constantinople. Throughout history, Greeks have never called Constantinople 'Istanbul'. Even today, no Greek will utter the name of Istanbul. Even the national airlines of Greece use the old name for the city on their destination boards.

Greeks can never forget the slaughter of Greeks in Smyrna in 1922, the burning of Constantinople's Greek neighbourhoods, the further persecution of Greeks in 1955, or the Turkish invasion and occupation of the northern part of Cyprus in 1974. This is partly because of the horror they felt knowing that when Constantinople fell to the Ottomans on 29 May 1453, it meant the end of Byzantium, and subsequently Hellenism, in the East. Constantinople was the centre of the ancient Greek world and the home of the patriarch, the most senior member of the Greek Orthodox church.

Even though Constantinople had a large population of Greek speakers, many were being removed and exiled to Greece. Most of these people were born in Turkey and their only crime was their religion. But many remained in Constantinople. Some were relatives of Debbie.

Bia and Debbie took the ship from Piraeus, and for the first time, Debbie met the other branch of the family. Although Greece had been decimated by the war, the Turks had remained neutral for its majority, so were unaffected. Unlike Athens, there had been no famine here. Debbie found Constantinople to be refreshing compared to the slowly recovering Athens.

It was love at first sight. Debbie – coming from a country still affected by the aftermath of war and used to people dressed in old and tatty clothes, everywhere the look of defeat – saw this confident, handsome young man standing on an ornate staircase, dressed in a fashionable suit and red tie. Zissis was the son of Bia's cousin, who was the local doctor. He was young, handsome, with an air of sophistication. Debbie was under his spell from the start.

Zissis had been privately educated in the German school in Constantinople and a university in Switzerland. His father had suggested he followed him into medicine, but Zissis was not interested in the long years of study and refused. As the family in Constantinople was wealthy, they had a stake in several businesses. One of Zissis's uncles had recently died, leaving a small factory making tin boxes. The family gave Zissis the responsibility of running the factory and signed it over to him as his own. As Zissis had never had to work for anything in his short life, he didn't see this as an honour but a chore. Until then, he was a carefree young man about town with no responsibilities. Suddenly he was expected to knuckle down and do a proper job, the first of his life. He did not enjoy getting up early in the mornings and enjoyed even less having responsibility for running a company. So, at the first opportunity, he sold the business at a reduced rate, took a bag full of gold coins and planned a European tour for a year or two.

Debbie had arrived just in time to spark his interest, so he decided to delay his trip to see what would develop.

In those days, they did not allow a young couple to be alone. Whenever they met, there was always a chaperone nearby. As the days passed, Debbie became more infatuated, and when the time came to leave Constantinople to return to Athens, she pleaded with her mother to invite Zissis.

She didn't have to wait long. In September 1955, a month after Debbie returned to Athens, the riots began in Istanbul.

The Istanbul pogrom, also known as the Istanbul riots of 6–7 September 1955, was a series of state-sponsored anti-Greek mob attacks directed primarily at Istanbul's Greeks. Various security organisations collaborated with the governing Democratic Party to stage the pogrom. A fake news story which stated that Greeks had bombed the Turkish consulate in Thessaloniki triggered the events the day before. To add insult to injury, this was the house where the Turkish hero, Mustafa Kemal Ataturk, was born in 1881. A bomb planted by a Turkish usher at the consulate, who was later arrested and confessed, incited the events. The Turkish press did not report the arrest; instead, it insinuated that Greeks had set off the bomb.

A Turkish mob, most of whose members were trucked into the city in advance, assaulted Istanbul's Greek community for nine hours. Although the mob did not explicitly call for the killing of Greeks, over a dozen people died during and after the attacks because of beatings and arson. The violence continued until the government declared martial law, called in the army, and ordered it to put down the riots.

The pogrom sped up the migration of ethnic Greeks from Turkey. Zissis's family realised there was no future for them in the city and left. They could see more trouble coming and being a wealthy family, needed to protect what they had left. This turned out to be a wise decision. In 1964, the remaining Greeks were told to leave.

Most of the expelled held Greek citizenship. They were ordered to leave the country within two weeks, taking with them only a suitcase weighing no more than twenty kilograms, and cash worth no more than twenty-two dollars. Any business interests in Turkey, together with assets, were frozen, and property seized.

When Zissis and his family arrived in Athens, they were among over one million Anatolian Greeks who had ultimately fled Turkey. Although the family were Christian and classed as Greek, they had Turkish passports. While some refugees enjoyed warm support upon arrival, many others found settlement in the unfamiliar country a painful experience. The Greek government was not ready for such a large influx of refugees. Greek people resented these new arrivals as they didn't see them as true Greeks. So not only did they have to suffer the indignity of being thrown out of Turkey, discrimination from their own people also confronted them.

So, Debbie's love had come to Greece. They soon got

together to continue the relationship begun in Constantinople and it flourished in Athens. Debbie was in awe of this exotic man who spoke five languages and, in her eyes, was a genuine gentleman. Debbie did not realise that Zissis was only here for a short while before leaving on his European tour. Most of the men she had known during her early years were family members, or rough sea-captain friends of her father. Here was a regal, almost royal man who had taken an interest in her, and she realised she had fallen deeply in love.

On their regular outings, the family would always send a chaperone to go with them. If no one else was available, then her brother, Vasilis, would have to follow to ensure no funny business occurred. But Vasilis was easily bribed and with a few coins pressed into his palm, would disappear to the local cinema, leaving the happy couple to continue building their relationship without the watchful eyes of the family.

Zissis was never a passionate man. He was subject to bouts of anger and had the unfortunate habit of treating those he felt were beneath him with contempt. Debbie had grown up with a happy, loving family and had felt hunger. She had lived through the great famine and witnessed people dying in the streets. She had seen with her own eyes the brutality of the occupying forces and appreciated her life as it was now. Zissis, being a privileged only child, never had to suffer starvation. He never witnessed the atrocities of the Nazi occupation and never had to deal with the consequence of his actions. But Debbie was in love and could not see this side of him. Bia was wiser than Debbie. She tried to warn her daughter that he was going to be a troublesome man.

Debbie and Zissis had been seeing each other for a while. They waited until Jannis was out of the country on a ship carrying cargo to the other side of the world, and approached

Bia. Debbie begged her mother to allow Zissis to move into their home, assuring her that nothing untoward would occur as 'Zissis was an honourable man'.

When Debbie's father returned, he was shocked to find Zissis living in his house. He called a family meeting and summoned Zissis's parents to the house.

Once all were assembled, Jannis asked Zissis in front of the family:

'So, what are your intentions, young man?'

'I am going to tour Europe,' he replied.

'Do you have any intention of marrying my daughter?'

'No,' replied Zissis.

Jannis asked Zissis to step outside for a private chat. Once out of earshot of the rest of the family, he looked into Zissis's eyes and spoke.

'Eísai sápio kréas.' (You are rotten meat.)

Zissis was taken aback. No one had ever spoken to him like this. His own parents had put him on a pedestal as an only child. For them, he could do no wrong. Now here was this rough sea captain calling him rotten meat. How dare he!

'Listen,' Zissis replied, 'I am not rotten meat, and to prove it, I will marry your daughter.'

This was not the fairy-tale romance Debbie had expected. She now realised Zissis was not in love with her and had only agreed to marry out of pride. But Debbie was deeply in love with him and was sure over time he would come to love her. She agreed to the marriage.

In Greece, it is customary for the parents of the bride to provide a home. If they were poor, then a space would be supplied for the newlyweds in the family home. If the family were better off, then they would build a house for the daughter to start her new life. In Debbie's case, the parents could allow her to choose the location and build a house for her to start her marriage. Debbie chose the village of Glyfada, just a few miles around the coast from her home in Castella.

Although under Greek law they could marry, Zissis, as an alien with a Turkish passport, could not work and had a time-limited visa. If Zissis was going to stay and work in Greece, he had to get full citizenship and a work permit. He would have to face intense bureaucracy or join the army for a period of national service. As someone who had never needed to do anything for himself, he was reluctant to join the masses of displaced Anatolian Greeks and negotiate the Greek bureaucracy to get the papers, and there was no way he was going to join the army and have someone tell him what to do. Months passed, and Zissis had still made no attempt to become legal in Greece, so Debbie, realising he was unlikely to make the effort to start the process, took it upon herself to deal with it.

One morning she took him to a notary who prepared a power of attorney which Zissis signed. It was a formal document allowing his now wife, Debbie, to deal with the visa and naturalisation process on his behalf. Months of mind-numbing bureaucracies followed as they passed Debbie from government department to government department until, finally, Zissis was granted full citizenship and a work permit.

As he was still receiving an allowance from his father, and still using up his bag of gold coins from the sale of his factory, he was in no hurry to get a job. Although it was enough to keep his lifestyle, it would not be enough to start a family and support a home.

Back in the UK, I checked my savings. It was not enough to pay for the land. I was working hard and long hours, but soon realised I could not make enough within the agreed time limit. I wandered around, trying to come up with ideas. Then I remembered. I had been paying into a pension for years. Being over fifty years old, I could cash some of it in. I called the pension company, who gave me a settlement figure. I didn't really like the idea of doing away with my long-term security, but I felt a little safer since we had the shop in Glyfada which would give us an income for our autumn years. I agreed to take it. This didn't quite cover the price of the land, but it was not too far away from the needed amount. But I had abandoned my weekly trips and remained working seven days a week to make up the difference.

Finally, I had succeeded. I arrived at Athens airport with the banker's draft in my pocket.

Alex was waiting at arrivals, smiling as usual. She ran over to me and jumped, wrapping her legs around me, and held tight. We had not seen each other for almost a month, and daily phone calls had done little to ease the loneliness we both felt. We jumped into the car and headed for home. In Glyfada, the first call was to the bank. We had to pay the cheque into our account so we could draw the money in Evia to complete our deal. The bank clerk took the draft and credited our account. I asked her to contact the branch in Evia to make arrangements for me to collect the cash there tomorrow. Next was a phone call to Anna, the estate agent. She had already arranged the meeting with a local lawyer who would liaise with the vendor and us. It was all set. Tomorrow we would buy land.

Then the bank called.

'There is a problem,' the cashier informed me. 'The draft paid in needs ten days to clear because it is a foreign bank.'

This scuppered our plans for tomorrow. I called Anna to

tell her about the delay. The line went quiet as she digested this information.

'But it's all set. The vendor has travelled from Northern Greece and the lawyer is all arranged.'

Unless I could come up with a solution, the deal was off. I had no way of getting hold of this amount of cash by tomorrow. The money was in the bank, but until the draft was cleared, there was nothing I could do. I didn't care about losing my deposit, but how would I break this news to Alex? She had set her heart on the land. Her lifelong dream of owning a home on a Greek island was about to be shattered. I was only due to stay in Greece for seven days and had to be back in the UK for business, which I could not postpone, so this delay could be terminal for the deal. I had always considered a banker's draft to be as good as cash but had not accounted for the international banking rules; and more importantly, I had not considered the older Greeks' distrust of banks.

I asked Anna to contact the landowner on my behalf to explain the situation and plead for a little more time.

'It won't work. She already has another buyer waiting. If you can't complete the deal, she will take the other offer,' she replied. 'Leave it with me. I have an idea. I'll call you back.'

With that, the phone went dead. I sat staring at the phone, wondering what idea she'd had. Alex was out shopping, and I hoped Anna would call before she came home. I really didn't want to give her this bad news until all options had been exhausted. We had both been working against all odds to earn enough money to buy this land. We had spent time apart, missing each other every day in our single-minded determination to move another step forward in our lives, and just as we thought we had made it, our hopes and dreams would be destroyed.

The phone had not completed one ring when I grabbed it. It was Anna.

'I explained your predicament to Yiayia. She said you are good people, so she will lend you the money.'

Yiayia had come to our rescue again. I have often experienced the kindness of Greek people, but this was exceptional. She was willing to trust us beyond our expectations.

'You give me a cheque for the amount, and I will collect the money from my bank,' she offered.

We would buy our land after all.

The next day, we had arranged to meet our lawyer, Michalis, at the ferry port of Arkitsa. He would accompany us on the short ferry ride to Evia while explaining the purchase procedure. We sat on the upper deck, enjoying the spring sunshine while we watched the green pine mountains approach. Today, we would own a piece of that island. Alex had prepared for the celebration by bringing along a carrier bag holding a bottle of champagne and two golden goblets. She opened the carrier bag to show Michalis. He looked at the contents and put his hand over the bag, quickly closing it.

'Show nobody this,' he warned. 'If people see you have that in your bag, they will think you're rich and try to charge you more for the land. And Peter, take off that watch, it looks expensive.'

I didn't want to tell him I got the watch from Glyfada market a few weeks ago for five euros. It was quite an honour to be told it looked good.

We arrived in the small market town of Istiea, a short drive from the village of Pefki. We found Anna waiting outside the bank, clutching a carrier bag. She smiled and opened the top, and we peered inside to see a large brick of cash tied up with elastic bands. She had been as good as her word. Michalis disappeared into a nearby office. He needed to check the title deed to ensure the land was truly owned by the vendor and had no mortgage or loans secured to it. After a few moments, he returned and told us with a smile that it was fine, and we could continue with the purchase.

We all followed Anna across the town square and into a dark hallway, climbed the stairs, and entered the lawyer's office.

A smiling lady was sitting opposite a stern-looking lawyer. They both rose to greet us and held out their hands in welcome. The lady introduced herself as Mary; the lawyer just nodded as we took our places on the spare chairs around the desk. Papers were passed around. We signed, Mary signed. Anna produced the bag of money, which was counted and a receipt given. The deal was done. We left with a folder full of documents and the precious deeds to our piece of this beautiful island.

Michalis shook my hand and kissed Alex as he wished us syncharitíria kai stous dýo (congratulations to you both) as he left for the port to catch the next ferry to the mainland. We waved Michalis goodbye, jumped into the car and drove straight to Pefki.

We arrived at the gate to our new land and released the padlock. A giant toad the size of a dinner plate watched us suspiciously as we invaded his field. This was no longer his, but ours. Holding hands, Alex and I picked our way through the brambles and parted the bamboo, trying to assess the land that we had just bought. A small lizard ran for sanctuary into the bamboo. A large tortoise ambled away from our feet, disappearing into the thick undergrowth, followed by the toad, who no longer felt welcome.

Alex took the bottle of champagne and two golden goblets from the car. We walked to the middle of the plot, sat on the ground, and opened the wine with a pop.

Champagne fizzed out of the bottle onto the ground and was sucked in by the greedy, dry virgin earth. We filled our glasses and toasted our success. We sat on that piece of earth for the rest of the afternoon, discussing where the house would go, how many bedrooms, even which trees we would plant in the garden. It was a wonderful dream, but we were just getting started.

For a little over a year, the land in Pefki remained just that. We still didn't have enough money to do anything substantial, and certainly not enough to even consider building. We just visited from our home near Athens some weekends to do a little gardening and carry on dreaming of our imaginary house.

One day, near our home in Glyfada, we were passing a yard selling caravans. Alex asked me to stop so she could look. She had the idea of towing a caravan to Pefki and siting it on the land rather than build a house. I followed her around while she stepped in and out of the caravans on show, opening drawers and checking the sizes. The salesperson was very persuasive, and Alex seemed to warm to the idea of a mobile home. Luckily, his phone rang, and I used the pause in his sales pitch to pull Alex away and explain the obvious downsides to this idea.

'What will happen in the summer? The temperature regularly rises above forty degrees in Greece. We would be pot-roasted,' I assured her, 'and in the winter we would freeze.'

I made excuses to the keen salesman and escorted Alex away to discuss this idea further.

'What about a tent, then?' Alex suggested. 'There's a shop nearby. We could buy one and camp on our land whenever we visited. That would be nice.'

Alex really wanted to progress with putting something on our piece of land, but was realistic enough to understand our financial position and didn't push her desire too much. We had already built our family home in Glyfada, which had used up all of our savings. We had managed to pay for the land in Pefki, so that was now ours, but time was running on and we needed to move forward.

At that time, like most Greeks, I was a smoker. Even though the European smoking ban for all inside areas had come into force, Greece complied by putting 'No smoking' stickers on taverna windows but leaving the ashtrays on the tables. We had just finished a meal. I took out my cigarettes and started to doodle on the packet.

'What are you doing?' Alex asked.

'Oh, I'm just designing our villa,' I replied.

'You are living in a dreamworld,' she scolded. 'We will never afford to build our house.'

This suddenly hit home. She was right. Just dreaming about it wouldn't make it happen; I had to move forward and do something. The time for indecision was over. If I had to wait until I could afford it, it would never happen.

Then and there, I decided. Somehow, we would build our new home. I didn't know how, but now was the time to find out.

During the past year, Alex and I had often talked about our dream home. Would it be wood construction like a log cabin? Would we build it traditionally using concrete blocks and cement? We would sit and dream. In Greece, over recent years, a new building method had become popular. It's called a Prokat. When I first heard about this, I hated the idea. A Prokat is a prefabricated house mostly built in a factory, then taken to the land on a lorry and bolted together. I had visions of the old asbestos prefabs built after the war in England to house people who lost their homes during bombing raids. I certainly did not fancy a flat-pack house. The last piece of furniture I brought from Ikea had lots of screws left over after I built it, and the legs fell off a month later. But clearly technology has moved on, which became clear when we visited a Prokat showroom. We were convinced. All pre-existing ideas of a prefabricated house fell away as we walked into the delightful show home. It was modern, light and sophisticated. The walls were constructed with thermal materials to keep warm in the winter and cool in the summer. It was clad on the outside with cement, which made it look like a stone-built villa, and inside was beautifully decorated with marble tiles on the floors. The kitchen and bathroom were ultra-modern, and the entire building looked magnificent.

We decided we would build a Prokat. We left the taverna and drove a short distance to a villa company we had passed many times, close to Athens airport. A big sign was displayed beside the main road with the name of the company emblazoned on a picture of an idyllic Greek villa. An assistant ushered us in to meet the owner of the company that bears his name. Mr Kofinas welcomed us into his office and asked how he could help.

I passed my cigarette packet to him and pointed to the tiny drawing.

'I want you to build that,' I told him.

Mr Kofinas smiled sympathetically as he studied my design. He called his draughtsman into the office, and they both examined my cigarette packet until the designer left, assuring us he would be back in a few moments.

During that time. Mr Kofinas explained the procedure. We would need an architect for the designs and necessary permissions required by the local mayor's office, and a local builder for the auxiliary work. His company would only deal with the construction of the villa. This would be built mostly in his yard in sections, then shipped to our land and constructed.

We would need to arrange for a concrete base to stand the

villa on. We would also need to provide drainage to a septic tank and arrange for water and electricity meters.

He would calculate the price of the villa per square metre and would include everything: kitchen, bathroom fittings, tiling, bedroom cupboards and decoration. We could choose our own colour scheme and whatever units we wanted from a wide selection. So, once he was finished, all we would need to do was connect the water and electricity.

This sounded perfect. It was simpler than we had expected, and all seemed doable. But then we were hit with reality. If we were to place an order, we would need to pay a deposit of 70 per cent of the entire cost. This was understandable. His villas were all made to order. He didn't have a showroom packed with ready-made houses waiting to be shipped out at a moment's notice; his factory had to make every one from scratch. Our dreams evaporated as we considered this impossible task. We had assumed we could arrange a monthly payment plan, maybe a hire purchase agreement. But although this would work for buying a car, no company would finance a villa without added security. And we had promised not to use our new apartment as collateral for a loan. It was still an impossible dream. He saw our disappointment and came to our rescue.

'Listen. There is no hurry. There is a lot of work for you to do first. I am happy to wait while you deal with the preparation and permissions. When you have done all that, come back and see me. This year, next year, no problem,' he told us.

But there was the issue of the design. For us to be able to get planning permission, and lay the concrete base and drains, we would need the complete villa design from his company. But he solved this with a wave of his hand.

'I trust you. I can see you are both good people. It would be my gift to you. Come back next week and everything will be ready.'

Mr Kofinas was as good as his word. The following week we left his office with a file holding architect drawings, structural calculations, full dimensions and everything we needed to apply to build.

If we planned this right, we could spread the procedure over a couple of years and pay for each segment as we could afford it.

We would start by employing an architect to start the procedure for the building consent. By the time this was done and paid for, we could then slowly arrange for the concrete base and drainage without stretching our pockets too much. We had decided to funnel all the rent from our shop in Glyfada into the project, and I was still working weekdays in London, so instead of using any excess money to visit islands and eat out, every penny would be devoted to the villa construction. But before anything else, we needed to get permission to build. So we had to get an architect. Mr Kofinas was happy to recommend someone who could help.

I was worried about getting the planning permission. Having experienced Greek bureaucracy first-hand and knowing how notoriously difficult it is to navigate. I had visions of years tied up in red tape until we finally gained permission to build. But Elena, our architect, removed my fears.

'You brought the land on plan,' she told us. 'The permission came with it. You are automatically allowed to build.'

We still needed to produce more detailed drawings, and they had to be approved by the planning office. But apart from that, we could go ahead subject to final approval and a visit from the forestry protection agency and an archaeologist.

We arranged to meet Elena at our plot of land for an 'autopsy'. She had already got the relevant maps from the planning office. Our plot was marked on the drawing in red. We still did not know the full size of the land, and the map was not very accurate. But Elena assured us that most of the unseen land was unimportant at the moment. She was only interested in the construction's position near the road. We could do what we liked with the garden once we had built the villa.

We weren't too worried about the forestry protection agency. In Greece, if you have any protected trees on your land, you may not move them, so it can be a problem to build. But as far as we could see, we didn't have any trees.

We were a little more concerned about the archaeologists. A stone's throw from our piece of land is the ancient village of Artemision, one of the oldest villages in Greece. This was a thriving village in ancient times. Off the coast in 480 BC a series of naval engagements occurred over three days during the second Persian invasion of Greece. The battle took place simultaneously with the famous land battle at Thermopylae, where three hundred Spartans bravely defended the mountain pass against over one million invading Persians. The sea battle was fought between an alliance of Greek city states, including Sparta, Athens, Corinth and others, and the Persian Empire of Xerxes I. The famous Battle of Artemision was named after this little village.

There had already been many finds of statues and other relics of that period in and around the village. If they found anything, we would never be allowed to build. The land would be confiscated, and a small sum paid to us which would not cover the original cost.

The day of the archaeologist's visit arrived. We watched from the road outside as a short, spectacled man directed another chap driving a huge yellow JCB. A trench over one metre deep was slowly cut across the earth, stopping occasionally to let the archaeologist jump into the trench to inspect the soil.

Soon he looked directly at us and asked, 'Are you the landowners?'

'Yes,' Alex replied.

'Well, go away and let me do my job,' he snapped. 'I don't enjoy working while being watched.'

Alex frowned and took a step towards him; she was about to pick a fight for telling us to leave our own land. Alex has never had any respect for authority, but I really didn't want her to upset this man. He already looked like he was having a bad day, and we needed a favourable report. I pulled her back.

'Please don't upset him,' I pleaded. 'Let's just let him get on with it.'

We left him and the JCB to continue digging up our land and went down to the local taverna for lunch. We weren't really concentrating on the food. We were far too worried about what they may find.

'How big a find would cost us our land?' I asked Alex hopefully. 'If they only found a small statue, wouldn't they just take it away and leave us to build?'

Alex reassured me it was unlikely he would find anything and to stop worrying.

Suddenly we felt a rumbling and the sound of the JCB passing the taverna. They had finished. We paid for our lunch and rushed back to the land. The archaeologist had gone, leaving enormous holes in the ground. We clambered over the piles of soil and investigated the excavations. My heart skipped a beat as I saw a pile of broken crockery at the bottom.

'Oh shit,' I said out loud. 'He's found something.'

Alex jumped into the hole, took a piece of the crockery, turned it over and read: 'Made in China'.

Either the archaeologist or the JCB driver had a sense of

humour. Realising we were worried he had thrown some old plates into the hole for a joke.

A few days later, Elena called. The forestry commission had sent their report: there were no protected trees on our land. The archaeologist had discovered no ancient monuments. The plans had all been cleared and final building permission was granted.

4

NAVIGATING THE STORM OF GREEK BUREAUCRACY

Sometimes we need to be reminded we are not living in paradise. It's necessary to be shot with a few arrows occasionally to wake you up. These arrows come in the form of Greek bureaucracy.

But it is slowly getting better. For example: now you can pay your tax online, avoiding the annual riot and bloodbath of queuing up for three days at the tax office, standing in the wrong line for most of the time and not having the right papers, then being turned away at the last minute because you forgot to tick the right box when you filled in your tax return. All this for the privilege of trying to give the government vast quantities of your hard-earned cash. No wonder that when the Greek crisis started in late 2009, triggered by the turmoil of the worldwide Great Recession, it dismayed Greeks to read in the world media that it was their fault for not paying taxes.

This change has come about mostly because someone in the Greek government realised that people were happy to pay the tax, but as the authorities had made it so difficult, most just gave up and went home. *'If they wanted it so badly, they would just have to come and get it.'* Some government departments realised there was a revolutionary new way to make extra cash by making it easy for people to pay their bills. Slowly but surely, the ancient, creaking wheels of bureaucracy turned. They introduced direct debits for water and electricity bills. It was all becoming automated.

Our architect would deal with all the necessary paperwork to secure permission to build our house. However, some details needed to be done by us. We had to arrange for electricity and water. This meant subjecting ourselves to the brutal Greek bureaucracy.

We had experienced this in many previous locations and were both dreading the saga to come. A simple thing like paying a parking ticket can take two days here. More complicated missions could take weeks of head-holding frustration. All Greeks must experience this regularly.

In the early days of our relationship, I wanted to buy a new car. So, we went to the local car showroom, chose our model and asked when it could be delivered. A knowing smile crept over the face of the salesperson. He went into his office and came out with a checklist.

First, he told us to go to the tax office to get a paper which needed to be officially stamped in triplicate, confirming we didn't owe any tax. Apparently, if you owed the government tax, you shouldn't be able to afford a car. The taxman wanted his share first. Luckily, we had finished that odyssey the previous month when we queued up for three days for the privilege of handing over a good proportion of our hard-earned cash, and we had a receipt to prove it. But the receipt wasn't good enough. We needed a special letter confirming our tax status and couldn't buy the car until we had it. This meant a visit to the tax office.

At that time, the tax office was close to home in Glyfada, within walking distance of our house. It was above a shop with a small door to the side at ground level. Inside was a staircase leading to a small window on the second floor, where we would need to ask for our papers. The problem was, it seemed everyone else in Glyfada wanted to buy a car that day, so the queue was outside the building and snaking around the corner. In those days, there was no ticket system employed by most government departments now; we had to join the end of the slow-moving queue and hope for the best. In three hours, we had moved about ten metres. After another hour, we were just inside the door. The queue extended up four flights of stairs to the little window at the top. We were still at the bottom and hadn't put our foot on the first step, when someone higher up yelled.

'Closed now, come back tomorrow.'

They even turned away people at the top of the stairs nearing the window as the shutter slammed down. The tax office never considered the possibility of allowing all the people currently in the building near closing time to complete their request. No, at two o'clock the shutters would be closed, and everybody had to go home and try again tomorrow. For three more days, we tried. On the fourth day, we did it. Armed with our letter showing we didn't owe any tax, we went back to the car dealer and proudly handed the salesman our precious document. He took a photocopy and handed it back.

'Now you need number plates,' he told us.

When you buy a car in most countries, the dealer takes care of the number plates. But not in Greece. We had to travel to the Ministry of Transport in Athens to get ours. After the wasted time at the tax office just to get a piece of paper, I was now panicking about getting a set of number plates and wondered what this would involve. At the risk of being boring and repetitive, I will skip the painful couple of days dealing with obnoxious bureaucrats and come straight to the point.

We had been battling with long lines of hopeful motorists for three days. We had visited the wrong office and been thrown out after lining up for hours. We had the door slammed in our face at closing time after hours in queues. So, we were sitting outside the ministry, trying to recover from another disappointing day, when we spotted a small group of people nearby. One detached from the group and walked past us holding a brand-new set of number plates. We went to investigate. One employee from inside the building had a roaring trade of shortcutting the officious system. If you gave him some cash, he would take your papers, go inside and return with your plates. This was worth every penny paid, and soon we had ours and we left. I think the system has changed now. It's likely that these errant employees were making so much outside the building, the government got jealous and made things a little easier inside. So we finally had our car.

Alex and I booked into a local hotel in Pefki. This would be used as our base of operations for the forthcoming saga. We had allowed two weeks to complete our tasks. We reasoned it would likely take a day or two to get the electricity meter ordered. Then another day to deal with the water connection. Meanwhile, we would look for a local builder to build the concrete slab which they would set the house upon, and the septic tank needed to be buried into the ground and connected to drainage. But we could do none of this until we had power and water.

The hotel was small and comfortable, with a central swimming pool and rooms spread around the perimeter so each bedroom had access to the pool directly from their small front patio. It was delightful, but I had no visions of being able to relax on one of those attractive-looking sunbeds under idyllic wicker umbrellas. We had work to do.

The water was arranged by the local mayor and I was told it shouldn't be too much of an issue, but the government-controlled power company had a reputation for being difficult. With the amount of unnecessary red tape in Greece, they had stiff competition. The electricity company comprised a small building on a backstreet of the village. Inside was a small Perspex box with a slot at the front, containing a cashier. They had drilled a circle of holes at mouth level to allow communication. A couple of desks covered with papers occupied the rest of the office, with two people tapping away on a keyboard. Behind the cash office was a window and beyond that, another office, with a man peering into a computer screen.

Alex tapped on the Perspex box and shouted through the holes.

'We want to buy an electricity meter, please.'

'Make an appointment,' he replied, and pointed to a telephone number handwritten on the wall. She took out her phone and dialled the number. A phone rang in the office behind the cashier. The man peering into the computer screen answered.

'I want to make an appointment to buy a meter,' she informed him.

'Okay, when can you come?' he replied.

'Is now a good time?'

I watched through the glass screen as the man put the phone on the table and took out a diary and checked his appointments. I could hear both sides of the conversation and was nowhere near a phone.

'I can squeeze you in later today,' he replied.

'But we're here now, turn around.' He turned and saw us both waving from two metres away. He put the phone down and waved us in. We gave our name, address and postcode. The details of our home in Glyfada flashed up on his computer screen. We filled in the forms for the new meter and exchanged them for an invoice, which he informed us needed to be paid from our bank with the details provided.

'Can't I just pay the guy in the box?' I asked.

'No. It must be by bank transfer,' he insisted. 'Come back when you've paid, and we can make an appointment to have the new meter installed.'

We went outside and called our bank to arrange an instant transfer. The next day, we went back to the office. The guy in the Perspex box pointed at the telephone number on the wall and told us to make an appointment.

'Can't we just knock on the door?' I asked.

He was having none of that. Procedures had to be observed. Alex dialled the number. The guy in the office two metres away answered, checked his diary, waved us in. We showed him the emailed bank transfer receipt; he checked his screen and announced that they had not received the money. Alex took out her phone and called the bank. The bank told her they had indeed transferred the money, but the electricity company sent it back. This we explained to the back-office guy. He checked our bank receipt and told us there were not enough numbers on the reference. That's why it was refused, and he told us to try again.

We went home, called the bank, arranged the transfer with more numbers and crossed our fingers. The next day back at the office, we wished the guy in the Perspex box good morning and called the number to make an appointment. The back-office guy answered the phone and let us in, then told us they had not received the money. We called the bank, who told us the electricity company had sent it back again.

'Please, can I pay the guy in the Perspex box?' I pleaded. 'Look, I have the money here.'

'No. It has to be a bank transfer. The bank put the reference number in the wrong box. Try again.' He grinned at us. He was obviously enjoying making our lives as difficult as possible. This seemed to be the favourite pastime of government employees, lightening their day and distracting them from their normal mundane activities.

We went back to our hotel, called the bank again. Sent yet another transfer. This time the tele-bank operator promised everything was fine and they would now accept the money. So we went to our favourite small taverna by the beach to celebrate over a pleasant lunch of calamari, Greek salad and home-made wine.

The next morning, before going back to the electricity office, we called the bank. The electricity company had again refused the money and had sent it back.

We returned to the office, called to make an appointment and went into the back office, where Alex finally exploded.

Until now, Alex's patience had surprised me while dealing with this particularly tough piece of bureaucracy. But enough was enough. This finally released my wife's Greek temperament. She slammed the pile of bank receipts on his desk and screamed into his face.

'You're enjoying yourself, aren't you?' she yelled.

'No, madam,' he stuttered. 'It's just procedure.'

'Screw procedure. You are just a bureaucratic malaka who enjoys wasting our time. We have paid you three times; three times you have sent the money back. What the hell are we to do now? Do you want us to go on our hands and knees and beg you to take our money?'

'But madam, it's procedure,' he tried again. He was beginning to look frightened.

By now, Alex was in full flow. If he had given her a silver-plated electricity meter on a golden platter, she would have still wanted to kill him. She leaned over his desk and put her face to his and poked his chest with her finger to illustrate each word.

'Give (poke) me (poke) my (poke) meter (poke). Malaka (poke poke).'

Then they threw us out.

Finally, we drove one hundred kilometres to the bank in Chalkida, electricity company form in hand. The bank teller revealed it was a common story, but she had the answer. Her sister worked for the electricity company, so she made a call, and between them they arranged the money transfer. It was done. The next day, receipt in hand, we went back to the electricity company, tapped on the Perspex box, called the number on the wall. Alex apologised to the back-office guy for the recent abuse and calling him a malaka. He was probably used to it, so hadn't taken too much offence. He checked the computer screen and announced our payment had been received.

They really didn't want our money. To them, it was a game. Bureaucracy in Greece had always been difficult and demanding, but with the advent of computers and bank transfers, which were supposed to simplify these procedures, it made it all a little more mind-numbing. But we had our power arranged. All we needed now was water. Time to visit the mayor.

We went to his office in Pefki. It was a small, informal place next to a taverna. The mayor was sitting at his desk wearing a grubby old T-shirt with a picture of a Greek flag on the front. He was leaning back in his chair with a telephone in one hand and a cigarette in the other. He finished his conversation and asked us to sit.

'Can we have water connected, please?' Alex asked.

'Of course. Do you have your water meter?'

We had intercepted this obstacle and had already been through this little piece of added bureaucracy. We had our water meter. All we needed was to be connected to the mains in the road. This was the mayor's responsibility.

'Okay. I will arrange it for tomorrow,' he told us.

The next day, nothing. The day after, they still hadn't arrived to connect our water. We went back to the mayor, who assured us it would certainly be done tomorrow. We were not convinced. Sure enough, the following day, no one turned up. We couldn't do anything on our land without a water supply and were getting desperate.

We went back to see the mayor. As we entered his office, the mayor turned his chair towards us.

'It's you again,' he said. 'Why do you keep coming here?'

Alex raised her voice.

'Because you told us we would have water connected by now,' Alex scolded. 'You keep forgetting and we need to start building. All you need to do is to dig a small hole and connect our meter to the mains supply. How hard can it be? I will even dig the hole for you if you like.'

She was getting angry now. I was seeing a pattern here. These visits to government departments always begin amiably. Then slowly, the official, seemingly deliberately, will put obstacles in your way to cause irritation and frustration. In Greece one in twenty people work for the government in some capacity. It seems to be policy to make things as difficult as possible, thereby extending the time needed to do anything. A simple procedure that should be achieved in a few minutes, with practice and determination can be extended for days or even weeks. This will then justify the existence of the government employee and everybody is happy, except the poor applicant who must take the brunt of the efficient time-wasting procedure practised here over generations.

Then finally, when you can take no more, they appear to be satisfied that they have caused the most amount of frustration. They wait for you to blow your top and finally relent – usually.

'Okay, okay,' he replied, 'you will definitely have water by tomorrow.'

The next day, still no water. So, the day after, we formed a plan.

It was well known in the village that the mayor was fond of his food. This time, we went to the office but instead of going in, we waited outside for the two o'clock closing time. At one minute past two, the mayor left the building and was just locking the door when we accidentally on purpose bumped into him.

'Oh hello,' Alex said. 'We are just off for lunch. Would you like to join us?'

The mayor checked his watch, then smiled and agreed. We walked next door to the fish taverna and took our seats. I thought this chap would need a little lubrication, so I ordered a kilo of wine, as is the way in Greece, and asked the owner to keep it coming. Meanwhile, Alex had been chatting with the owner and asked for the most impressive food he had available that day. She ordered a plate full of large, plump prawns, a selection of grilled fish, and copious amounts of salads and vegetables. Halfway through the meal, the mayor looked a little merry and was slurring. Alex reminded him about our water. He took his phone out of his pocket, pressed the button, barked a few words into it, and poured another glass of wine.

We left him there with another carafe of wine and went back to our building plot. By the time we arrived, we had water. They had erected a nice shiny pipe with a new tap. We turned it on and water flowed onto the ground. We were all set.

We had been in Pefki for nine days. So far, all we had accomplished was to have the electricity and water connected. But this was a great result as we would need this before the construction began. We had been saving furiously but still didn't have the full deposit for the house; however, we were well on the way, and Mr Kofinas was happy to wait until we had finished the preparation works and laid the drains and concrete base.

Elena had sent us the designs for the drains and the concrete base which the house would finally sit on. We needed to find a local builder for this.

In Greece, everything is word of mouth. If you need anything for the house or garden, the place to go is the local kafenio. These are always the centre of village life, and everyone knows everyone. This is where all the men of the village meet daily to drink their coffee, strong tsipouro spirits, and pass their time chatting and playing the national game of backgammon. It's common to see tractors and pickup trucks parked along the road. Fishermen moor their boats in the harbour, and once their nets are prepared and mended, ready for the night's fishing, they will spend the rest of their day drinking and munching small plates of meze with the farmers, local doctor and village priest.

To get information, though, is not straightforward. These kafenios are the equivalent of a private members-only club. They must accept you to be able to join them. We had two problems here. First, Alex was a woman and foreign. Although Alex is a true Greek, born and raised in a suburb of Athens, she wasn't born anywhere near this village, so was certainly foreign. Women rarely entered the kafenio. It's the reserved place for the men where they can be away from wives, mothers and children. A strange foreign woman setting foot on their hallowed ground was tantamount to blasphemy. Their eyes left her and focused on me. A blond, blue-eyed man with pink skin, a peeling nose from the sun, wearing a strange straw hat and knee-length shorts. If a little green man had left his spaceship outside and wandered in, they would not have reacted any differently to him. If anything, I was more interesting. All conversation stopped as we entered the dark, smoky room. The click of backgammon pieces ceased as they all watched us through the fog of cigarette smoke. A small cup holding a dice fell over. The dice rolled off the table and bounced onto the floor with a deafening sound in the vacuous, deathly quiet room.

Alex and I picked our way past the seated men and sat at an empty table.

'Geia sou Pétro, geia sou Alexándra,' came a voice from the kitchen.

A man with an apron appeared and held out his hand in greeting.

'What would you like to drink?' he asked.

Alex ordered two Greek coffees.

'Do you know us?' I asked.

'No, but welcome. We all know you have bought Mary's land along the road. Nothing happens in this village without us hearing about it first.' Then he looked into my eyes and asked, 'Are you German?'

'No, English,' I replied, 'but my wife is Greek.'

Slowly, the chatter in the room came back. The backgammon boards recommenced their clicking, and laughter erupted on a nearby table.

Alex called out to an old man at the next table. He was wearing an oilskin jacket and smelled of fish.

'Have you caught many fish today?' she asked him.

'Not many,' he replied. 'I grow the tomatoes in the village.'

The table erupted with laughter. But the ice was breaking. They all had miniature bottles of liquid in front of them and a bowl of ice. I watched as one of the men poured the contents into a glass and added three chunks of ice. The liquid turned cloudy.

'Is that ouzo?' I asked.

'No, tsipouro,' he replied. 'Here, try some.'

He passed the glass to me. The first sip hit my throat like a hammer. I felt like I had poured concentrated fire into my mouth. I suddenly got a shooting pain just below my earlobes as the horrible-tasting liquid burned my tongue and made my teeth ache. As I tried to gather the confidence to swallow, my throat tried to close to protect itself. But this seemed to be a test from the old men at the next table, which I was determined to pass. I resisted my body's gagging instinct to rid itself of this interesting flavour and swallowed. My throat burned as I felt it run down my neck and it settled on my chest and continued to burn. I have since heard that first-time drinkers of the ferocious spirit assume they are suffering a heart attack at this point, but it soon fades away, leaving you sweating and disoriented.

By this time, everyone in the kafenio was laughing and hitting their fists on the table, watching a new victim's first taste of the locally produced firewater moonshine known as tsipouro.

An old man came over from another table with a glass in his hand.

'Here, try this one. I make it myself.'

By now, the burn of my first glass had faded to a warm glow in my stomach. I was feeling happy and was keen to keep this experience going. So, I gladly accepted his offer and drunk another glass. This one didn't burn so much. The taste was still awful, but somehow smoother.

Alex kicked my leg under the table and whispered, 'Stop drinking – you may go blind.'

As a child, they often warned me of things that might make me go blind. But I don't remember being warned about drinking firewater in Greek bars being one of these sins.

'Look, we are making friends here,' I slurred. 'I'll just have one more.'

I accepted an offer from one more table and downed the cloudy spirit. This time there was no burn at all. I must have been getting used to it. That, or my taste buds had been stripped away and terminally damaged. Alex gave me a threatening stare.

'We are going home now,' she ordered.

I tried to stand. My legs didn't work. Alex helped me to my feet. My mind felt clear, but for some reason my legs had a mind of their own and had decided to stay for just one more drink. But Alex pulled me up. I put my arm around Alex's shoulder as she led me outside to the car.

Here's a word of warning. Don't. drink. tsipouro. This strange Greek spirit is the big brother of ouzo and gets your feet drunk first. You could be enjoying a meal and a glass or two, feeling relaxed and clear-headed – until you try to stand up. The tsipouro has attacked your legs and given them a mind of their own. You try to walk one way, but your legs have decided to go somewhere else. They make so much of this booze in the autumn that it is common to see sober men staggering around the village, arguing with their own drunken legs.

Before coming to this village, I had never heard of tsipouro. The traditional Greek spirit of ouzo is well known, as is raki. Tsipouro is another common home-made distillation. In Crete it's known as tsikoudia. Any cafe or taverna in this village will have tables outside filled with local men chatting and drinking this ferocious spirit. The bar owner will bring tiny bottles about the size of miniatures served during flights. It's common to see hundreds of empty little bottles pushed to the centre of the table until the bar owner sweeps them into a wire shopping basket and takes them away. He then sits at the back of his taverna with a large bottle and small funnel, and patiently refills every bottle and returns them to the table.

Most of the tsipouro is distilled in the village. Cheap stills can be bought at the local hardware shop. In the autumn, grapes are picked and used to make wine. But there is quite a lot left over from the wine production: grape skins, stalks, substandard grapes. These are not thrown away and wasted; they are all mashed up, fermented and distilled into the local spirit. The very best tsipouro is made by a priest, up in the mountains. Some villagers will take barrels of the by-product after the winemaking and give it to this famous priest, who will distil it into the most exceptional product on the island. Tsipouro made by this priest will command the highest prices and is only for the connoisseurs. Most just settle for the cheaper version and consider the risk of blindness an acceptable hazard.

I spent the rest of that afternoon with my head down the toilet. Once I had finished vomiting, I passed out in bed and awoke the next morning feeling like I had died and gone to hell.

We only had a few days left to arrange a builder to deal with our concrete base and laying drains. The previous day's visit to the kafenio only resulted in me being poured into our car after getting completely drunk with the locals. But we had made friends and introduced ourselves to the village. I still felt delicate. The light hurt my eyes, but there was no sympathy from Alex for my self-induced hangover. She reminded me she had warned me to be careful, so it was my fault. I mumbled an apology and took some aspirin, put on my dark glasses, and we set off back to the kafenio.

This time, they greeted us with smiles and handshakes as we walked in. I must have proved myself yesterday by joining them and sharing the local moonshine. I had promised Alex that I would not join them at a drinking party today. They were obviously used to the terrible liquid, and I was only a novice. I politely refused the offer of another glass. I felt sick just looking at the miniature bottles spread over the tables. This time we ordered coffee and slowly my headache subsided to a light thumping, making me feel a little better.

For years I have been struggling to speak Greek, and still find it hard. I seemed to be okay with normal conversation when in Athens; I could follow most conversations, and even contribute. I was fine with ordering food, drinks, and going shopping on my own, happily chatting with shop assistants in my broken Greek. But this village was different. I could only understand one in ten words. It was like listening to a completely new language. If we were going to live here, my education had to begin all over again. I had been learning Athenian Greek and certainly was not ready for the regional accents and dialects of the islands. Here, I sat and listened to conversations around me and felt I'd learned nothing from my years in Greece and found myself struggling to understand the most basic phrases.

Most of the words appeared to have a nasal *nya* added, so instead of the normal Geia sou Pétro, it was pronounced Ny-eia sou Pétro (Good morning, Peter). This was most confusing for someone with only a basic understanding of the language.

I had experienced this as a kid. My grandfather was from Tyneside and had a broad Geordie accent.

'A ye gannen the match?' (Are you going to the football match?)

'Gan canny or we'll dunsh summick.' (Please drive carefully.)

I didn't understand a word until I was twelve years old, and even then, struggled to understand him for the rest of his life.

So here was another new language I needed to get to grips with. Even Alex was struggling a little and she is pure Greek, so what chance did I have?

I listened as Alex chatted with the old men. I could understand most of what Alex was saying but relied on body language and tone to get an idea of the replies.

We left clutching a piece of paper with the name of the best builder in the village and a telephone number.

That afternoon, we were waiting on the road outside our plot of land. Stamos arrived in a rusty grey pickup truck with scaffold poles tied to the top of the cab with string, hanging over the back with a red rag tied to the end.

He jumped out of his truck and held out his hand. He was a short, stout man with a shaved head, wearing a blue polo shirt with the name of his building company emblazoned on the front. A cross on a gold chain swung across his chest. I took the offered hand and noticed his sandpaper grip. This guy is a worker, I thought.

'Welcome to our village,' he said.

We explained what we needed, gave him a copy of the plans, and asked him if he could do it.

'Yes, of course. It's easy,' he replied. 'But why don't you let me build the house too? I have a full team of workers; I could build you a beautiful house here, and quickly.'

It was tempting, but we had already made a deal with Mr Kofinas in Athens, and the plans had all been approved. If we changed the builder now, we would have to do it all again. And although it would have been nice to use a local chap, Mr Kofinas had always been honourable and we were already indebted to him for trusting us.

Stamos accepted this with a smile and started to measure up the land. He would need a JCB digger to level the land where the house would sit and to dig for the drains and septic tank. The concrete base would need to be reinforced with a network of steel to stop it cracking, and we would need to wait until autumn to lay the concrete because if it cured too quickly in the scorching sun, it would crumble.

We didn't mind. We now had water and temporary electricity. We had Stamos to deal with the preparation works. We were still saving every penny of our rent received from our shop in Glyfada. I was still working in London and saving. Alex was working in Glyfada, so our savings were growing. This temporary delay would allow us to build more capital.

We paid Stamos a deposit to get started and agreed to stage payments for each part completed. We were progressing towards our dream.

5

GRAND DESIGNS IN A GREEK VILLAGE

L ate in November, Stamos called me while I was working in England. He had finished the work on our land. The drains were done, the concrete base laid. He assured us it looked good and asked us to come to see. I was due to take some time off from my work in mid-December and spend Christmas with the family in Greece. Friday morning, I arrived at Athens airport and went straight to Glyfada. Alex had been working on

Debbie to convince her to get behind us on our project. She already saw the struggle we had endured to buy the land; she had watched as we counted our pennies to have water and electricity connected. She had taken an interest in the building design and was getting involved in choosing the colour scheme of the kitchen units and bath tiles. Debbie could see that we were not just talking about it but doing it, and without borrowing money or putting our Glyfada home at risk.

Debbie had never seen her daughter show so much determination and was proud of her.

I remember her words when we first approached her with the idea.

'Peter, you are a dreamer, and so is my daughter,' she told me.

Yes. Alex and I are dreamers. But it never ends there. Alex and I talk. Not just conversations about the weather, or what to cook for lunch. No, we discuss philosophy; we talk about life; we study each other's interests, hopes and dreams. We arrive at a decision through long and in-depth discussion and thought. But once we have agreed, we are unstoppable. We will unite to not just dream but focus on turning our dreams into reality. Alex's brother once commented on this.

'You two always seem to agree on everything,' he told me. 'My wife and I will argue for a week about buying a mirror, and which wall to put it on. You two just get on with building an entire house; no arguments, you just get on with it and always work together.'

Before we got together, we both had difficult relationships. We had both married young to the wrong partners and had each suffered in our own way. Alcoholism afflicted my first wife, and she died young after a long and difficult addiction. Our relationship consisted mostly of meaningless alcohol-fuelled fights and arguments as I misguidedly thought I could cure her affliction. I didn't realise the error of my ways until I attended a local group for relatives of alcoholics. There I learned the three Cs.

You did not cause it.

You cannot control it

You cannot cure it.

As a forty-year-old widower, at first I blamed myself, but as time went on, I realised I had not lived. My life comprised two jobs. One, making a living, the other, a full-time carer, with nothing in between.

Alex also suffered. Her Italian husband didn't consider working an honourable occupation and often told Alex, 'Only fools work.'

He would spend his time in the bars and cafes of Glyfada mixing with the wrong people, wheeling and dealing with one scam or another. He never provided an income to the family, and frequently items from the home would disappear as he took the TV or VCR to sell in payment for one of his debts.

Alex's life comprised trying to support a husband who promised her the world and gave her nothing. So, she committed the ultimate sin for a Greek family and divorced him. No one in her family had ever divorced. Marriage was sacred. You had made a promise to God. She became the talk of the village and the subject of local gossip for years afterwards. But although this hurt, it was better than living an uncertain life where there was no future.

So, Alex and I came together after experiencing life the hard way. I often wonder if we would have made it as a couple if we had not suffered as we did. Would we truly have appreciated each other if we had never felt the lash of our lived experience?

Philosophy teaches us we can never experience true happiness unless we have suffered. In our case, this was so true.

Right from the start of our relationship, I have never lied to Alex. She has never lied to me. I would promise nothing I felt I could not do. Alex initially felt a little insecure with me. Her past life had taught her to be on her guard: not to fall too deeply in love, not to give the ultimate trust. I had to earn this honour by deeds, not words.

'Don't listen to what I say, just watch what I do,' I would tell her. And this I kept to and still live by it now.

So yes, we are dreamers. But we have also had nightmares.

I had also noticed that Debbie had changed a little with me. She had always been incredibly kind and supportive and had invariably shown me the utmost respect as her son-in-law. But I always detected a little fear in her eyes. She had never seen a husband and wife work together so well as Alex and me. Her father had always been the decision maker in her family. Her mother would just accept anything he said and obediently comply. Here was a genuine couple, both pulling in the same direction for a shared dream, both equally hard-working and determined. The fear had lessened her in her eyes and had been replaced by a look approaching respect.

Debbie had always been the worker in our family. Her marriage to Alex's father had never gone smoothly, and she feared the same for Alex. Her wisdom was not in doubt, but because of her own lived experience, she feared we were putting ourselves in too deep and risked losing everything. She had watched over the years as her father's legacy had slowly eroded away and all she had left was our home in Glyfada. She had owned property in Athens, which she had to sell to keep the family safe and pay for Alex's and her brother's education. She had sold another to finance a failed business project for her husband. Only now was she beginning to feel that she could at last have peace in her old age and didn't want the worry of another building project in the family.

Debbie had finally secured all the paperwork Zissis needed to live and work in Greece. Zissis was content to take an allowance from his father and let Debbie's salary support herself. This was not the partnership Debbie imagined when she first met this sophisticated, attractive man. It was not turning out to be an ideal marriage. The house where they would spend their life was nearing completion in Glyfada. Debbie was teaching full-time at Athens University, but Zissis spent his days sitting around the house or visiting friends for coffee. The family were becoming increasingly unhappy about Zissis's lack of motivation. They wanted to see their daughter enjoying a normal life and start a family. Something had to be done.

Debbie's father, Jannis, invited a friend to the house one Sunday afternoon. Stavros was a large man and the owner of two hotels in Athens. Stavros also ran a tour company, taking tourists to see the sights of Athens. The tourist industry in Greece was becoming buoyant after the war years and he needed employees. As Zissis spoke five languages, this would be an ideal job.

Zissis was under pressure from the family and agreed to take the job. With their combined salary, they found a small apartment to rent near Sigrou in Athens and moved out of the family home. Debbie at last felt like a housewife and her life was changing for the better. Zissis took to his new job with enthusiasm and was soon promoted to take a more active role in running the tourist side of Stavros's business. In those days, Debbie saw very little of Zissis. He would leave home early, stay in Athens during the evening, and sometimes didn't come home at all. Debbie didn't mind as at least he had a good job and would be able to support a family once they moved into the Glyfada house. Finally, the house was ready. Debbie made plans to move in and spent her days off visiting furniture shops with her mother. One evening, she suggested to Zissis that they should give notice on their small apartment and move to Glyfada.

Zissis disagreed. He had been to Glyfada and inspected the new house, and didn't like the idea of living in a village with earth roads. He had been born into a wealthy family in Constantinople in an excellent area and felt village life would be below him. He complained Glyfada was too far away from his work and flatly refused to move, suggesting Debbie should live there. He would stay at weekends. Although this arrangement was not ideal, it worked to a certain extent, and Debbie went about setting up home alone. Some weekends, Zissis would visit. But he mostly led his own life from his apartment in Athens. As he was now doing well with his job, money started to come to Debbie. With this extra cash, she could work a little less and make the Glyfada house into a home. But Zissis still refused to live there, even though Debbie announced she was pregnant. As the pregnancy progressed, Debbie found she was tiring easily and in the latter months, gave up her job to prepare for the arrival of the baby. On a sunny October day, the world became a brighter place. Alex was born. Zissis took little interest in the new baby. After all, it was not a son, only a daughter. So Bia moved into the Glyfada house to help Debbie. Two years later, Debbie gave birth again, this time to a son.

As Debbie had warmed to the idea of our new building project, we decided to take her to the village and see for herself. We called our new friends at the local hotel. They had closed for the winter but agreed to open just for us.

We arrived in Pefki, checked into the hotel and went straight to the land. We had never seen anything other than weeds and bamboo there, so were keen to see the progress. It was amazing. Where before there was just bumpy ground, now there was a smooth concrete structure shining in the winter sun. It was huge, much bigger than we had expected. We walked over the new concrete with the plans to our house held in front of us in outstretched arms. I stood in our bedroom while Alex explored the imaginary kitchen. Debbie went into one of the imaginary bathrooms and inspected the waste pipe protruding from the floor. It was still only a slab of concrete in a jungle, but it was *our* slab of concrete in *our* jungle. Alex and I stood on this grey slab of concrete and realised this was going to be our new home.

Debbie asked about the size of the garden. We had still not seen all of our land; most of it was still a tangle of thorn bushes and tall bamboo. Without a machete and a few days to spare, we still had to guess the full extent. But this didn't matter yet. We were progressing with the house now, and the garden would come later.

I walked out of the gate and onto the road outside. I looked down. Instead of walking on the earth road, I was standing on a new tarmac road. I was so engrossed in seeing the progress on our land, I hadn't noticed it on the way in. It was jet black and smooth, leading all the way down to the beach five hundred metres away. Wow, that was progress.

Debbie and Alex came towards the car. I pointed to the road and smiled.

'That's because the English lord has come to the village,' Debbie joked.

Debbie wanted to see a little of the village, but being

Christmastime, it was mostly closed for the winter. A few tavernas were still open near the harbour, so we left the car to walk the short distance. As we got to the beach and turned left towards the harbour, a moped stopped beside us. It was the mayor.

'Geia sou Pétro, geia sou Alexándra. Pós eísai símera?' he asked.

'We're fine. How are you?'

Alex introduced her mother. Debbie smiled and shook his hand.

'We are going for lunch. Would you like to join us?' she asked.

'Love to,' he replied. 'I'll see you there.' He turned his moped and with a sound like an angry wasp, was gone.

We continued our walk along the deserted beach. Although it was midwinter, the air was warm and the sun was shining. We stood on the shingle by the sea and gazed out over the flat calm, stunningly blue water. I pointed out the island of Skiathos. We could just make out the shape of the next island, Skopelos, in the distance. Debbie's smile widened. I could see that she was also beginning to fall in love with this village. Debbie had also been born and grew up in a fishing village, but hers was the village of Castella, a suburb of Piraeus. There was always someone about. The roads and harbour were always busy year-round. Glyfada, being an up-and-coming city, was also lively. But here, standing on a deserted seashore, looking along the three-mile beach with not another human in sight, was a strange experience for her. She was used to people but found the calm and peace of the place intoxicating.

We continued our walk to the harbour. Costas had already arrived, and his moped was propped up and leaning on a tree opposite the taverna entrance. The heat from the log fire warmed our faces as we walked through the door and were met by the owner.

'Welcome, Peter and Alexandra. Costas is keeping your table over there.' Costas had chosen a table with a beautiful view of the harbour and colourful fishing boats. He insisted on sitting with his back to the view to allow Debbie to sit opposite to appreciate the beauty through the window.

'What do you think of your new road?' Costas asked.

'It's lovely,' Alex replied. 'Are you resurfacing all the earth roads in the village?'

'No, only yours,' the mayor said. 'We want you to feel welcome. We were resurfacing the main road and had some tarmac left over. Most of the people here have tractors or four-wheel-drive trucks, so they can easily drive on the earth roads. You only have a car, so you need to be comfortable.'

This amazed me. The mayor, whom we had to fight with to get water, had not only connected our supply but had given us an entire new surfaced road, just so we felt comfortable. This was incredible kindness, but only a minor example of things to come.

The taverna owner came over with a basket of fresh baked bread, a large red tin jug of wine and five glasses. He took one glass, filled it from the jug and held it up.

'Stin ygeiá sas and welcome,' he said, before swallowing it in one gulp and refilling it. 'What food would you like today? I have fresh shrimps which I can grill on charcoal, fish Yannis over there caught this morning' – he waved his glass towards another table nearby – 'and we have lovely calamari.'

We were all hungry so ordered a portion of everything. That lunch lasted three hours. By the time we left the restaurant it was dark outside. We had met new lifelong friends, enjoyed one of the best meals we had ever eaten, and Debbie now fully understood why we wanted to build our new home here.

The next day, we were back in Glyfada. We had arrived tired from our trip the previous day. Debbie came to our apartment and made some coffee. We sat around the table holding our cups and chatted about Pefki. Debbie had loved the village, she loved the people she had met, and all her concerns seem to have evaporated. She held her cup between her chubby hands and looked into my eyes.

'I am sorry, my son. I have misjudged you. You are not just a dreamer, you are definitely a doer,' she told me. Then she surprised me by asking, 'Can we go and see the villa company?'

'Of course, Debbie,' I replied. I was so happy she was taking an interest. 'We will go now. We would love you to see one of his villas.'

We drove the short distance to Mr Kofinas, the villa company. He came out and shook Debbie's hand and complimented her on her daughter. Debbie asked to see the computer picture of the villa, and discuss the colours of tiles, and the kitchen.

Then, once she had seen everything, she smiled and asked, 'So, how much more deposit do you need to start work?'

We had been steadily paying money to his villa company, but there was still a considerable sum outstanding. He told Debbie the amount.

'Okay, I will pay the balance. When can you start work?'

Alex's eyes filled with tears. She grabbed her mother, hugged and kissed her. She was overcome with her generosity. But although I saw the happiness in Alex's eyes, it conflicted me. I had never asked or expected anything from anyone. Alex and I had decided to build our home through our own hard work and determination. I had already promised Debbie that I would never ask her for anything and never put her at risk with our new venture. Now here she was, giving away her life savings to help us finish our dream.

I looked into Debbie's tearful eyes and loved her for doing this. I looked at the enthusiasm in Alex's eyes. Even Mr Kofinas was mopping away tears.

'Sorry, Debbie, I can't let you do this,' I found myself telling her. 'You have already given us too much. We live in a new penthouse apartment in Glyfada, the most expensive part of Greece. You have given us a shop which gives us an income. Now you are offering to give us everything else you own. Sorry, Debbie, I love you for this, but we cannot accept.'

Debbie looked at me with tears still in her eyes and squeezed my hand.

'You are my son, and the husband of my daughter. I gave you the old house built by Alexandra's grandfather, which was falling into ruin. You and Alexandra created what we all have now. You both ran the building project. You dealt with the architect. I know the trouble and suffering you both endured building the beautiful apartment block we now have. If they had left it up to me, I could never have achieved what you both did. All I am doing is to give you a small seed to grow another beautiful tree. Please, take my daughter and build your dream.'

Since ancient times Greek mothers have always been the stronger parent, something rooted deep into the Greek culture. Trying to change their opinion once they have made their mind up is almost impossible. But here, Debbie was showing me she was cutting the 'umbilical cord' connecting her to her daughter at last.

She reached out and held Alex's hand.

'With our mother's blessing, we say take your mother's blessing and climb all the mountains.'

Alex looked at me and nodded. It was agreed. Debbie paid the balance of the deposit. Mr Kofinas agreed to give us extended finance on the balance once he had completed our house, so we were ready to build.

It would take two months to have the house panels built in the factory before being shipped on lorries to Evia. Once on site, it would take another month to complete the construction. We would need to arrange a hotel from mid-March to mid-April for the workers. So, we contacted our new friend who owned the hotel in Pefki. As it was off-season, he agreed to open the hotel especially and ensure the cheapest rates. We were all set. In April, we would have a new home.

There was nothing more to be done. Alex and I went back to normal life while we waited. I continued my schedule of working weekdays in England, while Alex ran her beauty therapy and physiotherapy business from Glyfada. We needed to work as much as possible now to chase our dream, so I restricted my visit to one weekend every month. As winter turned into spring, the building in Pefki began.

We resisted the temptation to see the building progress during my monthly visits to Greece. We didn't want to see it half done, and Mr Kofinas had asked us to stay away and leave his chaps to it. He had obviously dealt with difficult owners in the past who had seen their properties half-constructed and got under the feet of his workers, delaying the project. We were determined not to be one of those difficult clients.

On the fifteenth of April, Mr Kofinas called to tell us our house was ready.

When the call came, I was still in England. I finally arrived at Athens airport two days later. The weather was warming up and the Greek spring was underway. Alex ran across the arrival hall, and in true Alex style, jumped and wrapped her legs around me. We had been apart too long, but we were desperate to see our new villa. This time, we did not go to Glyfada but turned out of the car park and headed for our new island home.

We drove up through the mountains of Evia. Today it seemed every tractor and painfully slow truck had been let loose onto the single-lane road heading north. Our excitement built as we were frustratingly held up by mile after mile of slow-moving vehicles, with no chance of overtaking. But after what felt like the longest car journey ever, we finally turned the corner into our road.

Then we saw it. It was enormous, much bigger than we could possibly have imagined. A red-tiled, centrally pitched roof towered against the blue sky, supported by gleaming white timber supports extending from the front of the house over a terrace of sand-coloured mosaic tiles. The front door was set up a few steps and flanked by two large windows. Another two doors from the front bedrooms opened onto the terrace, just a few metres from the road. It was magnificent. We had seen drawings and computer-generated reconstructions, but none of this prepared us for the sheer size of this house.

Alex and I stepped through our front door for the first time and our eyes were filled with beauty. The first thing we saw was the incredibly high ceiling. It had followed the contours of the roof and was like a barn. White supporting timbers spread from the side, with two king post trusses to make up the effect. The living area had the new kitchen; rosewood cupboard doors gleamed in the sun shining through the new windows. There were two bedrooms on each side of the villa, separated by bathrooms: one decorated with blue tiles, the other with warm pink. The bedrooms, two at the front and two at the rear, all had windows to the side and doors opening onto the patio. Fitted silver-grey cupboards and drawers had been installed in every bedroom. The floors were tiled throughout with matching sand-coloured ceramic. The rear of the house had French windows leading to the back-garden jungle. It was perfect. We had no boundary walls – the house sat in the middle of a jungle of bamboo and thorn bushes – but we didn't care; this would all come in time.

All we needed to do was move in. We had ordered the furniture to arrive in the next day or two. Meanwhile, we had an inflatable bed, a loaded fridge and a kettle. We slept that first night in our new home with the windows open, listening to the sound of the crickets in the nearby trees. It was perfect.

On our first morning in our new house, I woke up to the sound of scraping on my bedroom door and tinkling bells. I pulled my dressing gown on and sleepily looked out of the window. A large goat looked back at me. He was standing upright with his front hoofs tapping on the glass. I opened the door to the garden, and he watched me suspiciously as I stepped onto the patio. Rubbing the sleep from my eyes, I patted him on the head and wished him good morning. A voice came from further away.

'Kaliméra.' A shepherd was waving at me. He was holding a long staff, and a small white dog sat by his side, its tongue lolling out of the corner of its mouth. Scattered around my garden, there was an entire flock of goats happily munching on my land.

'Kaliméra,' I replied. 'Coffee?'

'Yes. five sugars, no milk,' he replied, 'and some feta with a little bread.'

I went back into the house to make his coffee and cheese sandwich while wondering why he had brought his flock of goats to visit. Perhaps he was trying to sell me some?

Soon I was back in the garden with his breakfast. I didn't ask why he had visited – maybe this was a village custom that I was unaware of – and instead complimented him on his goats and discussed the weather while he sipped his coffee and finished his sandwich before leaving with his flock close behind.

I later discovered that before I built my house, the goats would graze on this land every day. 'That will not end just because you built a house on it,' the locals informed me.

Alex and I dressed and stepped out into the street. We stood back to admire our house in the morning sunshine.

'Kaliméra, welcome,' came a voice from behind us.

It was our neighbour standing at his gate. He introduced himself as George. He had lived in the village for the past few years after returning from Australia. George used to have a karate and boxing school in Athens, but gave it up to live a peaceful life here. Although George was semi-retired, he still ran a small boxing school from his garage. A few locals would arrive most Thursday evenings to spend a couple of hours learning to box and punching each other.

He was happily reminiscing about his life in Australia, his karate school in Athens and his move to this village, when his expression changed and a serious look spread across his face.

'Be careful of your river,' he warned us. 'In the wintertime, it floods and runs down the street and into my garden. There is water everywhere.' He put his hand near his knee to emphasise the height of the flood water.

'We have a river?' I asked.

'Yes, over there at the end of your garden.' He waved his hand in the direction of the wall of bamboo to the rear of our land. I was delighted. I had no idea that as well as buying a piece of land, we now also owned a stretch of river. This was great news. I had always wanted a house on a river. I could buy a boat and make a little jetty. I could pass warm summer evenings sitting on my riverbank with my fishing rod. It would be perfect, if only I could find it.

We had only cleared enough of our land to build the house. The rest of the land was unknown and hidden by gigantic walls of bamboo and head-high barriers of prickly brambles. Walking through the impenetrable jungle was impossible.

The next day our furniture arrived. Alex hung curtains while I spent the day assembling the flat-pack furniture. By the evening, it was done. We had beds, basic furniture, and cupboards ready to be filled. We stood back hand in hand and looked around at our creation. We had done it.

We were far too exhausted to grasp the reality of what we had done. We just wandered around the house, silently staring into space, waiting to wake up from this dream. Since we arrived the day before, every moment had been taken up by working to make our home liveable. We had been far too busy to look past the next box that needed opening, or the missing screws from the bed frame that had rolled under one of the crates. But here and now, the reality hit us. We had a villa on a Greek island. We both needed that short period of silent reflection to stand back and appreciate the enormity of our achievement. But it was short-lived. After all, we were not finished yet.

First had to be the clearance of the land and, for the first time, seeing what was hidden under the dense jungle. We could then plant a few trees and perhaps a build a seating area. We still had a muddy patch of earth leading to the steps up to our front door. We still needed a wall around the land and a gate. But this could all come later. Alex was keen to get the garden in order but has a fear of snakes so great that she refused to go into it, her fear being fuelled by local gossip about how many snakes they found in the village and being told not to leave milk outside for the cats because it attracts them. I finally persuaded her to venture out by buying a set of angler's waders that were held up by thick rubber braces and covered her feet, legs and belly.

The Greek word for snake is pronounced feeth-ee. It is a hated creature. But it hasn't always been this way. Indeed, the recognised sign of Hippocrates is a snake wrapped around a staff to show the powers of healing. In ancient Greece, snakes represented wisdom and eternal life and were used as part of the healing process. In some temples, non-venomous snakes would freely crawl over their sleeping patients, licking them along the way. It was believed that contact with the snakes, as well as being licked by the reptiles, would help cure the sick.

Not in our village. This unfortunate creature does not benefit from the usual kindness shown to the furry type of animal and is killed on sight. Drivers will swerve across the road to run one over if spotted, and the locals will always kill one if it's found anywhere near them.

The sight of Alex walking around the garden wearing green waders and a bikini top keeps me giggling at the memory. I finally dismissed some of her fears when we went to see the old man who sold trees.

The chap was in his nineties and had sold plants to the village all his life. While browsing around the nursery looking for ideas for our garden, Alex casually asked the old man, 'Are there many snakes in this village?'

This was a make-or-break question. A wrong answer would probably mean selling the house and moving back to the safety of the city.

I stood behind Alex. Unknown to her, I was wildly gesticulating at him, shaking my head and mouthing *Nooooo*, and praying for the right answer to save our home. The old man understood and looked into her eyes.

'Madam, I have lived in this village for ninety-five years, and I can assure you I have never seen a snake.'

I could have kissed him!

Our garden was still an untidy field of weeds, brambles, and large holes in the ground that the archaeologists made to ensure we didn't have any of the missing Parthenon marbles buried there. I was keen to find my river, so we set about trying to clear the land.

Alex, wearing her fisherman's waders up to her armpits to protect herself from the dreaded snakes, and a bikini on top in case she got hot, hacked away for hours with a machete, creating a small clearing further up the garden, while I chopped a path towards the elusive river. Apart from the small weedless area, it was just a field with no boundaries. Every time we stood back to admire our work, it seemed like more weeds had grown and we were back at square one.

We stopped for a break. I went inside the house and made some coffee, dragged a couple of chairs from the kitchen, and we both sat and sipped our coffee while looking at the mountainous task ahead of us. It was getting hot and the sun was beating down on my head. 'Let's rest today,' I suggested. 'We can carry on tomorrow.'

'I think we need a bulldozer,' I joked as Alex came to sit next to me. She smiled and nodded with a familiar glint in her eye. I had inadvertently given her an idea.

I erected a makeshift canopy and sat to read a book. Alex rarely sits down and busied herself with dusting the new house, arranging furniture, and generally pottering around while I read under my shade. After a while, Alex appeared from the house wearing her anti-snake fisherman's waders and bikini top with her machete in hand, ready for some more gardening. I apologised. Although it was still May, the temperature was rising as the hot Greek summer approached. It was touching thirty degrees and felt even hotter in the full sun. It was still a little hot for me to help with the hard digging.

Being blond with blue eyes, the midday Greek sun caused a rapid sap of my strength. If I even walked to the end of the garden, I would melt into a puddle and likely evaporate into nothing. I suggested we leave it until later when it cooled down and we could do it together. Alex agreed and went back into the house, leaving me to continue my reading.

I hadn't heard Alex for an hour and was wondering what she was up to. Alex is like a small child. When you can't hear them, they are usually up to something naughty. The reason everything was temporarily quiet revealed itself a few moments later when I felt the ground shake, accompanied by an increasingly loud rumble as a huge yellow JCB entered our garden with a smiling Alex hanging off the side.

'Look what I found!' she yelled over the noise as she jumped to the ground.

'That's nice,' I shouted over the sound of the engine. 'Where on earth did you find that?'

She ran over to explain. She remembered seeing the JCB parked outside a house nearby, and she went and knocked on the door. The old lady inside told her it belonged to her son who was working in Athens, but assured her a friend of his could drive it.

'You can find him near the harbour. He always goes there for his coffee in the morning.'

Alex, determined to surprise me with a bulldozer, went down to the harbour to find the driver. The sight of an attractive woman searching all the local cafes wearing angler's waders and a bikini top, asking for a bulldozer driver, must have been a first in this village. But Alex didn't care, and she eventually found him.

For the next two hours, the JCB rumbled up and down our garden, eating everything in its path. He had bulldozed all the brambles and weeds, together with tons of earth, old metal frames and rusty feta cheese tins.

Suddenly Alex waved at me from the end of the garden.

'I've found the river,' she yelled.

I rushed to where Alex was standing. I looked down into the dry riverbed. This was disappointing. The 'river' was only a small ditch, about two metres wide. There was no water, just a few dry stones and weeds sporadically growing at the base. A small frog watched me as I jumped down the bank and stood on some pebbles. My vision of a small pontoon and a little boat tied up to it evaporated. I could no longer imagine myself sitting on the banks on warm summer evenings, catching local trout from this ditch. But now I was in the riverbed, I decided to explore.

I turned right and walked upstream away from the sea. As I turned the bend, it became wider, and the banks higher. Ahead of me was a bridge. I went into the dark tunnel and emerged to see a hamlet with a bakery on the corner above me. By now the river, although dry, was at least ten metres from bank to bank. I could see the evidence of water. There were no longer weeds growing on the pebble bed. The bank had been replaced by high concrete walls on either side. There was a tide mark above my head which showed this had recently been a raging torrent. But now, because of the lack of rain, it had become dry and dusty. This would be a threat to my house. My neighbour's warning had been real, and if this river filled, it would be a danger.

I turned around and followed the riverbed the other way towards the sea. It narrowed still more as I passed the end of my garden. A few metres on, the banks levelled out, and the river seemed to end at a large white wall. Someone had built a house on the riverbed. So, the enormous river in the nearby village would take the water from the surrounding mountains, past my house, then come up against a house built in the stream and go no further. Physics dictates that if it could go no further, it would all back up and come my way. Never mind about a pontoon and a little boat; I was going to have a lake every winter.

So while the JCB digger was here, we arranged for the earth to be piled along the bank to form a barrier. We could always plant flowerbeds on it to make it look nice. But I still had a worried feeling that the bank would not be enough to prevent the flooding. Summer was here, though, so I assumed that I didn't need to worry too much yet. There were lots of other things we needed to do first. But I would certainly be proved wrong about that soon.

When it finally finished the mass destruction of our garden, the JCB trundled back up the road, carrying its driver off to continue his coffee while we surveyed our flattened land. It was enormous. We had never seen it without the towering weeds and bamboo plants, and had never walked around it because of the brambles, which were like prickly walls. We had no idea how big it actually was. Now we were standing in the middle of a freshly ploughed field almost devoid of any vegetation and looking like the surface of the moon, with only an apple and an olive tree left standing, which we didn't know we had. The apple tree had a few sad-looking fruits hanging from its sparse branches. It was completely bare of leaves at the base, and there were just a few at the top where it had found some sunlight. The olive tree looked to be over a hundred years old, with a hollow trunk and only a few leaves sprouting from the top where it had fought for its share of light with the rampant bamboo. They both looked sickly, but they were ours and needed to be protected and nurtured back to health.

As part of our planning permission, it was necessary to have the land inspected by the Greek equivalent of the forestry commission to ensure there were no protected species on the proposed building plot. They missed these poor specimens because they had been hiding in the undergrowth. If the inspector had realised we had an ancient olive tree on our land, it may have been a problem getting permission to build. But it wouldn't have mattered anyway. As soon as the olive tree received its long-overdue sunshine dose, the shock was too much and it promptly died and fell over.

So, we now had an enormous field of dust and earth which somehow we needed to make into a garden. Being English, my first thought was grass. The problem is that lawns are very rare in Greece. After asking around, trying to find a turf supplier, we were getting a reputation in the village. They had all heard about our spot of gardening with the bulldozer and were keen to see what we would do next. I was sure I'd overheard the words 'Mr Bean' more than once, and coming from Athens, Alex had no chance; the people in the next village are only tolerated because they have the same accent. The locals are always polite and friendly, but a conversation usually ends with them wandering off, shaking their heads in amazement at these strange xénos (foreigners) who built a house here.

In villages everything has a purpose. A dog is not a pet, but there to guard the home or help with the goats or sheep. A cat may live in the area because it's useful for catching mice and dealing with the odd snake that slithers by. Vehicles are usually pickup trucks or tractors, and trees are planted for fruit or shade. They grow vegetables and fruit for the table; flowers are grown to be picked to decorate the local church or to be exchanged for useful products like olive oil and eggs.

So, this strange foreigner has become the subject of local discussion. I was asking where I could buy flowers because they would make my garden pretty and smell nice. Stamos, the local builder, had shared with the village my idea of building a lattice frame in the garden to support nothing, and plant orna-mental trees that don't produce fruit.

So, when I decided to plant a lawn, the gossip increased. I was told that grass won't grow properly here, it will attract mosquitoes, and snakes can hide there – not to mention the amount of water needed to keep it green.

Undeterred, I finally found some grass seed and got fifty kilos, which should be enough. After all, the odd snake bite, or losing a litre of blood here and there to the savage insects, is nothing compared to looking at a nice green lawn.

I spent the day toiling under the scorching sun, tilling the soil, throwing generous handfuls of seeds on every patch of bare earth until I was satisfied that every inch of exposed soil was covered. I went to bed dreaming of my nice new stripy lawn, imagining sitting on a ride-on lawnmower. I had always wanted one of those.

The next morning, I woke up keen to see if any of the seeds had germinated. I checked the earth. Yesterday, I had thrown so much grass seed on the ground that it was no longer a muddy brown but had a nice yellow sheen of seeds sitting on top, covering the whole garden. Now, the garden had somehow transformed back to earth. Not one seed was visible. I searched the garden. All gone. But where had they gone to? It hadn't rained last night, so they couldn't have been washed away. The weather was still, with no wind, not even a flutter of the trees next door, so they couldn't have blown away. I needed to solve this mystery of the disappearing seed. Crawling over the earth with my nose to the ground, I looked for at least one. Out of the corner of my eye, I noticed something. I focused, and there it was. One grass seed. But it was moving. I looked more closely and saw that it was being carried by a tiny ant. I looked further; there, disappearing into the distance, was a line of ants stretching as far as I could see. Each with one of my precious grass seeds on its head. Following the line, I saw a hole in the ground with an army of more ants stuffing them down into the nest.

I sat on the ground and watched as they kept busy. My mind wandered. Grass seeds must be rare in this area, so how did they know they were good to eat? Also, which ant had the bright idea, and how did that enterprising individual spread the word to the millions of other ants in the area and get them to all work together? I can't imagine trying to get a million humans together for a single purpose; that would certainly be a challenge.

This must be the ultimate act of democracy in the land that invented it. Perhaps the ancient Greeks had the idea while trying to plant a lawn. Either that, or pure communism. Anyway, I didn't have time for any more philosophical discussion with myself. I had to buy some more grass seed.

6

USELESS BIRDS OF GREECE

By now, I was spending less time in England. I found I could deal with most of my work remotely and concentrate on finishing our house here.

We were getting to know our neighbours. At first, it was just a wave or a smile of recognition as we passed, then people started to stop and chat, or arrive at our house with baskets of lemons or oranges as a gift from their gardens. Others left eggs on our doorstep. One day, we were sitting in the garden and heard a voice from the front door.

'Kaliméra. Boró na bo?' (Can I come in?) she asked.

Alex opened the door while dragging a chair out for her. 'Fysiká, éla mésa, kalós írthes.' (Welcome, please come in.)

She introduced herself as Maria, a short, red-faced and cheerful lady, who smelled of lavender and wore a black dress, her grey hair tied into a bun. She looked to be in her early sixties and was struggling with an enormous basket of oranges and lemons. They looked and smelled beautiful and were obviously just picked as the leaves attached to the green stems were still fresh. I relieved her of the burden and thanked her for such a lovely present.

'Apó to dikó mou déntro ekeí péra.' (They are from my own tree over there.)

She waved her hand towards the nearby village as she squeezed herself onto a chair at the table. This was the last time Maria asked permission to enter. After that, she strolled in and out of our house freely, as if it were her own.

'Welcome to Artemision,' she said.

I was a little confused. I thought we had built our house in Pefki.

'Surely we are in Pefki?' I asked.

'Well, your front garden and kitchen are in Pefki, but your living room and back garden are in Artemision,' she informed us. We had built our house on the border between the two villages. I liked this idea. We owned property in two Greek villages.

We'd been so busy planning and building in what we thought was Pefki, we had completely ignored the nearby village of Artemision, which was just two hundred metres away from the back of our garden.

I made some coffee and put a cup in front of her.

Maria turned out to be a mine of information and knew everything about everyone in the village. She had been born here and had never travelled further than the local market town of Istiea, ten kilometres away. She didn't see the point. Everything she knew was here. Maria had no dreams of exploring the world; she was far too busy with the fascinating goings on in the village. Although the village looked sleepy on the surface, it turned out to have hidden depths.

We got to hear about the local loose widow who refused to dress in black – Maria was sure her husband died while trying to satisfy her insatiable appetite in a vain attempt to prevent her granting favours to the other men of the village.

She told us about the local priest who also ran the mall supermarket with his three children. A conspiratorial look spread over her face, and she looked left and right to make sure no one else was listening before she revealed the worst part.

'And he's divorced,' she confided.

There was the local alcoholic, her second cousin, but also the chief of police. She put her finger against the side of her nose and assured us if we ever had any trouble, he would help us.

There was another cousin, the local teacher, who often played truant to take tourists on boat trips.

Then we sat open-mouthed as she told us about the coincidence of Nikos, the local carpenter, who had just married a girl less than half his age.

'It's such a romantic story,' she insisted.

Alex quietly translated the difficult words so I could keep up to speed with the story.

'Twenty years ago, Nikos had a girlfriend. He was very much in love with her. She was from another village four kilometres away, but despite that, she was a good person. Then Nikos found a local girl and called off the relationship because the other one lived too far away and he wasn't keen on a long-distance relationship.'

Alex and I, too, had a long-distance relationship. But ours was a little more distant.

She continued her story.

'So Nikos never married. He had a few girlfriends over the years, but they didn't last long. When he realised they were no good at cutting wood and loading his truck, he would end the relationship. Then a year ago, he met his dream girl. She was strong, could carry a fifty-kilo bag of cement and was fantastic at cutting wood. She also lived in a village four kilometres away, but he was definitely in love this time and would give her the bus fare to visit him instead of walking.'

'That's romantic,' I said to Alex in English.

Alex stifled a giggle and refused to look at me in case she burst out laughing.

Maria continued.

'They announced their engagement. Nikos hadn't yet met her parents, though, so he had to travel to meet her mother in the village. Her father had left many years ago, before the girl was born. But guess what? And here's the coincidence … Her mother was his ex-girlfriend from twenty years ago. Isn't that romantic?'

The coffee I was sipping suddenly found itself spat over the table. I looked at Alex, who had not yet seen the fact of this romance which was staring her in the face.

I apologised to Maria as I mopped up the spat coffee with a tissue, trying to keep a neutral look on my face. I could feel the laughter rising and tried to ignore my shoulders, which were shaking as I tried to breathe without giggling.

'Yes, that is romantic,' I told her. 'By the way, how old is the girl?'

'She's only nineteen, but strong and fit.'

Alex suddenly caught on to my thinking and sat with an incredulous look on her face.

Maria took this to mean that Alex had realised the romantic coincidence, and smiled.

Maria was obviously a very pure woman who would never have considered the possibility that perhaps Nikos was about to marry his daughter.

We were not going to pop that particular bubble.

By the time she left, we were exhausted and beginning to suspect we had built a house in a very interesting village. I had spent the last half hour mopping tears of laughter, which Maria took as my sensitive confirmation of her 'romantic story'. We wanted to know more, but needed to finish our home first.

It was Sunday. A church bell ringing woke us to announce the morning service in the nearby village. It was a nice day, so we thought we would take a walk to the church and light a candle. As we entered the dark building, we saw it was full, with standing room only. All eyes turned to us, and everything went quiet. Even the priest paused his song to look at the strange foreigners who had just wandered in. I watched nervously as people looked at my feet to see if they were smoking as I was standing on holy ground. They needed to see if they were likely to catch fire. People nudged each other and whispered together. I felt like I had just walked into a saloon in a Wild West movie where the piano player stops. There were no hostile stares, just curiosity. In the short time we had been in our home, from the kindness of the few people we had met, we were already feeling part of the village, but obviously, nobody ever thought we would be part of the congregation. People began to smile and nod as they recognised us. The priest recommenced his prosefchí while we stood at the back and watched as the service continued.

After the service, we left the church together and were greeted with smiling faces and handshakes. Even the priest came over to welcome us. On that day, I started to feel even more at home.

Since our visit to the church, we had noticed a difference in the village. People greeted us by name and made a point of crossing the road to chat rather than strolling past with a wave and smile.

Maria turned out to be the local Yellow Pages. Whatever we needed, she knew someone. If we needed a plumber, electrician, the best place to eat, best fruit supplier ... anything we needed, she had a contact.

As we were expecting to spend time away in Athens and the UK, we needed someone to take care of our growing garden during our absence. Maria suggested her nephew Dimitri. That afternoon, he arrived smelling of fish. He keeps his family by doing odd jobs around the village, a little gardening and plumbing. But his genuine passion is fishing and hunting. He owns a small rowing boat, which he takes out most mornings, and a twelve-bore shotgun that he keeps in his pickup truck in case he sees anything worth shooting.

Dimitri followed us around the garden and made a few suggestions. He agreed to return to take care of it during our absence and would come the next day with a few plants.

'My young wife is also very strong. She is always available if you need any cleaning while you are away. It would keep your lovely house fresh,' he suggested.

The next day we woke up to a strange noise of loud chattering coming from our garden. We went outside to find the source and there, perched on the overhead cables, were hundreds of colourful birds happily sitting and squawking loudly, having a conversation with each other. They were beautiful. All had green chests, red crowns, and a patch of yellow under their beaks. It amazed us to see so many of these exotic birds in our garden, but we had no idea what species they were. I rushed into the house, found some bread, and was throwing some around the garden to feed them when Maria arrived from the village. She saw us staring up at the show.

'What are they?' Alex asked her, pointing up to the beautiful birds spread along the telephone cables.

'Oh, they are useless xeni (foreign) birds. They come once a year on their way somewhere,' she replied as she waved her hand towards the sea. 'They don't taste very good though.'

Everything in the village must have a purpose. As these creatures were not very good to eat, the villagers ignored them.

I rushed into the house, grabbed my laptop, and found them on Google. They were bee eaters. These migratory birds had stopped off in my garden for a rest from their long journey south. I was quite pleased they were not tasty, otherwise every hunter in the village would be rushing to my garden to share in the harvest.

By nightfall they had all left to continue their journey after a day spent ignoring my bread and chatting amongst themselves.

The next morning, Dimitri arrived with a box full of plants for the garden. He had already heard about our strange fascination with these useless, inedible birds.

'I hear you like birds,' he told us.

'Yes, we have a bird table in our garden in England. We watch them from our window,' I said.

'So, you shoot them from your window?' he asked.

'No, we hang bags of nuts and watch them eat,' I replied.

This made no sense to Dimitri. He could not understand why we would just look at them without eating any. With that, he went out to his van and returned with a string of several dead blackbirds, all with bright yellow beaks. He laid them on the table.

'Now these are proper birds, and they are delicious. My wife cooks them stuffed with cheese. She can prepare some for you if you want?'

Alex and I looked at the unfortunate collection of blackbirds laid out on our dining table. Their little eyes were open, and some were lying with little yellow feet in the air. Alex nudged me to not show disapproval. She didn't want to offend Dimitri. To him, they were precious, and it was an honour to be offered such a valuable gift. But I really couldn't see myself plucking and cooking any of these poor creatures. We politely refused his generous gift. He simply shrugged his shoulders and put them back in his van, muttering about how strange we were not to like his birds. It was a little rude of us to refuse such a gift, but he didn't take offence.

The selection of birds in our village is small. Apart from the seagulls who hang around the harbour, and the tiny opportunistic sparrows who make their living stealing bread from taverna tables, there are few species left. We have a few members of the crow family hanging around our garden, magpies being the most common. The villagers call them karakáxa as they make an annoying sound like old women gossiping. There are also the occasional large black crows hopping around the lawn. Fortunately, they don't taste very nice either, so the villagers ignore them.

But sometimes even 'useless' birds can make a difference.

And on one island, a bird nearly started a war.

We recently went to Mykonos for a long weekend. It's a beautiful island, best known for jet-set lifestyles, celebrity visitors and all-night parties. But we went off-season, so it was a little quieter than in the summer. It was still warm enough to sit outside a beautiful taverna in the town, overlooking the harbour, and enjoy a leisurely lunch. We ordered our food and wine and sat to admire the view. It was a lovely atmosphere. The bougainvillea were still in bloom, climbing up the bright white walls of nearby houses. Window boxes stuffed with blood-red geraniums provided a contrast to the blue-painted windows. We could hear the sound of the waves gently lapping against the harbour wall and soft bouzouki music emanating from a radio inside the restaurant. Further away, we heard a canary singing. The cage was golden coloured and hung from a balcony so the little bird could observe the view. He sounded happy. So were we.

We could smell the fragrant food before it arrived: a sweet aroma of fresh fish grilled over charcoal, so reminiscent of all Greek islands. Greeks much prefer their fish cooked over charcoal.

We were tucking into our meze when I felt something brush against my leg under the table. I was used to the local cats. Every taverna in Greece has their resident population who are fed titbits from the tourists and locals, so one brushing against my leg was normal. I ignored it. I would give the little beggar a piece of fish soon. If I fed them too early in the meal, others would realise I was a soft touch and arrive trying to shame me into giving my lunch away. Then I felt a powerful push under the table, and the corner lifted and dropped back onto the cobbles with a thud. That's a strong cat, I thought.

Suddenly a giant beak appeared from under the table and slapped onto my knee. This was no cat; it must be a bird. If the rest of this creature was in proportion to that beak, we were in trouble. We must have a dinosaur-sized thing under our table.

I jumped back to get a better look. It was a pelican. It stood higher than my waist, looking at me with its small beady eyes. I reached to my plate and grabbed a small chunk of fish, which I offered to this enormous bird. It ignored it and carried on staring at me. The taverna owner came out and offered it a whole raw fish. The pelican opened his cavernous beak, took it, lifted his head and his whole body shook as he lifted his head to swallow.

We had met the famous pelican of Mykonos.

Petros the pelican (the Greek word 'pétro' means stone or rock, but can also mean grumpy and old) had been adopted as the island's mascot, although pelicans are not native to Greece. Petros was a white pelican, who was found hurt off the coast in 1958. He soon became a popular resident and tourist attraction of the island.

Early Christians considered the pelican a symbol of the crucifixion. They believed that young pelicans, when they push their beaks deep into their mother's pouch, are drinking her blood. In fact they are eating regurgitated fish, but because of those beliefs, pelicans have always been looked upon as objects of piety.

Other islanders took Petros's appearance as a sign of good luck and decided he should stay. One of the fishermen, Theodoris Kyrantonis, formed an immediate friendship with Petros and converted a large oil drum for him to sleep in next to his house. Petros learned to jump onto Theodoris's shoulder on command. The two communicated in a combination of Greek, squawks and grunts, and developed their own unique language. He and Petros were soon inseparable and fast became a popular attraction for the early tourists of Mykonos.

Petros did indeed bring good luck to the island. More tourists began to arrive, boosting the local economy. Most had come to see Petros.

Petros continued to lead a peaceful life, spending his days with his friends Theodoris and Nikita, a stork that lived on the island, and followed Theodoris everywhere he went. He was often seen sitting beside his friend in the local tavernas.

Then one day, Petros disappeared.

To the religious islanders of Mykonos, Petros's arrival was a sign that God had heard their prayers for help. Greeks at that time didn't usually keep pets. Dogs had a purpose: hunting, and keeping prowlers away. Cats would keep rodents under control so were useful. Petros was an exception. He had become everybody's pet; he had already gained celebrity status and was soon missed.

That morning, Petros had been out swimming and followed a boat to nearby Tinos, where he was instantly recognised. They decided to keep him. Using fish as a lure, they coaxed him into a nearby taverna and locked him up, clipping his flight feathers to prevent his escape. The islanders of Tinos considered the visit as voluntary migration, so now he belonged to them.

The authorities in Mykonos demanded they return him. The Tinos islanders refused. After all, they did not kidnap him; he had decided to come. Petros would stay if he wanted to. After all, he was just wandering around the port and wasn't being held captive.

There followed a bitter legal battle. Nothing of its like had been seen since the abduction of Helen of Troy. Neighbouring islands were going to war.

The Mykonians were outraged. The mayor contacted the prime minister of Greece and was told to settle the matter in the courts. The villagers were not prepared to wait that long. So, led by Petros's friend Theodoris, they assembled an armada of twelve fishing boats and set off for Tinos, where they were greeted on arrival by the mayor, a priest and the chief of police, and reporters from Athens who had been alerted to the impending war.

The mayor denied their pelican was Petros but agreed to bring him out. The pelican was produced from a cafe. Theodoris shouted, 'Come, Petros!' The bird at once lashed out with his powerful wings and bit the cafe owner's nose. The man yelped in pain and dropped the bird, who ran to Theodoris and jumped on his shoulder. The Mykonians cheered and the people of Tinos were embarrassed as they realised they had been caught out, and the Mykonians boarded their boats and returned in triumph with their mascot.

Petros's entrapment in Tinos was the first court case in Greece where the custody of a bird was decided. When finally Petros returned to Mykonos, there were celebrations in the streets with music and dancing and a public feast, and all the church bells on the island were rung.

For many years, Petros was seen strolling around the harbour and streets. Tourists and film stars would have their photographs taken with him. He had gained worldwide celebrity status.

Petros was a confirmed bachelor. They offered him several female companions over the years, including two pelicans sent by Jacqueline Kennedy, but they died a short time after they arrived. Irini, a pelican from Louisiana, was sent to be his bride, and they held a wedding. But Petros showed no interest in his new bride. He preferred his friend Theodoris. So, the marriage was never consummated and remained platonic. Irini never forgave Petros and just lived her life, snapping at tourists unwise enough to come too close.

The day before Easter in 1975, he was sitting near Theodoris, who was drinking wine with friends in a cafe. Suddenly, Theodoris slumped over in his chair and died. It is said that Petros remained next to Theodoris's coffin until they buried him. His son, Yorgos, carried on his father's love affair with the bird and cared for him until he died.

In the thirty years Petros was the mascot of Mykonos, rumours that he had died circulated from time to time, but the islanders swear there was only one Petros over that time. It would not be unusual: some pelicans have lived over fifty years.

The people say they can never replace their Petros, but in time, another pelican probably will be found, for there is a saying among the people of Mykonos: 'Only if you have seen the pelican will you return to the island'.

Petros was killed by a car on 2 December 1985, after more than thirty years on the island. Hamburg zoo donated a pelican, also named Petros, and some years later another wounded pelican found itself in Mykonos, where it was cared for by locals, who renamed it Nikolaos. Today there are at least three pelicans roaming around freely in Mykonos Town.

Petros is not the only curiosity in the birdlife of Greece. We have also met some surprising residents of another island.

We received an invitation from Panagiotis, a resident of the tiny island of Agistri. He asked us to visit and perhaps write an article about the island which could be included in the local newspaper or sold to help the island school buy some new computers. We were happy to visit and help if we could.

We had recovered from yesterday's hair-raising Athenian taxi ride and interesting cruise in the Flying Dolphin. But it was certainly worth it. I sat on the hotel balcony with a steaming coffee, watching the glittering sea, and planned the day.

First, breakfast overlooking the pool and the beach beyond. Then a leisurely stroll around the village and perhaps a coffee near the church. Maybe a nice fish lunch at the charming taverna overlooking the bay. Then a lazy afternoon reading. That was my day sorted.

But Alex had other ideas. She wanted to hire a bike to explore the island. I wasn't too keen as there were a lot of hills around, and being rather lazy, I didn't like the idea of sitting on a razor-blade saddle with my knees around my ears, trying to follow her up a mountain. But when my Alex puts her mind to something, I will never put her off. So, no leisurely, lazy day for me. I was going on a bike ride.

We went to see the guy who hires bikes to tourists. I was delighted; he had electric bikes. We never had those when we were kids. No furious pedalling for me; I would just let the motor do the work while I sat back to enjoy the scenery. All I had to think about was steering and not falling off.

But I failed at both.

We set off towards the next village. Alex sped off into the distance. I turned my dial to maximum power and followed. It was a strange experience. I simply pressed the pedal and off I went. I soon caught up as she turned towards the mountain road. There was a church at the top she had seen and decided we should visit. I didn't care. The bike was going uphill with almost no effort, so I happily followed. But as the road became steeper, I found I had to peddle a little more to compensate for the weak electric engine.

I was getting out of breath and my legs ached. Now I was suffering. Suddenly, there was a grinding sound, a puff of smoke, and the bike came to an abrupt halt. It was like hitting an invisible wall. With no forward motion, the bike tipped, and I fell off and rolled down a grassy slope, closely followed by the smoking bike. Alex, being far up the mountain ahead of me, had disappeared into the distance, leaving me lying on the ground with a spinning front wheel by my ear. But it was peaceful. I wasn't hurt, so I lay on my back and looked at the clear blue sky while I struggled to get my breath back. Then I felt it. A little tapping on my feet. I looked down, and there was a fully grown male peacock with a long, colourful tail, investigating my shoelaces.

I sat up as another approached me, then another. Three beautiful birds surrounded me and were curious to meet this strange red-faced, puffing creature who had rolled into their field. A few moments later, Alex returned to find out why I was no longer around. There I was, sitting in a field with three magnificent peacocks and a black chicken, with a still-smoking bike around my neck.

We had met the wild peacocks of Agistri.

Nobody knows where these birds came from. They just arrived and slowly grew in number. They now occupy the entire island. These feral birds make a nuisance of themselves. They squawk throughout the night and most of the day; they wander around the tavernas terrorising the local cat population. But for me they were an incredible sight. Peacocks are magnificent-looking birds, but they are also extremely loud. I have heard them before in England in some private estates, but there are usually only one or two ambling around making a noise. This is nothing compared to when there are lots of peacocks and peahens together all over the island. Their high-pitched noises sound like a baby crying or a cat meowing shrilly. They also produce a honking noise, which is also loud.

Agistri is a tiny but interesting island. As far as we could make out, it only has three villages: Megalochori (the capital of the island), Skala, which is less than a mile away, and Limenaria to the south. It has a population of around 1,200, but this swells to more than double in the tourist season.

The next day, Panagiotis, our guide, who doubled up as the island taxi driver, arrived to take us around to explore the island. Being tiny, it didn't take very long, but we visited all three towns, two beautiful, secluded beaches backed by pine forests, and a small church, which he claimed was haunted. He stopped the car outside but refused to enter with us. Saint Varvara is where St Nectarios of Aegina was sanctified. Alex tried to explain that this man was a saint, so he should not worry. But he remained in his car, clutching the steering wheel with white knuckles in case we tried to pull him out.

That afternoon, he introduced us to some of the older residents of the island. One lovely chap was in his late nineties but still ran the village shop. He remembered when he was a boy working in the fields. They did not pay him with money – that was no use on the island as there was nothing to buy. No, they paid him in olive oil. This was more valuable than currency and could be easily traded. Alex and I listened as he shared his memories.

When he was a young boy living in Skala, the residents of the next village were their mortal enemies. Although only a mile away, they would each keep to their own territory and never met unless they were throwing rocks at each other. This changed when someone from the nearby island of Aegina stole a donkey from the port of Megalochori and took it away. Being the only female donkey on the island, there was uproar. A meeting was held between the warring villages and a truce was agreed, and they combined forces to get the donkey back. After the brief war and victory over the raiders of Aegina, the donkey was recovered, and the new-found peace held, leading to the long-lasting friendship which remains today.

He did not know where the peacocks came from, though. According to him, they just arrived and became the local pests they are today. I didn't ask why I hadn't seen peacocks on any menus. Perhaps they were also useless birds that didn't taste very nice.

Dimitri would have thought he had reached paradise if he knew about Agistri. We didn't tell him because Agistri was noisy enough without the boom of twelve-bore shotguns added to the peacock cries.

'Okay, you don't like birds. Do you like fish?' he asked.

I was a little hesitant to answer. I wondered what strange aquatic creature was next to be pulled out of his pickup truck.

'Yes,' Alex replied, 'we love fish.'

This time, instead of rummaging through his truck, he told us he was going fishing the following morning and asked if we would like to join him on his boat.

I loved the idea. Alex, too, was keen. Over our years together, Alex had readily taken an interest in my fishing hobby. In England, we have had several deep-sea fishing trips on a charter boat and Alex had proved to be a natural. The first time we went was on a breezy day on the south coast. Alex was among me and eight other men, all experience anglers. As we motored out to the fishing grounds, they nudged each other and made private jokes about the 'dolly bird' and how perhaps she would use lipstick for bait. But as we started to fish, Alex pulled a five-pound cod over the side of the boat before anyone had even had a bite. This continued for most of the morning. Alex was catching three cod to their one. There were some rather depressed-looking faces on board, not only because they were being beaten by a woman, but as we set out from the harbour that morning, we had all put twenty pounds into the pot, and the one with the most fish that day would take all the money. Alex was way ahead and sure to win. She was pulling out her twentieth fish of the day when she called over to me.

'I can't pull this one up,' she yelled.

'Okay, I'll take over,' I assured her. The other men sniggered; it had proved them right. This girl was okay catching five-pound fish, but when a bigger one came along, she wasn't up to it.

I took her fishing rod and pulled. The fish pulled back. Line screamed off the reel as I tried to stop the fish running. Suddenly there was an almighty splash as a huge black fin appeared out of the sea, followed by a large, pointed nose and very sharp-looking teeth, and a five-pound cod in its mouth. It was a shark. While Alex had been pulling up her fish, a passing shark saw an easy meal and grabbed it. I pulled again, but the line went loose as the monster casually swam away. I pulled again and recovered the head of the cod. It had been bitten in half when the shark struck. After that experience, Alex was keen to take any opportunity to go fishing again.

The next morning, the sun was still below the horizon as Alex and I met Dimitri at the harbour. We boarded the small boat, and Dimitri rowed us out to his favourite fishing spot.

A short distance away from the harbour, he lifted the oars from the water, picked up a small hook-shaped anchor and dropped it over the side. He took out some fishing poles and handed one to each of us. We were about two hundred metres from the shingle beach; I could see the beachside restaurants busying themselves, preparing for the day as the sun reached above the mountains and flooded sunshine into the calm water.

All was quiet until we heard a sudden splash nearby. A huge grey dolphin leapt out of the water and landed on its back a few feet away. The boat rocked as the wave created threatened to tip us, and we held on to the side to steady ourselves. Then another leapt and splashed back into the sea. Soon more arrived, until there was a pod of these magnificent creatures playing and leaping in the short strip of sea between us and the shore. We sat open-mouthed watching this incredible display. However, Dimitri did not share in our enthusiasm. He wound in the fishing line, pulled up the anchor and swore under his breath.

'Bloody dolphins. No bloody fish today. We may as well go home.'

Alex and I sat there, amazed. I was tempted to jump into the sea and join them. I had seen dolphins before but only in an aquarium, performing trips for audiences. Here were wild dolphins playing and frolicking around our boat, so close to our village. It was a wonderful experience, but Dimitri didn't see it that way. To him, they were useless creatures who only upset the fish.

It reminded me of a TV documentary I once watched where a tribal warrior was being interviewed in Africa. The chap was being asked about the effect of tourists visiting his land for guided safaris.

'They are strange people,' he told the interviewer. 'Only interested in useless lions. They should look at my lovely cows.' He walked away, shaking his head.

Dimitri was the same. He had no concept that people would come for miles to see this sight. To him, they were point-less animals that served no purpose.

7

GREEK JUSTICE AND DUCKS IN THE GARDEN

W e had only been in the house for a few weeks, but had juggled our finances and were ready to build the wall around the house and fit gates. We called Stamos, who arrived quickly in his grey pickup truck. It still had the scaffold poles on its roof, with the same red rag tied to the overhanging bits.

We walked around the side of the house. He stopped in his tracks.

He hadn't seen the garden since the bulldozer had flattened the land. The last time he had seen it, it was a tangle of thorn bushes and bamboo and an impenetrable jungle.

'That land is enormous,' he said. 'We can't build a wall around all of that. It will take forever, and the cost.'

So, we agreed to just build a wall to the front, and either side of the house. There would be a wrought-iron gate leading to the front door, and a larger sliding gate across the driveway entrance. The rest of the land could have chain-link fencing erected around the perimeter. We also needed a patio as we were still stepping out of our back door onto bare earth and wanted to set up a table, some chairs, and perhaps an umbrella to protect us from the hot Greek sun. We took our red ball of string and, together with Stamos, marked out the area. His labourers set to work, levelling the ground and building a shut-tered wooden frame.

A team of labourers dug the foundations for the wall. They nailed together a lattice of timber to make a frame and erected shuttering. Then a concrete truck arrived and pumped its contents into the space between the shuttering and over the ground at the rear to form our new patio for our seating area.

Stamos stood back to admire his work and told us to wait for a week for the cement to cure, then he would return, remove the wood from the wall and patio area, and fit the gates.

All seemed to be fine with the wall. The cement was hard-ening nicely and looked ready for the shuttering to be removed. The patio looked good, but we were still tripping over the wood shuttering and would be glad when it had gone. While we were waiting, we decided to drive to the next village of Istiea to buy a patio table and some garden chairs. We left the house as the sky darkened. Clouds began to thicken and blot out the sun. A storm was coming. As we drove towards the next village, the heavens opened. It was not just a rain shower – this was a tropical monsoon. The windscreen wipers had no effect as we tried to drive through the sheets of water. It felt like someone had turned a fire hose on to the windscreen, and all we could see were sheets of water with a defining sound of rain and hail hitting the car. It was impossible to drive any further in this storm and we considered turning back. That, too, was pointless. It didn't matter which direction you were travelling, it was the same. We had to stop driving and wait for the visibility to clear a little, but the rain and hail continued. We watched as if day had turned to night, the darkness only punctuated by loud claps of thunder and frequent flashes of lightning.

An hour later, we were still sitting in our car, with no sign of the rain abating, when I squinted through the side window. The road was no longer there. Instead, there was a gushing river, and it was rising. I looked down and saw water seeping into the car through the base of the doors, and pools appeared around the pedals. We had to get to high ground. I started the engine, wound down the window, and put my head out. Alex did the same and shouted instructions as we crept along the road. We finally navigated through the river and up a shallow hill. The river was still running down the road in torrents but was not gaining any depth. We were both soaked, but as we were on higher ground, we were safe for now. We waited a little longer as the rain eased from a wall of water to fat drops splashing over the bonnet. Luckily, our destination was slightly uphill, and the windscreen wipers were clearing our vision. We recommenced our drive. We drove past abandoned cars; motorcycles were lying on their sides where the riders had left them to run for cover. The road was still mostly flooded by the time we reached the next village, so we found a taverna to have lunch and wait for the rain to stop and allow the flood waters to recede. It was late afternoon by the time we had negotiated the flooded roads and driven the short distance home.

As we opened the door to our house, it confronted us with water across the floor. Rugs were floating, and a stream was pushing itself through the back door. We ran around the house into the back garden. The rear of the garden nearest the river was a lake. The water had come either side of the earth barrier and flooded half of our land. It hadn't reached the house, so it was a mystery how so much water had got inside. Then we saw the reason. When Stamos had laid the patio, he had sloped it towards the house, so instead of the rainwater running happily away onto the ground, it was all coming backwards and flooding our new home.

Alex was furious. She called Stamos, who promised to come straight away. He turned up the next day – I think he was waiting for Alex to cool off before showing his face. Meanwhile, we had mopped the water out of the house, taken the rugs outside to dry in the sun, and assessed the damage. The house was generally fine, but some of the plasterboard looked a little stained at floor level and the entire area felt damp. But after leaving the windows open, it soon dried in the hot Greek weather. The lake in the garden had shrunk a little, but a few seabirds were hopefully poking around in the shallow water, looking for lunch.

I know that every Englishmen's house is his castle, but I would rather not have a moat. This episode focused our minds on the real danger of the river during the winter. My neighbour George had been right. Something had to be done.

Stamos looked at the patio, scratched his head, and suggested another layer of cement should be applied to level it up and make it slant the right way. But he was far too busy now with the recent flooding. There were people in the village whose houses had been severely damaged by the storm, so we would have to wait. Alex was still angry with him, but we had no choice. No more rain was expected, so he left after a good telling-off, with his tail between his legs.

We were still worried about the river but didn't yet have enough money to build a wall to protect ourselves. It was still summer and the recent storm had been exceptional; even the locals had never seen its like. So, while waiting for Stamos to return to finish our front wall and new gates, we decided to do some gardening.

It was still early, and we had the whole day ahead of us. The grass had grown at last; I had finally beaten the ants, and instead of a ploughed field, we had green shoots covering our garden. The floodwater had taken most of the new grass away near the river, leaving mud and soggy ground, but a few more grass seeds germinated readily in the soft, damp soil.

It was time to buy some trees. We wanted to plant a few lemon and orange trees, and Alex really wanted a willow. She had always admired these majestic trees, but they were almost unknown in Glyfada and Athens because of the hot climate. Here, being more northerly, they seemed to be common. Our village does not have a plant nursery, but the growers sell plants and trees. We had already met the old man of the village who sold all the trees in the area, so we went to see him. We drove into his yard and parked near his hut. The old man wandered out to greet us and showed us the best trees for our needs. Suddenly Alex stopped, put her face near the man's, and sniffed.

'Have you been drinking?' she asked accusingly. 'You realise it's only nine o'clock in the morning.'

'Of course I've been drinking,' he replied. 'I make about five hundred litres of tsipouro every year. I can't sell it all, so I have to drink the rest, don't I?'

This makes sense, I thought. I didn't care about the old

man's drinking habits. I continued to amble around looking at the saplings while Alex continued to lecture the old man about how too much booze wasn't good for him.

'Look, I'm ninety-seven years old, so if anything, my boozing habit has preserved me,' he replied.

Alex finally stopped her attack on the old man and joined me to inspect the trees. We bought four orange trees, two lemons, two fast-growing trees for shade, and a fig, together with a small willow. They were all delivered that afternoon, and we set about digging holes to plant them in. I took the small willow to the end of the garden. I thought it would look nice by the river. All willows I had seen in England were planted by water, so not being a gardener and knowing nothing about trees, I simply followed tradition. As I dug the spade into the ground, I hit something solid. I dug around the obstruction and finally loosened it from the soil. I pulled it out and examined my find. It was a large piece of pottery. It looked old and must have been in the sea at some point because it had old barnacles fossilised into the surface. I turned it over. The surface was painted with an intricate wave design of red and yellow. By the shape, it looked to be part of an old pot, and it was certainly ancient.

This was both fascinating and worrying. I was please to find something so old and clearly a relic of ancient Greece. But I was also concerned that if the archaeologist had found this during his investigation, would I have been allowed to build? Now I had found it on my land. What would happen next? Would we lose everything?

It tempted me to rebury my treasure, but I came clean. If anyone found out I had been hiding ancient relics, I would be in big trouble. Having only just finished building, was this going to be a major problem? I showed Alex, who turned it over in her hands.

'It doesn't look ancient,' she said.

I pointed to the fossilised barnacles on the other side, which seemed to confirm the age. I had seen pots with similar designs in museums. So, we took it to the mayor's office.

'What do you want me to do with it?' the mayor asked. 'Can't you throw it away yourself?'

'But it looks ancient,' I said.

'We find this stuff all the time,' he said. 'It doesn't mean anything. These bits and pieces just come down with the river. I guarantee there are no important relics on your land.'

'But the archaeologist, he spent ages digging; and he had a JCB, so it was serious,' I told him.

'Yes, only because it's the law. He knew he would find nothing,' he said. 'It's part of the bureaucracy here.'

He gave us a history lesson.

'At the time of the Battle of Artemision, the small village near your house was thought to have been the harbour. At the same time was the famous battle of the three hundred Spartans over there at Thermopylae.' He waved his hand towards the distant mountain across the sea. 'At that time, Thermopylae was next to the sea. But over the last two thousand years, the sea has retreated and is now a few kilometres inland. So, your land would have been under water. There is no chance you have any ancient buildings there. You may have pieces of pottery washed down the river, and there may have been things thrown overboard from passing boats, but rest assured, we are not interested in any bits of pottery found.'

We were both relieved at this news. We had heard so many stories of people losing their land because of historic monuments being found during construction and were certainly worried. But now we were in the clear to carry on planting our trees.

The next morning, I was pottering around the garden. But

something was not right. The new lawn was growing – I had set sprinklers to activate during the cool nights and trimmed the edges with kitchen scissors. I was getting ready for the first mowing with my nice new machine when I walked around for a last inspection. To my horror, it was covered with earthy hills. My new lawn had chickenpox. A mole had arrived, and he had brought friends. I had no idea moles lived in Greece – I would have thought the ground to be too hard and dry. But then I realised that my persistent lawn watering had made the soil soft, which created an ideal environment for these little furry miners. This was depressing. I had spent ages fighting with ants over the grass seed. Every time I planted it, the ants arrived in their thousands and carted the seeds away. I only managed to grow the lawn eventually by laying a trail of fig juice to my neighbours' tree to distract them long enough for the seeds to germinate while they weren't looking.

I did a quick Google search and read that they were blind and quite fond of worms, and the best way to get rid of them was to stuff something smelly down into their burrow. I couldn't think of anything that would smell worse than a worm. I needed local knowledge.

I walked down to the village to find the old men. In the village, anything plant or garden related, the old men knew about it. Living in the village all their lives, what they didn't know about horticulture wasn't worth knowing. There they were, as usual, drinking the local firewater from miniature bottles while putting the world to the rights.

They shuffled together and made a space at their table. I ordered a round of drinks and explained my problem. One of the oldest locals told me that coffee was the answer. 'Just open a hole near a molehill and bury coffee grounds,' he instructed.

'No, that won't work,' another local piped up. 'Just put a firework into the hole and blow it to bits.'

'You need a cat,' another contributed. 'That will get rid of it.'

'No, plant a prickly bush and the roots will cage it in, then you can kill it,' the oldest local added.

The conversation was becoming animated and now tempers were flaring. I was no longer included in the conversation as the old men shouted at each other. Not wishing to be part of a bar fight, I left to go home and study my lawn. I had nothing personal against the mole, so I didn't really want to harm it. I just wanted it to dig somewhere else. Perhaps I could catch it, put it in a box and drive it to the mountains, then let it burrow up there.

I dragged a garden chair over to the freshest-looking mole-hill, sat with my fishing net on a stick, and waited. After two hours, I heard a faint sound of scratching. I looked in the sound's direction and saw a little furry head pop out of the ground and sniff the air. It was really cute. I thought about scooping it up in the net, then had second thoughts. This was his home as well as mine. What right had I got to take him away? He might have a mole family down there, all as cute as him. Okay, I would like a nice lawn, but not at the expense of evicting this little guy. So I did what most other soppy Englishmen would do and gave it a name. I still have a lumpy lawn, but my family is bigger with my new pet Digger the mole.

Summer was with us. The next thing on our list was to repair the patio so it didn't flood our house every time it rained, and finish fitting the gates. Stamos arrived. His men took away the wood cladding from the wall, leaving a beautiful, smooth concrete. He set about fitting the wrought-iron gate to the entrance, and the larger one across the driveway entrance.

Although our wall and gates looked nice, we didn't really trust Stamos to deal with our defective patio, and we were not keen on the idea of bare concrete. We were still stepping out of our back door into puddles and thought we could build up the patio at one end using stone paving, which would also keep the water away from the house. We would lay the patio ourselves. How hard could it be? We soon found out.

Alex's grandmother would always tell her that unless you have built, you have not experienced life. In Greece, this is even more appropriate than other parts of the world. During our recent project in Glyfada, we couldn't really have claimed any part of the actual building process. We did learn rather a lot about protecting ourselves, but material quantities were still a mystery.

I did a quick calculation and worked out a couple of jumbo bags of sand and ten bags of cement should do it, but thought we would check with the builder's yard. They would know better.

We went to see the local building material supplier. I went for a walk around the yard while Alex tried to explain that we needed to cover twenty square metres with stones. The owner did his calculations and assured us the delivery would be with us that afternoon.

We went from the yard to the seaside for lunch. When we returned, the delivery was on the road outside our house. A line of giant white bags, all overflowing with sand, extended along the front of our home and into the distance. There were over twenty-five enormous bags, along with several pallets of cement. This was obviously a mistake; we had enough materials to concrete most of the village.

We went back to the merchant.

The owner held up his hands in defence as Alex stormed into his office.

'Why have you sent so much material?' Alex raged.

'You told me you wanted twenty cubic metres. That's what we sent.'

Instead of asking for enough sand to cover twenty square metres, Alex had forgotten to use the word for square and asked for twenty cubic metres.

We now had enough for the world's biggest sandpit, or we could create our own beach and wait for a little more global warming. I understand sea levels are rising, so we could soon have a waterfront property. We certainly had enough sand.

A lorry arrived and took away the excess sand, leaving us just enough to do our job. Being a loving, considerate husband, I didn't want Alex to mix concrete by hand, so I took her to choose a cement mixer. She was delighted and chose a bright yellow one and a matching wheelbarrow.

The paving consisted of different-sized flat stones of varying thickness. It looked good and very natural. It would certainly be better than just looking at poured concrete. We would just have to sink some of the thicker ones deeper into the concrete to keep the level. We started up the yellow mixer and set to work. First, we mixed a batch of cement, poured it onto the patio and set some of our stones on top. They sank below the surface, leaving only a few bubbles; the cement was too wet. We made another mix with less water, poured it onto the ground and set some stones on that. The cement dried too quickly, leaving the stones sitting proudly on top of the base. This wouldn't have been too much of an issue if we had used standard-thickness paving, but natural stones were of various thicknesses, some less than one inch, others over four inches. Okay, we thought.

'Let's just lay the stones on top of the drying cement and sort it out later,' we agreed.

We went ahead and finished the patio. It looked awful, rather like the surface of the moon only with more craters.

'Let's just fill in the gaps between the stones,' Alex suggested. 'That will level it out.'

That didn't work either. We were beginning to feel seasick walking across our finished patio. It was rather wavy. But overall, we were happy with our work. All we needed now was to cut the chair and table legs to make them level so we could sit and have a meal without the food sliding off. But the ultimate test was with the hosepipe. We waited until the cement had cured, and soaked the entire patio. We watched with relief as we saw the water run away from the house and soak into the ground. There were still lots of pools because of the uneven way we had laid the stones, but thankfully nowhere near the wall of the house. So at least we were safe from flooding inside.

Next, we would build a roof over it. But before then, we had a pressing worry about the river. We had seen first-hand that when the rain came down, the roads in the village became a torrent and most of our land became a lake, with the odd visiting waterfowl in search of fish.

So before winter came, we needed a solution. We had no choice. We had to call Stamos. He arrived, took one look at our patio and doubled up laughing. He took his phone out of his pocket and took a photograph.

'Who the hell laid these stones?' he said, laughing.

'We did,' Alex replied. 'It was to deal with your cock-up, so don't be too happy.'

'Sorry.' Stamos looked sheepish. 'I was going to deal with this for you, but you didn't call.'

'We've asked you to come to talk about the river,' Alex said.

'It floods and our garden turns into a lake when we get heavy rain.'

'Yes, I know about that. Someone over there built his house in the river. That's why.'

'How did he get permission to build there? It's not even beside the river, it's on it. He must have built it in the summer,' I said. 'When the rain came, the water had nowhere to go, so it filled up and flooded our garden, and the surrounding countryside.'

'Yes, but I think he has friends in the planning office,' Stamos replied, putting his finger to the side of his nose.

'I bet you built it for him,' Alex said. 'You are the only builder in the village.' He didn't answer, he just looked away innocently.

I did not feel comfortable getting involved in village politics to ask why this idiot had built a house on my river. But we needed to find a solution. I thought about sending Alex to visit him to demand he removed his house. A raging Alex would make anyone think twice, but a full house demolition seemed unlikely. So instead we decided to build a wall along our side of the riverbank and on both sides of our land. This would prevent flooding in my garden and send the water somewhere else.

We were due to travel to London on business for a few weeks and left the details to Stamos. After two weeks, we received the first photograph of our nearly completed wall. It looked huge and sturdy. There was no way our garden would flood again. But trouble soon came.

We received a call from Maria. She told us our usually peaceful garden was now full of screaming people and six police officers looking for us. Stamos had run away, and the police had put out an arrest warrant for him and us.

Someone had seen our new wall being built. As flooding

was a big problem for most of the houses in the area near the river, word had spread, and the owners assumed that our building a wall was likely to cause them even more problems and reported us to the police.

We took the next flight to Greece. Stamos had gone to ground and was not taking our calls. We didn't know what laws we had broken, but it must be serious.

In Greece, the police deal with planning offences. So, if you build something on your property without the necessary permission, you could be on a long diet of bread and water, peering through bars. Stamos was so keen to get a nice building job, he conveniently forgot to tell us we needed approval from the mayor's office before any work could be done.

Maria met us as we arrived home.

'It was terrible,' she cried. 'There were police everywhere. Stamos has run away, and I didn't know what to do.'

Alex put her arms around Maria.

'It's fine, we will sort it out. Please don't worry,' she told her.

Rather than wait to be arrested, we went to the police station to turn ourselves in. I wasn't looking forward to this. I had already had a brush with the law in Glyfada when I built a Parthenon on our roof there. Like here, someone reported us for an illegal construction. I only escaped arrest by agreeing to remove the offending bits to comply with the law. But here we had built an enormous wall and apparently it was completely illegal, and the police appeared to take it very seriously this time.

Our village does not have a police station, so we drove to the nearby market town of Istiea to give our confession there.

As we walked up the dark stairwell to meet our fate, Alex and I held hands. In our hearts we knew we had done the right thing to protect our new home. Our palms were sweating as we walked towards the uniformed officer standing behind the desk.

'Oh, so you are the ones we've been looking for,' announced the officer. 'There is a warrant out for your arrest, you know.'

This didn't look good. We had no idea we were breaking any law; we were just trying to protect ourselves from the river.

Alex took over. 'Are we under arrest, then?'

'Technically, yes, but you must go to the main planning office and see them. They will tell you what to do. They will give you a paper which you must bring back here. If you don't come back, we will come looking for you.'

Me being a foreigner seemed to help. After all, how was I supposed to know about the local rules? Alex, being Greek, should have been more aware; a foreigner may be forgiven, but a Greek should have known better. I think they were a little hesitant to arrest us as it may have provoked a diplomatic incident and the paperwork would be horrendous. But nonetheless we were in big trouble.

Although we were under arrest, we were still free of handcuffs, which was a good sign. The young police officer appeared to be more concerned with filling out forms and applying official stamps rather than throwing us into the cells. He stamped the paper one last time and handed it to Alex.

'Off you go then,' the policeman said. 'Take this paper to the planning office, and have a nice day.'

We were free. Our vision of spending the night in the cells and being dragged into court the following morning to receive our punishment proved unfounded. With relieved smiles on our faces, we crossed the road, entered the planning office and presented our police paper. A young girl asked us to follow her into a small office to discuss our crime.

It appeared that four people had lodged complaints to the police about our wall. She went on to explain that we would have been okay to build a wall in another part of our garden. We might have received a small fine, but we could have kept it. Our crime was more serious. We had built a wall near the river. In Greek law, this is forbidden. It had to be removed at once. We would still pay a fine, but for every week the wall was standing, the fine would double.

In Greece, being the home of democracy, if someone makes a complaint, you have a right to know who reported you, and where they live. We were interested in finding out who had made the complaint. Perhaps one of them was the person who had built his home in my river. That would be interesting. We tried to explain that the reason for the flooding was that somebody had not only built a wall in the river but finished it with a complete house. But in her eyes this was no defence. In a few days, we would find out more. Meanwhile, we had more pressing matters. We had to get rid of our wall, and quickly, so we drove to the next village in search of Stamos. We found his truck outside the cafe. He saw our car and rushed out to meet us. He wrung his cap in his hands as he stuttered an apology and promised us he would help as much as he could.

'Do you have a bulldozer?' I asked.

'No, but I know someone that does.'

'Okay, get it and meet us at home,' I demanded.

An hour later, a big yellow bulldozer trundled into our garden. In another two hours, they reduced our precious wall to a pile of rubble on the lawn. A lorry appeared with a grab and took away the debris, leaving the riverbank in its original condition. It looked as if the wall had never existed.

The next day, neighbours arrived throughout the morning, some bringing baskets of figs, and other with gifts of freshly laid eggs or honey from their hives. All were keen to assure us it wasn't them who reported us. Finally, Maria, the local gossip, appeared with a smile. She had visited a friend in the mayor's office and proudly revealed she now knew who the guilty parties were.

'It was the foreigners who reported you,' she announced.

'I thought I was the only foreigner in our village,' I told her.

'No, it's the real foreigners. The ones from Athens. It's the ones who have holiday homes here. They are not real villagers.'

She was so happy that none of the real villagers had reported us; if she had found this to be the case, she would have made their lives a living hell. But the foreigners, being from Athens, didn't know any better, so they could be forgiven.

Although Maria offered to tell us who the guilty parties were, I asked her not to tell Alex. I didn't want an ongoing feud with the 'foreigners'. Alex would certainly never have forgiven them and would likely have attacked them in the street. It was all over now, so best to forget it, keep our freedom and move on.

Stamos wasn't expecting to be paid, but we settled his full amount anyway. He was amazed.

'I've never met people like you two,' he said. 'Everyone in the village considers you to be heroes, and you have certainly gained their respect.'

Even the mayor arrived and told us we were right to build the wall. He shook his head as he assured us that no villager would ever have reported us, but these people bypassed him and went straight to the police. For a few weeks, our wall was the talk of the village. After all, it was the most interesting subject in the area. Even now, over a year later, we are introduced to strangers as 'the couple who built the wall'. Everyone knows that story.

Our garden still floods. The house in the river is still there. But the village is peaceful. I just need to adopt some ducks and grow lily pads rather than lawn.

8

VICIOUS CREATURES OF OUR VILLAGE

Our first cat arrived as the bulldozer left. It was a thin tabby who meowed at me and wrapped itself around my legs until I went to the fridge, found some ham and passed it to her. She ate it and came back for more. I filled a bowl with water, and she drank thirstily, then went to investigate the dog's empty food bowl. She was clearly hungry.

I didn't have any ham left, so I went to the small village

supermarket, got some cat food, and returned home. By the time I entered my garden, one cat had become three. She had obviously spread the word and told friends about the kind person who gave her ham. Filling a bowl with dry cat food, I left them alone to eat. My two dogs were on the other side of the garden, watching intently with anxious looks on their faces.

When our dogs first arrived in Greece, they were used to the natural order of things. In the country they were born, they were used to going out for their walkies, chasing a cat up a tree, then trotting off wagging their tails, feeling pleased with themselves. Their first encounter with the local feline relative of the leopard in Greece did not end well. My Labrador, Jack, saw a cat while ambling along next to me on the beach and gave chase. The cat saw him coming but didn't run away and turned to face him. Slowly, Jack realised this creature would not run away, so reduced speed and approached suspiciously. As he reached out his head to sniff it, there was a sudden blur of claws and fur as it attacked Jack, who turned and ran with the cat in close pursuit. Soon the cat broke off the chase. It had achieved its aim of terrifying my trembling mutt, who returned to my side with blood soaking into his fur from a badly scratched nose. After that, whenever he saw a cat he would cross the road to avoid another encounter. Now, the dogs were in their own garden with three scary predators eating from their bowl.

Here, birds chase cats, and cats chase dogs. The wildlife in Greece has a pecking order established by many years of each animal developing their own skills independently from the rest of the world.

First is the seagull. These flying eating machines are always on the lookout for food. Fish, being their favourite, comes mostly from the local boats that anchor in the bay before returning to port. Fishermen use this period to clean and pack the fish before entering the harbour and tying up at the dock to unload their catch. Sitting at the harbour coffee shop, we watch these seabirds squabble and fight for every scrap thrown overboard before being shooed away by the fishermen once in port. With no more fish to grab, they turn their attention elsewhere. This is usually my plate of fried calamari. Be on guard when a seemingly innocent seabird is sitting on the wall near your table, pretending to be looking out to sea. Suddenly, in a flash, and flurry of wings, it will swoop down, grab your lunch and make off with it, followed by its cronies, all wanting to share.

Next on the list of feathery beggars are the sparrows. They sit in a group watching food being delivered to the table. When they spy something that takes their fancy, they will hop onto the table and steal from under your eyes. Commonly, they find the half-loaf of bread they have just stolen is too heavy to fly with, so they drop it onto the floor to be devoured noisily by several more of the flock of these tiny birds.

The third in the pecking order are the cats waiting under the table. They are afraid of the sparrows and huddle behind table legs until the birds finish the feast and fly away. Then they emerge to wrap their bodies around your legs while purring loudly, in the hope of being offered a morsel of fish.

Last in the order of priority are the dogs. They are afraid of the sparrows and the cats. They sit watching from a safe distance until the sparrows have gone and the cats have had their fill and ambled off to sleep in the sun. Then these lovely creatures come over and rest their chins on your lap and wait patiently. They all have scratched noses from encounters with the local cats and will quickly run away if one comes too near.

I have always wondered how this complete reversal has occurred. Where I lived in England, the cats chased birds, and the dogs chased the cats. This is the natural order of things. But not in Greece. Charles Darwin would have loved it here. He would certainly have needed to revise his theory of evolution.

The next visitor to my garden was a tortoise. In the summer, they roam around the village, chewing on the plants and shrubs. Whenever I find them, I hand-feed them with a juicy slice of tomato.

It can be a risky business for the tortoise. The cats just ignore them and pretend they don't exist. But this tortoise was not wandering freely in the garden. It was in the mouth of my dog. My pet must have found it, sniffed it, realised it was not a threat, so it must be food – and decided to eat it. She was there on the lawn, legs outstretched, happily chewing around the edge of the shell, trying to get inside. Luckily, I got there before the main course.

In our village, we share a vet with most of northern Evia. But on this day we were lucky as he was holding a surgery in the next village.

At the veterinary clinic, there was a guy with a poorly looking dog curled up at his feet, a pleasant, smiling lady with an unidentified creature wrapped in a blanket, a young boy with a goat on a piece of string, and me with a nibbled tortoise, all waiting for the vet. He declared my patient fit and healthy, with no lasting damage. He gave me some cream to rub onto its nibbled bits, so after a few days of convalescence in a box, I drove him to the mountains and left him with a packed lunch of sliced tomatoes and lettuce.

Often during our drives in the hills, I'll see one on the main road, ambling across the tarmac. I always stop the car, pick it up and carefully place it in a nearby field. The problem is that I don't know where they have been, or where they intend to go. I just don't want them to get run over, so I pick a side of the road and leave them there. But every time I get it wrong. As soon as I have placed him on the grass verge, he decides this is not the side of the road he wants to be on and turns around to cross the road again. I was sure they were just being difficult or playing a game with me. So, one day, I tested my theory.

I found a tortoise in the middle of the road, picked him up and put him on one side. He crossed again. I picked him up and put him on the other side. He didn't like that either and turned around and went towards the other side. This went on for a few more moments until I realised he just wanted to be in the middle of the road. I think that's why they are becoming rare.

The next pet arrived quickly. We were sitting on our wonky patio when a dog walked over from near the river, taking a wide arc around the cats, sat at Alex's feet and held up a paw. She was a strange-looking dog. She was rusty red with a round body and a docked tail. Her face was reminiscent of a boxer. She wasn't wearing a collar but looked well fed and healthy. Alex found a bowl and gave her some food. Because of her colour, we gave her the name Korky, after the colour red in Greek (kókkino). She introduced herself to our dogs. They seemed to get on well together. The cats just sat on the wall and ignored the dogs, and the dogs did likewise. So, we had three cheerful dogs and an uneasy truce with the cats. Korky stayed with us for the whole day. When we took our dogs for a walk, Korky followed a respectable distance behind, as if she realised she wasn't really part of the family and felt hesitant to intrude. When we returned, she followed, and in the warm afternoon, snoozed under the table. Then, as the sun set, she got up and left.

As darkness fell, Alex and I moved from the back of the house to the front porch. We enjoyed spending evenings there because the heady smell of jasmine would begin after dark. We also had the chance to say hello to passing friends and neighbours. We were sitting drinking a glass of ouzo when Korky came back. But this time, she wasn't alone. Following her were three tiny pure-black puppies, and one more with a white bib and a white-tipped tail. They were lovely. As her family followed her onto the porch, I picked up the one with the white tail and stroked her head. She was beautiful. She jumped down to join her brothers and Alex poured some milk into a bowl. They drank together around the bowl with their tails raised in the air and wagged them in time to the sound of lapping.

Our new family stayed with us for a few days. Most of the puppies looked to be well, but the smallest was my personal favourite, the one with the white-tipped tail. She wasn't eating as much as her brothers and sisters, and looked a little delicate. I gave her special attention, and when we fed the rest of the puppies, I would sit her on my lap and hand-feed her the best bits of food. One afternoon, we were watching our dogs and the puppies playing together in the garden, when my little favourite collapsed onto her side and started shaking and foaming at the mouth. She was having a fit. By the time I got to her, she had stopped moving. I picked her up and her body was limp. She had died.

We wrapped her in a sheet and brought her lifeless body into the house away from the other dogs. We were both sad at her passing, but nature always favours the strong; she was clearly the runt of the litter, so we had to accept it. I decided to dig a small grave at the base of our willow tree, so took my spade and excavated the loose soil. The rest of the puppies were oblivious to the tragedy and continued playing. I put my spade down to collect the body for burial, but when I turned away from the small grave, in front of me was a little puppy wagging a white-tipped tail. She was not dead after all. She had woken up and bounded into the garden to see what I was doing. It was lucky she woke up when she did. I was sure she had died and would have buried her. I wanted to get her checked by the vet, but he was out of town, so we separated her from the rest of the brood and made a bed inside the house for her to recover. Over the next few days, she recovered quickly, and by the end of the week was as boisterous as her siblings.

A few days later, we had to leave. We needed to deal with some things in Glyfada, then go to England for two weeks. Our dogs, Jack and Bella, would stay with Debbie and Zissis in Glyfada while we were abroad. Zissis loved dogs and was always happy to walk them around the town. I was concerned about Korky and the puppies, so asked Maria to take care of them and feed them every day, which she agreed to do. I went to the supermarket and purchased a month's supply of dog food. At the pet shop, I bought a large plastic kennel and set it beside the house, and we reluctantly left Maria in charge as we drove away.

Two weeks later, we had finished our business abroad and returned home. Alex set about opening the shutters and airing the house while I wandered around the garden to check on the progress of our trees and lawn.

Whenever we arrive home, it's not long before the local wildlife turns up. First to arrive are always the cats. It starts with the arrival of one poking his head around the corner to make sure it's us. He then disappears for an hour, spreads the word, and returns with most of the cat population of the village. They all know where the Friskies live. But I couldn't see Korky or her puppies.

Maria arrived within a few moments. She always seemed to know when we were at home. Although she lived nearby in a small house in Artemision, there was no line of sight from her house to ours. I think she may have a complex radar system to alert her to our arrival.

'The puppies left,' she told us. 'It was the day after you went to Athens. I went to feed them, and they were gone. I haven't seen them since.'

I was sad that the puppies had left. But they didn't belong to us. They probably had a proper home nearby and were just visiting. We did all we could to have them taken care of during our absence, but there is no way we could have taken them with us. We had to accept we were not destined for any more dogs just yet.

Dimitri had been busy during our absence. He had cut the lawn, planted a few more trees, and had arranged four old feta cheese tins at the end of our wonky patio. He filled them with light-green basil plants. The tins looked a little old and rusty, but Alex loved them. She thought they added character to the garden. Throughout Greece, they use feta tins as plant pots, buckets on building sites, to carry water for animals, and many other things. There is never a shortage of these handy objects. Every meal in Greece has feta as an accompaniment. Greek salad would not be Greek without feta, so they give these tins away to anyone in the village who can use them. But why were our feta tins full of basil plants? They use very little basil in Greek cooking. If it were oregano, I would not have been surprised. This is used on everything from salads to barbecued fish and meat. Most food in Greece tastes of oregano. So why basil?

Basil, or 'vasilikos' in Greek, is a herb found all over Greece. It had a prominent role in Greek culture long before it became an ingredient for cooking. In fact, most Greeks still don't use it in food despite how well it grows here.

Basil is a member of the mint family and a native plant of the Mediterranean. It grows abundantly throughout Greece and has been cultivated for over five thousand years.

Basil has carried symbolic meaning throughout Greek

history. For ancients, basil was associated with hatred, but they are said to have placed the herb in the hands of the dead. They thought it would ensure safe travels to the afterlife and the opening of heaven for them.

Basil has significance in the Greek Orthodox religion as well. It is used to sprinkle holy water. It is said that in 326 AD, Empress Helene found the original cross they had crucified Jesus on, and basil was there as well, growing in the shape of a cross. She named the plant 'vasiliki', which means 'of the king'. In fact, the word 'basil' comes from the Greek word 'basilias', which means king.

There are still many Greeks who will not eat basil as it is associated with the raising of the cross. In Greece today, basil is used ornamentally and in some religious rituals is a symbol of fertility. They commonly hang it on doors to bring good luck and wealth. Some Greeks will bring basil as a gift to the church and may also ask their priest to bless their basil for the health and prosperity of their home.

But the most important use in our garden was to keep the pesky mosquitoes away.

I had noticed that recently I had been scratching more than usual. It was summer, and we were spending more time outside enjoying the warm evenings. We find these little bloodsucking beasts in all hot countries, but luckily here they only annoy. In other, less fortunate places, they can kill you. This is no comfort when all I seem to do on warm summer evenings is scratch bits of me that have been feasted upon. During the feeding season, I cope by spreading vast amounts of citronella all over my exposed parts, which seems to deter them until it wears off. The only downside is that I have become known as the local xeno who always smells of lemons. It's a price I'm willing to pay. If I stepped foot out of the door in the night-time hours without my lemony protection, I would likely invoke a feeding frenzy, leaving painful, itchy red lumps on my painful, itchy red lumps. Alex is unaffected by the bites and claims that I'm such a baby – it's probably a nappy rash.

The mosquitoes appeared to love the feta tins full of basil, and happily swarmed around the tin before seeking out some juicy exposed flesh.

I tried everything. Lashings of super-jungle-strength repellent, small plastic bracelets, sonic devices which claim to rid your home by emitting tone, but these all seemed to attract them. I would spend most evenings sitting on the warm patio wearing long-sleeve jumpers, a bobble hat, canvas trousers and wellington boots.

Eventually I got to grips with mosquitoes. I knew where they lived, and sensitised my hearing so much that I could hear their high-pitched whine from a hundred metres away. I could even pick up the dog whistle when the local shepherd called his mutt. So imagine my surprise when I got bitten after all my recent precautions. Had mosquitoes suddenly developed stealth mode? My old dad swore that during his recent package holiday, 'the bloody mosquitoes had developed headlights'. Of course, he mistook fireflies for mosquitoes.

No, in my case, I was being bitten by something else. Sitting in the garden one evening, busy scratching exposed parts of bitten flesh, I mentioned to Alex that I was still being eaten but there were no mosquitoes around. She looked up from her iPad and waved away my comment.

'They are only sknípa,' she casually informed me.

'What are they?' I asked. 'You never told me about those.'

'Tiny insects. You won't see them. They are far too small, but they bite,' she explained. These are also known as 'no-see-ums', and you can't see um. These are sneaky, tiny bugs. There is no point covering your arms and legs with long trousers and sleeves; these vicious little predators bite straight through the protection, and they love insect repellent. This is not fair. At least when you are attacked by real mosquitoes, you can hear them whining in your ear before you get savaged. These little pests are invisible and silent. Great. This was a revelation to me. After all my effort avoiding mosquitoes, I was now being attacked by an invisible predator that I couldn't see or hear coming.

Alex, being Greek, seems to have built up a resistance to mosquitoes and sknípas. She does occasionally get bitten, but unlike me, she never reacts. Every bite I get swells up and causes days of irritation before the next attack, and another few days of scratching.

The villagers take a more laid-back approach to the local insects. They are not really interested in what species is around. It's a little simpler here.

We were having lunch at a nearby taverna, sitting outside under the shade of the trees. Something green and nasty was buzzing around my head. It had long legs, big red eyes and was the size of my thumb. I used the napkin from the table to wave it away, but this only enraged the little monster to start dive-bombing me. The taverna owner saw me flapping my napkin and assumed I needed more wine, so he came to the table with a brimming jug and placed it on the table.

'What else do you need?' he asked.

I pointed at the flying creature and asked, 'Ti eine aftó?' (What's that?)

'Einai móno mia mýga,' (It's only a fly) he informed me, and wandered off.

In the village, nobody bothers with the finer details of entomology. The species of local insects fall into one of only three categories.

If it bites, it's probably a mosquito (kounoúpi).

If it stings, it's a wasp (sfíka).

If it does neither, then it's a fly (mýga).

So, being only a fly, I was assured that this savage-looking creature would not bite or sting me, so I should be happy.

Villagers are practical people. As long as they have identified the threat, they are not really interested in the details of what it actually is. But I was still wary of the local insect population and needed to find the threats for myself. After all, I had discovered a new biting insect which I had never been told about. Maybe there were more pretending to be innocent flies. I was sure the noisy crickets and cicadas in the nearby trees were fine; at least they had never bitten me. I had received a painful bite near the beach from a horsefly, though. Was this, according to the villagers, a wasp? I felt I wasn't getting all the information to protect myself, so decided to investigate further. The more I looked, the more biting creatures I discovered. Ants bit, so did some species of spiders; obviously mosquitoes, and my newly discovered sknípas. Some beetles were known to nip. We had horseflies, hornets, sandflies, ticks and bees, and of course several species of wasps … and a very worrying giant centipede had crawled over my foot yesterday. I was beginning to think I had built my house in an Amazonian rainforest.

That morning, I sat on my patio watching a large green insect sitting on the table, studying me. It was a praying mantis. I knew these were famous for eating their mates during copulation. I sat and sipped my coffee, hoping this one didn't fancy me. I was beginning to get a little paranoid about the biting creatures, so later that evening I put mosquito tablets around the house and burned blue foul-smelling spirals in all the outside areas. Alex coughed as she came out to sit with me.

'I can't smell the jasmine with all these things burning,' she complained. 'It smells like a bonfire out here.'

For me, this was a small price to pay. I would rather choke for a while than scratch painful lumps for a week.

I was getting sleepy. It may have been insecticide poisoning or carbon monoxide from the spirals, so I decided to leave Alex and go to bed. As I left the porch, Alex extinguished all my little bonfires and settled down to enjoy the rest of her evening.

I climbed into bed, snuggled under the covers, stretched my arms over my head and touched the bedhead with my fingers. Suddenly I felt a searing pain, like being stabbed by a hot needle. I quickly pulled my hand away and tried to look for a wound. Other than a little reddening around my fingertip, there was nothing to see. I got out of bed and went to get some sympathy from Alex. While she was looking at the swelling finger, I felt it go numb. Then the numbness spread from one finger to my hand. A few seconds later, it started to spread up my forearm. I was a little worried about this creeping affliction and wondered where it would stop. After another minute, my arm was numb all the way to my elbow. After an hour with no further spread, some feeling came back, starting with a slight tingling and the return of a painful finger.

We went into the bedroom to look for the creature that had attacked me, but found nothing. We pulled the bedcovers off and shook them. Still nothing. I crawled around under the bed with a flashlight. Nothing to be seen. I was a little concerned about going back to bed with the unknown vicious creature lurking around somewhere, but it seemed to have gone. My finger was still a bit sore, but the feeling in my arm had come back. Even so, I still felt worried as I drifted off to sleep.

The next morning, Maria arrived with some fresh bread from the bakery. I told her about my being attacked in bed and asked her what it could be.

'Oh, it's probably a scorpion,' she said. 'We get lots in the summer. They don't hurt much though.'

Great. Not only did I need to worry about the assortment

of biting insects who had moved in to feast on me every evening, now I had to be careful of scorpions.

'So how do I keep scorpions away from my house?' I asked her.

'Oh, the cats do that. They eat them. They also keep snakes away,' she added.

Alex's ears pricked up at that. Her fear of snakes was even greater than my fear of mosquitoes and scorpions. We looked at each other and simultaneously announced:

'We need more Friskies.'

9

NO, I WILL NOT COOK FOR YOU TODAY

By now we had a moving population of between ten and fifteen cats. Some stayed with us permanently, others just wandered off and were replaced by others who moved in. They all enjoyed their daily diet of dry cat food, which we bought weekly by the sack, but were much keener on the table scraps from our regular lunches at one of the nearby tavernas.

We had got to know the wonderful local tavernas and

discovered all their specialities, and we had become friends with the restaurant owners. All were small family businesses. The owner would cook, and sons and daughters would wait on tables. A family restaurant produced a real family atmosphere. We always ordered a little more food than we could eat because the cats greeted us on our arrival home and we didn't want to disappoint them.

Pavlos's taverna was the closest restaurant to our home and only opened at weekends. He was well known for his special calamari, thought to be the best on the island. He served his own home-made wine and cooked fish soup the traditional way. He would boil a whole fish with carrots, potatoes, local herbs and spices. This would be simmered for hours before the soup was served in a bowl and the boiled fish served on a separate plate with the head still attached. This restaurant was always full of locals occupying his tables inside and outside under the shady trees. His prices were so low it was difficult to understand how he made a living. He only charged one euro for a large jug of wine. When that was finished, the next one or two were usually free. He didn't attract many tourists as the type of fare wasn't really to their taste, but the locals loved it, as did we.

We usually went there for lunch on Saturdays and Sundays. We had already enjoyed a great lunch with him yesterday, but because of the excellent food on offer, we ordered a little of everything. We had gone slightly mad with over-ordering and realised this when Pavlos's son had to bring an extra table to fit it all on. The food was, as usual, incredible. A large Greek salad, glistening with olive oil poured over a slab of pure-white feta cheese and sprinkled with oregano, was wedged beside a plate of small fish dipped in batter, fried to perfection. Two plates of barbecued octopus sat at each end of the table. There was a mountain of fried potatoes, a dish of plump pink grilled shrimps, a whole grilled fish, and portions of tzatziki, hummus and taramasalata, with a basket of fresh bread to mop up the juices. The home-made, ice-cold white wine served in a red tin jug was heavenly and tasted better than the most upmarket French vintages. As one jug emptied, someone would take it away and replace it with a new full one, with condensation dripping off the outside. Although we had spent more than three hours over lunch, chatting to locals, eating, and drinking wine, we still had far too much food left and asked for it to be put into bags for the cats.

Today we were going for his famous calamari. We arrived, sat at our usual table, and waited for Pavlos to come out to take our order. Normally he would wander out of his kitchen, sit at our table, pour himself a glass of wine from our jug and tell us what was good to eat today.

He is a large, imposing man with a strict demeanour and a rough, booming voice. He never wears a shirt, and has an apron tied so tightly around his waist that the strings disappear into the folds of his flesh. Although he gave up smoking years ago, he always has an unlit cigarette in his mouth to remind him of the pleasures of life now denied. But being the best cook in the village, his clients are happy to ignore these little habits and focus on his amazing food.

His father originally owned the restaurant and, like many Greeks, when he was young, left the village to seek his fortune. He was a sailor, a gambler and a seeker of the good life. But when his father passed away, he left it to his two sons. Pavlos's brother ran the restaurant initially until Pavlos returned from his travels, at which time his brother left, leaving him to run it alone.

This time, he did not sit down at our table. He remained standing, looking at us with a disapproving expression. No wine had arrived at our table, which was unusual. Normally, a jug of wine would arrive as we took our seat, and more would keep coming as it emptied. But not today.

'I will not cook for you today!' he said in a strict voice.

We sat staring at him, knife and fork in hand, ready to tuck into a sample of his famous calamari.

'There is no point in cooking for you today. You never eat it all, and then you take my food home and feed it to the cats.'

'But we are starving today,' I told him.

'I promise the cats will go hungry today,' Alex assured him with her fingers crossed behind her back.

I saw his face soften a little, then his resolve returned.

'Look, I spend all day in the kitchen making the best food in the village. I cook for people, not cats.'

'Perhaps we ordered too much yesterday,' I said in my defence. I could smell the delicious aromas emanating from the kitchen, which made me feel even hungrier.

He seemed to waver. The people at the next table giggled, then abruptly went silent after a look from Pavlos. They didn't want to be told that they couldn't eat here either, so looked away quickly.

'Your food is so good, we want to try everything,' Alex added. 'You are such a superb cook.'

'Okay. But only if you promise to eat everything. And I will choose the food for you today.'

We both nodded in agreement.

He disappeared into the kitchen. Alex looked at me like a naughty schoolgirl.

'I think we upset him,' she said.

I reminded her that we did order rather a lot yesterday. There was no chance of us eating all of that food. We hadn't even considered it would offend him if we didn't eat everything. We thought he would be happy to sell a lot of food to one table.

But to Pavlos, money meant little. He cooked for the love of it. If his food wasn't eaten, he took it as a personal offence.

This time, when the food arrived it comprised a plate of delicious-looking fried calamari, a plate holding whole barbe-cued sardines, a Greek salad and an enormous pile of boiled shrimps. The meal was still huge; he had been generous with the portions. We had eaten our fill, but there was no way we could leave any and risk a lifelong ban. So, we filled our pockets with sardines and chunks of calamari and bread, clearing every-thing. Alex took the clean, licked plates into the kitchen to show Pavlos. A worried look spread across his face.

'Oh dear, you've finished everything. I didn't give you enough, did I? Sit down, I will bring you more.'

That day, the cats were not disappointed. We waddled out of the restaurant with fish heads sticking out of our pockets and bread stuffed down our shirts. We would never disappoint Pavlos again.

Manya's taverna is a different story and more typical of the picturesque, idyllic restaurants found in tourist brochures. The building is set back from the quiet beach road and built from whitewashed stone, with a whitewashed wall separating the courtyard from the road. There are tables set under shady trees with branches spread to make a beautiful green canopy. A short walk across the road is the beach, with a view of Volos opposite and the island of Skiathos.

We had first met and fallen in love with Manya when we arrived in the village. Hers was the first taverna we got to know well. Her restaurant was spotlessly clean, and she did all the cooking herself. She catered to the locals and tourists, so hers was one of the very rare tavernas with a printed menu. Being local now, and an honorary villager, I never bothered with them. I just asked what was cooking, or wandered into the kitchen to look. This was a lovely, friendly place, and some villagers almost lived here. There was Claude, the old Frenchman who sat at the same table every day, drinking local wine while smoking his smelly Gitanes cigarettes. It didn't appear to have done him much harm, as he was well into his nineties and looked healthy. Claude was born in this village but left as a young man to seek his fortune. He ended up as a successful business owner in Paris and made his money there. But as with most Greeks who leave to find a better life, he always dreamed of returning to the village of his birth for his old age. He was happy. Whenever we went there, he would smile at us and speak to me in French. I never understood a word and reminded him he could speak to me in Greek or English, but not French. He would then switch to English, allowing us to chat for a while. This happened every time we met. One day he said to me:

'I know you are Greek, but where is your wife from?'

'I'm more Greek than you. You're just a French tourist,' Alex teased, and gave him a cigar. We always kept a few in the car for when we met him.

Claude's story is common. So many Greeks leave their cities and villages in search of a new life. The lifestyle seen on social media and TV tempts young men of the villages. When old enough, some turn their backs on the family farm or local business and head out into the world 'in search of a better life', leaving the farms and fields to decay and homes left to rot and become swamped in the rampant bamboo. But although some become wealthy, some have thriving businesses and trophy foreign wives, there is always the dream of returning to spend their autumn years and taste the water of home. Greece being a seafaring nation, many young men of the islands are expected to take work on ships and sail away to exotic international locations. Although they see the most beautiful places in the world, they usually return to their village, back to the simpler life they dream of.

Some, like Claude, finally achieve their dreams. Others will never see home again.

Greece seems to cast a spell on anyone who spends time here. As someone born far away, I have no wish to return to my original home. I have tasted another life and Greece has become my home. Other expats also feel the same. I have many friends who stumbled across Greece during their travels and went no further. One day, I was chatting with a local fisherman who was born in this village.

'Haven't you ever wanted to travel?' I asked.

'Yes, I arranged a trip to Athens once,' he told me. 'But when I drove to the top of that hill over there' – he pointed up – 'I stopped my car, looked back, and thought about it. Where could be better than here? So, I turned the car around and came back home.'

In the taverna Manya did all the cooking and had two helpers to serve and wait tables. There was Michalis, a polite young man whose father was the local butcher, with a shop nearby. While not working here, he would help his father by making village sausages, cleaning the shop or making deliveries on his moped. He spoke a little English and was always keen to learn more. When the restaurant was less busy, he would come and sit at our table and speak to us.

The other server was Eleni. She was a beautiful young girl, full of life and always with a genuine smile. Whenever she wasn't looking, Michalis would stare in her direction with soulful eyes and a wistful expression. We were sure that he was in love, but Eleni never appeared to notice. She was a thin girl with an angelic face and blonde hair. She never seemed to stop moving as she rushed between tables, balancing huge trays of overloaded plates and delivering wine to hungry clients. Eleni had a crush on Alex and looked upon her as a role model. She began to dress like Alex, changed her hair to Alex's style and spent as much time as possible asking about the city of Athens, which she has always wanted to visit. But as for all youngsters, the grass is always greener on the other side of the fence, and Eleni had not appreciated what she already had in this perfect village.

One day, we were there for lunch when Eleni excitedly came rushing over to us.

'We have live music tonight. They have asked me to dance. You will come, won't you?' she pleaded. 'I need to have someone with me who knows how to perform Greek dancing. We will start the show.'

Alex was always up for dancing. Whenever she heard music, she was always the first on her feet.

A few days ago, we visited another taverna by the harbour. This was where the old men, farmers and fishermen came to eat and drink. Although a lot of tables were taken, we found one and sat down. It was remarkably quiet. The only sound was mumbled conversation and the occasional click of worry beads being wound around an old man's wrist.

All eyes turned to Alex as we took our seat.

'Kaliméra,' she yelled into the kitchen to wake up the sleepy cook. 'Ti fagitó écheis símera?' (What food do you have today?)

A sleepy-looking man sauntered out of the kitchen, spread the tablecloth in front of us and recited the menu. We ordered our lunch and Alex stood up to walk around the restaurant, admiring the pictures on the wall and chatting with the old men.

She noticed one chap had a bouzouki case leaning against the wall beside him.

'Do you play?' she asked, pointing at the instrument.

'Yes, but it's only a hobby,' the old man replied. 'I'm not very good.'

'Doesn't matter, we're all friends here. Let's hear it,' Alex said.

A group of old men on the next table woke up and clapped their hands in encouragement until the bouzouki player unzipped his case and strummed a few cords to tune up.

'Any special request?' he asked.

'Yes,' Alex replied, '"Agalma Poulopoulos", if you know it?' The song held wonderful memories for Alex. She and her brother would play it whenever they had difficulties in their early lives to give them courage. It was their inspirational song.

The music began as our food arrived. We sent a jug of wine over to the old man playing and listened to the sweet music as we enjoyed our lunch.

The door opened, and a man walked in carrying a tom-tom. He sat next to the bouzouki player and tapped the drum in time with the music. Alex could resist no longer. She sprang to her feet and started to dance. The old men clapped as she performed a classical fisherman's dance in the middle of the previously sleepy taverna. As she twisted around in time to the music, I saw tears in her eyes. For Alex, this was not just dancing; it was a solitary experience of remembrance and thought.

Alex has always had trouble hiding her emotions, and everyone realised what the dance meant to her. As she finished and sat down, the old men clapped and cried out, 'Bravo kopelia.' They had appreciated her performance and wanted her to continue.

Soon, the cries of 'Opa' radiated around the room. One man got to his feet and started dancing. Alex remained seated and clapped in time to the rhythm. The taverna owner, who had been watching the show with a smile, got up, rummaged in a cupboard, and found his instrument. It looked like a goat with its legs sown up. It was a tsambouna, Greek bagpipes. So, we had a band.

As the sun set, lunch became dinner. Families from the village had heard the music and streamed inside to join the fun. We arrived home after midnight, after leaving the party in full swing but with more wonderful memories of our Greek village.

For Alex, this is normal. Wherever we go, she always has people dancing. Her spirit and love for life infect even the most formal-looking characters. They always end up smiling in the end.

Recently we travelled to Greece the long way, having decided that rather than fly as normal, we would drive and take the scenic route. We drove to Folkestone and took the Euro-tunnel to France. After an overnight stop in Champagne and another stop in Switzerland, followed by Lake Como, we spent three days in Venice. One evening, we were walking around St Mark's Square as the sun was dipping below the historic buildings. As usual, it was crowded with people taking photographs. Vendors with enormous bunches of balloons mingled with the crowds, and there were pop-up stalls selling picture postcards and traditional ceramic masks. As we strolled around the square, we noticed one of the pavement cafes had an orchestra to entertain their clients. I had heard that this area was the most expensive place in the world to sit for a coffee, but we were only there once so braved the expense and sat to soak up the atmosphere.

Wherever we go in the world, Alex, being patriotic, always carries a small Greek flag. Today was no exception. Alex loves Venice. There is a bond between Greek and Venetian culture, and many of the towns spread around the islands and mainland of western Greece have similar architecture and character. We took our seat at a table near the orchestra. It had a pure-white linen tablecloth and a vase of fresh flowers as a centrepiece. She took out her flag and planted it into the vase of flowers on the table. An immaculately dressed waiter wearing a starched white jacket, black waistcoat and matching bow tie appeared instantly and took our order.

We sipped our coffee while listening to the orchestra playing soft Vivaldi music and looked around at the majestic architecture. It was such an honour to be in this beautiful square in this beautiful city. We finished our coffee but did not feel like moving on. We were enjoying this experience, so ordered another. The orchestra had finished their recital of *The Four Seasons* and had taken a break. As the conductor climbed back onto the small stage, he looked at our table and saw Alex's flag.

'Are you Greek?' he called.

'Yes,' Alex replied, and took her flag from the flowerpot and waved it in the air.

He turned and waved his baton, and they began to play. Gone was the sweet music of Venetian composers. Gone were the sweet tones of a classical violin. They were playing 'Zorba the Greek'. Alex clapped her hands in delight and stood up and began to dance slowly, her arms outstretched in time with the slow music. I watched as she entered a trance-like state and swayed with the soft, slowly increasing tempo. It was as if no one else was there. She had entered her own world of dance; this was where she felt comfortable. As she danced, a girl from another table joined her, linking arms across her shoulder, then another, until there were several girls dancing in time to the rapidly quickening music, with Alex waving her flag. I noticed crowds of people had funnelled from the rest of St Mark's Square. Other cafes with their own bands were emptying as crowds diverged to watch the performance. Soon, there were hundreds watching and clapping in time with the beat. It became too much for Alex's dance partners, who one by one dropped out, laughing and exhausted, leaving Alex dancing alone. There she was, leaping in time to the music, waving her flag and having a wonderful time while her appreciative audience was still swelling. People were clapping and whistling and cheering at this impromptu show. When the music finally ended, there was an almighty roar of approval from the whole of the square as people clapped and cheered. The orchestra stood up and bowed to her as she rejoined me at the table.

So, after dancing on a world stage in front of thousands of people in Venice, she had no fear of performing with Eleni in our small village taverna.

That evening, we arrived and were met by an excited Eleni. She showed us to our reserved table and disappeared to get ready. The restaurant was already packed with locals and tourists keen to experience some Greek culture. The band included a drummer, a bouzouki player, a bearded man holding a violin, and another with a clarinet. They had set up microphones and lighting directed at the band. They were ready.

Most visitors to Greece consider 'Zorba the Greek' to be the traditional dance of Greece. This is not the case in most villages and islands. Zorba is a type of dance known as Sirtaki. It's probably the most famous Greek dance known around the world. However, Sirtaki only dates to the nineteen sixties; the Greek musician Mikis Theodorakis created the dance for the movie *Zorba the Greek*. By alternating slow and fast steps from the Hasapiko and Hasaposerviko dances, Sirtaki was born. They danced it in a line or circle formation, with hands placed on their neighbour's shoulders.

Each region has its own unique folk dances. No one knows them all. Most villages dance a Syrtos – it's a name used to describe a vast collection of dances, typically line dances that form a semicircle. Most areas of Greece have their own variation, tailored to match their own traditions, and it is danced at most Greek festivities and weddings. The most well known of these dances is the Kalamatianos, which uses the same steps as the Syrtos, though the former is more upbeat and faster paced. They typically regard it as the national dance of Greece. This was going to be the main dancing style tonight.

They taught traditional Greek dancing in schools. This is where Alex first developed her passion as a small girl. Over the years, she honed her art so much that she will leap up and dance whenever the opportunity arises.

Greek dancing is always a combination of tears and smiles. 'Zorba the Greek' is a perfect example of smiles, where the pace goes from very slow to furious until everyone collapses in a heap, giggling and happy. Other dances are pure emotion.

The first dance was to be performed by Alex. It would be the Zeibekiko. It's a difficult dance, mainly because it has no set steps, no particular rhythm requiring an inner intensity, as it is an improvised movement that expresses the feelings of the individual. These are mainly feelings of sadness, life's despair and unfulfilled dreams; after all, its origin is in Asia Minor, the place of displaced Greeks, a homeland long lost along with lives and fortunes. So, it is almost a religious experience and not to be taken lightly. Alex's family had suffered deportation and sadness, and it was important to remember the suffering of her ancestors. This was her way of remembering them.

For me, this seemed to be a strange beginning to an evening of dance. Most parties would begin with upbeat music and build up the fun from there. But this was different. It would be a very sad, almost religious dance to remember the suffering of the Greeks and the sadness inflicted upon this brave race.

Alex took her position as the band played. She swayed gently, and slowly increased the intensity of her moves. One moment she was sitting forlornly on the floor; the next, she had sprung up and was gazing at the ceiling with her hands pressed together in prayer. By the time the music stopped, there was absolute silence. I looked around the room to see tear-stained faces with expressions of joy. Someone clapped, then another, until everyone present was on their feet clapping and cheering for her performance.

Alex came and sat beside me. Her dance had also affected her, and tears were rolling down her cheeks.

The music started again. This time it was brighter, and uplifting bouzouki played rapidly, signalling the beginning of the festivities. Alex remained seated as Eleni went around pulling people from their chairs. A circle formed as they danced, holding hands around the floor, led by Eleni. The music played as more people joined the growing group. Alex pulled me up, and we went to join in.

It was a wonderful, emotional evening, starting with sadness and ending in the early hours of the morning with smiles and companionship. Everyone went home happy. This was our village, and we couldn't love it more.

10

VISITORS TO OUR HOME

O ur home was built. We still needed to deal with a few extras, like painting the wall, putting the garden in order, and generally getting everything as we wanted, but it felt good to know we had done it and were recovering financially.

Owning a house on a Greek island attracts visitors. Alex and I are always happy when friends or family come. But some are more welcome than others.

I have spoken to many people who have visited Greece and asked them if they enjoyed it; I am always keen to hear their impressions of my beautiful adopted country. But I am often disappointed.

'Yes, the pool was wonderful, the weather was glorious' is the usual reply.

They had spent two weeks meandering between the hotel bar, restaurant and pool. They didn't set foot outside, but they had a wonderful time. Greece, Spain, Turkey or any other sunny European resort could have been their location. Would they have known the difference?

When asked why they chose Greece for this adventure, the reply is usually 'Because I love Greece'. But the only part of Greece seen was the route from the airport to the hotel, and back again two weeks later.

Many hotels have realised this and anticipated the needs of these travellers. Fully self-inclusive hotels are arriving. These insulate travellers from any culture outside the walls of the compound. This is such a loss. Tourist resorts have sprung up catering only for British people, with pubs selling British beer, and British soaps beamed directly to bars to be watched during happy hour while munching on fish and chips. But not in our village.

A friend of mine called me to ask if his brother could come to visit us; he was holidaying in Skiathos with his family. After all, it's only a short boat ride to Pefki. We had never met them but had no problem if anyone wanted to visit.

'Sure,' I said. 'Come and stay for a few days. You'll love it.'

The next day, he and his wife arrived. We greeted them at the gate and showed them to their room. They walked through the house into the garden, looked at me, and asked, 'Where's the pool?'

'See that big blue thing over there? It's called the Aegean Sea. That's our pool,' I told him.

'Sorry, we can't stay anywhere without a pool,' he said.

Alex could see I was getting a little angry with these people and put a calming hand on my shoulder. Being a perfect host and full-blooded Greek, she was concerned that people coming to visit were not satisfied. In the genuine spirit of philoxenia (kindness to strangers) she made a call to the hotel next door and arranged a room for them next to the pool, and paid the bill. We never saw them again.

Then came the call from Alex's brother, Christos. He was arriving in Athens with his family and was keen to visit our new home. He was a welcome guest.

He is not just a brother-in-law to me; he is like a real brother and a genuine friend. We share the same humour, and whenever we meet we spend our time laughing with tears rolling down our cheeks.

We call him the absent-minded professor. Being a genius engineer, he was one of the first inventors to bring automation to Greece. After he completed his degree in England, he secured a job in a fruit factory in the north which gathered crops of apricots and soft fruit from all over the region and sealed them in cans. It was a laborious task and very labour-intensive, until he designed a system whereby the fruit was poured in at one end of the factory and emerged at the other end fully sealed in tins, labelled and automatically packed in boxes. Instead of every stage being done by hand, all that was required was for one person to press a button. The owners loved his work, the employees were given other jobs such as quality control and administration, and the growers delighted because their crop would be canned quickly while it was still fresh. The buyers of the fruit were happy because production increased, and everyone was making a better living.

But living in the isolated village, the only entertainment was the village kafenio. Christos, being a sensitive person who loved being with people, missed his family and had trouble coping with the loneliness. This led to finishing work, then spending every evening and weekend with nothing else to do but become addicted to alcohol, which was freely available.

This took a terrible toll. The loneliness and guilt over-whelmed him. He cut off contact from Debbie and Alex as he plunged deeper into his drink-fuelled abyss. Debbie's and Alex's attempts to contact him failed. He didn't want to talk any more.

So, Debbie and Alex took the car and drove to his village to find him.

They drove around the small village, not knowing where he lived. They found the factory on the outskirts, but it was Sunday, so closed. The last place to try was the kafenio to ask if anyone knew him. All the men of the village were there, but not Christos. Unknown to Alex and Debbie, he was nearby in his small room, recovering from another hangover. The men were drinking coffee or tsipouro as they entered.

'Does anyone know my son, Christos?' Debbie called out. Everyone went quiet. One man stood up from his chair, came over and knelt at Debbie's feet.

'Please let me kiss the belly of the woman who gave birth to the saviour of our village,' he begged.

Before Christos, the village was dying. Young people had left in search of a better life. The only industry in the area was growing or packing fruit. It was a scant and unreliable income, leaving the village in poverty. Not only did Debbie's son bring automation to the factory, but it was now prosperous and people were returning to join in the bounty. Families were reuniting. People had more income, and the life had returned to the village. But at what cost to Christos?

After a long fight with alcoholism, and the loving care of his family, he finally overcame his addiction. Christos now lives in Holland with his Dutch wife, Jaqueline, and two children: Darwin, and Despina, named after his mother Debbie. He is still an inventor and works every day with cutting-edge technology, which he shares with the world. He has never drunk since.

Christos is well known for being highly intelligent, but unfortunately fails in the mundane things in life. He has trouble tying his shoelaces, and frequently arrives home by bus because he forgets where he parked his car. He has the forward-planning ability of a headless chicken running around a farmyard. He lives his life from one crisis to another and has no sense of direction. So, we decided to drive to the airport to get him. He would never have found us otherwise.

We met the family at the airport. Darwin had brought his new Dutch girlfriend, Britt, a beautiful, tall girl with long blonde hair and a comfortable smile. Britt had never visited Greece, and Darwin was looking forward to showing her his heritage. Despina was also in a relationship and had brought her girlfriend, Cecile, a short, dusky girl with cropped hair, but unlike Britt, there was no smile. Christos picked up a hire car and followed us to our home in Glyfada, where he would spend a few days with us, Debbie and Zissis before the trip to Pefki.

While the youngsters did their own thing, exploring Glyfada and relaxing on the nearby beach, Christos wandered around Glyfada, tutting with disapproval.

'In Holland, the trains and buses run on time, and they are spotlessly clean,' he told Alex. 'The drivers here are terrible, the road signs make little sense, and where are the cycle lanes?'

He criticised everything about Greece: the lack of organisation, stray cats and dogs, graffiti, and anything else that wasn't like Holland.

Alex sat and listened patiently without a flicker of her usual anger when her country is criticised.

I would never have got away with this. If I ever show the slightest disapproval of her beloved country, I am in real danger of physical harm, usually with her weapon of choice, a slipper or a mop, or even more scary, the laser-beam stare.

So how come he could get away with it? He had not been hit, not once. She hadn't screamed at him or threatened his life. This restraint wasn't like her at all. The only reason I could think of was that she had made allowances for him living abroad and becoming institutionalised. After all, he was still Greek, and still her brother.

An uneasy peace fell upon the house. I could see Alex was upset and something needed to be done to lift everyone's spirits. So, on the third day of his visit, I insisted we left for our trip to Pefki to help him become Greek again.

On the first day, he walked down to the harbour and joined the old men for coffee. When he returned, his expression had changed. He looked calm and peaceful. His eyes had been opened to the beauty and the kindest people in the world around him. It was as if he had woken from a dream where everything in his life was organised and robotic. Now he was free. Now he was Greek again.

Here, life is simpler. If you miss a bus, there's probably another tomorrow. Things run in a different time zone. People are more relaxed; there's no pressure to rush and keep appointments, and everyone is happier for it.

Christos was back to his old self. We spent a delightful few days laughing until we cried and enjoying the village and surrounding areas as he got himself reacquainted with Greek life after living in a more formal country. But his son Darwin seemed to be as dizzy as his dad.

Darwin was born in Holland and has adapted to the efficiency of Dutch living. But when he arrived in Greece, his Greek side surfaced. The family spent their sunny days here lounging on the beach, eating at laid-back seaside restaurants. Life had slowed down.

One day, Darwin went shopping with his Dutch girlfriend. He stopped at a petrol station to fill up, but his credit card didn't work when trying to pay for the fuel. They didn't have enough cash, so he left his girlfriend at the petrol station as security while he came home to get some money. On the way home, he passed Pefki beach, saw a friend and decided to join him for a quick coffee. An hour or so later, he arrived home and went to have a shower. He came out of the bathroom wrapped in a towel.

'Hi, Darwin,' I said. 'Where's Britt?'

A look of realisation spread over his face as he remembered leaving her at the petrol station hours earlier. We all jumped into the car to rescue her.

We arrived and found her sitting under a canopy beside the forecourt at a long table, eating lunch with the owner's family, a forkful of stuffed tomatoes in one hand and a glass of local wine in the other. As we approached, the family set a few more chairs around the table and invited us to join them for lunch.

Britt forgave Darwin, and we had a lovely lunch with our new friends.

Two weeks passed in a flash and we enjoyed every moment of their visit, until the very end. Alex and I were sitting with Christos on our patio having breakfast.

'Have you all had a good time?' I asked.

'Yes, we did, but the kids' partners were not very happy,' he told us.

That was surprising news. We had done our best to make them feel part of the family.

'Why is that?' Alex asked.

'They say everyone here is false and too polite, especially you two,' he said. 'It makes them feel uncomfortable.'

Alex did not receive this news well. She slammed her coffee cup on the table. 'So, you want us to be pigs, do you? We are living our normal lives here. We all love and respect each other. We are never false or over-polite, we are just who we are. You can all take it or leave it,' she told him, and stomped off.

I think it was just a clash of cultures. Northern Europeans tend to be more insular and reserved. Greeks are happy, loud people who show their hearts, their passion in life, and love to share it. Perhaps this makes some people feel uncomfortable. Never mind, we were happy this way and would not change.

We bade farewell to Christos and his family, promising to meet again soon and agreeing not to be too nice next time.

Our next visitor was my friend Mike who brought his family. They would only stay a couple of days and we had warned them that the house was still a little basic, but Mike was a good friend from England, and had followed the progress of the building and was keen to see it for himself. Mike is a surgeon, with a stressful lifestyle, so a visit to our sleepy village was just what he needed. He planned to show his family the Acropolis and other sights of Athens, and had booked a hotel near Glyfada for a two-week holiday. They would break this up with a quick visit to us.

That morning, Mike and his family arrived. They loved the house, but Mike, being a keen gardener, looked at the state of our garden. The lawn was growing well around the molehills. The few recently planted small trees looked okay, but otherwise it was rather bare.

'Why not plant a vegetable patch?' Mike asked. 'You have lots of room and you could grow really interesting things here, even melons in this climate. But you certainly need cucumbers.

They would grow really well.' We agreed we'd see what we could find at the market the following day.

We took our guests on a pre-lunch tour of Pefki. Mike loved the village. He had never been to a Greek island before. He was more used to holidays in exotic locations, white sandy beaches and high-class hotels with twenty-four-hour room service. This was something different for him and his family. There are no five-star hotels decorated with crystal chandeliers or red carpets. It's a pure, traditional village which lifts the heart and makes you feel part of it and its people.

For lunch we took them to a friend's fish taverna near the beach. It's a simple place. Niko runs it with his mother, who does most of the cooking. He speaks English well, so we thought it would be good to introduce them so Mike could have another friend in the village. We sat down at the table. Adonia, Niko's mother, saw us arrive and rushed out with a wide smile and open arms. She grabbed Alex and hugged her. Then it was my turn. I felt the breath leave my body as her arms enveloped me and she squeezed. She greeted Mike and his family and ushered us to a table overlooking the beautiful harbour.

'We have something special today,' she proudly announced. 'Wait, I will show it to you.'

She disappeared into the kitchen and returned with a large black slippery cone. It was around one metre long, broad and circular at one end and tapered to a point. She proudly laid it on the table and asked us to smell its freshness.

Mike poked it to see if it was alive.

'What is it?' Alex asked.

'It's a swordfish nose,' she told us. 'It's delicious grilled and makes wonderful soup. My husband caught it this morning. It's the talk of the village. But I knew you were coming, so I saved the best bit for you.'

Mike grinned. I was planning on ordering a typical Greek

meze, but the swordfish nose sounded too good to miss. His first meal in Greece would include a swordfish nose, and he was delighted. When the prepared swordfish nose arrived from the kitchen, it had been skinned, deboned and fried in batter. Succulent chunks of were piled on a plate surrounded by cut lemons freshly picked from Adonia's tree. As the rest of the meze kept coming, Niko brought another table to hold the bounty. We enjoyed our leisurely lunch while watching over the calm water of the harbour as the sun dipped, casting golden ripples onto the perfect Aegean Sea.

The next day, Mike and I went shopping for plants. My Greek language was coming along well, but I was still having trouble with the regional accents, so going to the market for supplies was still a challenge. Alex had also given me a shopping list. Top of the list was bread. I had already suffered with this one. When I first started to learn Greek, she sent me to the baker's asking for psoli (penis). I should have asked for psomi (bread), but Alex always loves to embarrass me.

When on our island, we tend not to shave every day, so we both looked a little like hobos. I wore an old T-shirt and shorts, and Mike dressed in his normal tatty surgical scrubs stained from yesterday's lunch, his belly protruding below the hem. But in the village, there is no formality or dress code, so we felt comfortable driving the short distance to the local market dressed as we were.

At the market we browsed the stalls selling local plants. We bought some watermelon, aubergines and tomatoes, but could not see any cucumber plants. So we had to ask.

I called Alex.

Alex slowly and phonetically told me what to say.

'You must ask for écheis agorákia,' she said.

I remembered the word for cucumber was angoúri, so it sounded right. I didn't really trust Alex as she had got me into trouble before, but this sounded okay so I memorised the phrase.

I went to the plant vendor and in my best Greek asked, 'Écheis agorákia?'

The man looked at us two scruffy, unshaven foreigners. His face darkened and he told us: 'No. Go away.'

Well, that was uncharacteristically rude for a Greek, I thought, and we moved on to the next stall and asked again. This time, the vendor shot us a withering look and turned away without replying.

Alex had played yet another game on me. Instead of asking for angoúri (cucumbers), these two dirty old men had been wandering around the market asking for agóri. It sounded the same, but to my embarrassment meant something completely different.

We had been asking for little boys.

I decided not to buy any cucumbers that day and went home to sulk.

Mike was still looking shocked when I explained the mix-up and the deliberate plan of Alex's to get me into more trouble. I told Mike about my early Greek lessons from Alex: getting me to ask the petrol attendant to fill me up rather than the car; sending me to the pharmacy to ask for 'nappy rash cream to spread onto my sore buttocks'. It took me ages to learn that phrase – I thought I was asking for vitamin pills. She would take every opportunity to teach me Greek until I realised the best way to learn the language was to ignore her. But not all language mishaps are Alex's fault. My brother, Jon, came back from his Athens holiday in a strange mood.

'Did you have a delightful time?' I asked.

'No, I bloody well did not,' he replied. 'I don't want to talk about it.'

This was surprising. I thought he'd have had a lovely time

in this beautiful, warm and welcoming country. After a little probing, all became clear. My dear brother, along with thousands of other tourists, had learned his first Greek word.

Malaka is the most common word in the Greek language. Tourists learn it before they learn to say good morning. It's used with a variety of different meanings by men and women, but it literally translates as 'man who masturbates'. While people typically use it as an insult, its equivalent in English being 'wanker', the meaning alters depending on the context. It can be an exclamation of pleasure, an expression of horror, a cry of anger, a declaration of affection, or something else entirely.

Finally, I got the story.

He explained.

'On the last day of my holiday, I went to the kiosk to buy a packet of cigarettes and he called me a malaka. I am never going to Greece again because they are rude.'

Jon had fallen into the trap of the Greek tone. The chap in the kiosk had only asked him if he preferred a hard packet of cigarettes or soft (mal-a-ka or ma-la-kó). The word is similar, and to our non-Greek ears sounds virtually identical, but the pronunciation changes the meaning completely. I could see Mike making a mental note.

The family spent their days swimming from the beach while Mike sat at a table and sipped his cold Mythos beer, enjoying the relaxation. He had made friends with some people in the village and was communicating using some recently learned Greek (not from Alex), body language, and pictures drawn on napkins. He was just finishing his drink and ready to bring his family back when Niko came running out of his restaurant.

'Mike, my mother has cut her hand. Can you help?'

Adonia had been cutting a fish when the knife slipped, leaving a gash in the back of her hand. Mike sprang into action and wrapped her hand in a towel to ease the bleeding. He called me to bring his medical bag from the house, and he set about repairing the damage. He stitched and bandaged her hand, then sat with her until she felt better. A moment later, Niko came running in.

'My friend Costas has just got off his boat. He has a big fish hook stuck in his hand. Can you help?'

The next day, Mike left the house early with his medical bag. He didn't come back at lunchtime. He wasn't answering his phone, so I went to find him. There he was at Niko's restaurant, sitting at one of the outside tables, surrounded by a group of people. He was holding surgery, with Niko translating, and having a wonderful time.

Mike cancelled his booking at the five-star hotel in Athens and spent his entire holiday with us, but he spent most of his days at the taverna. He removed fish hooks, advised people on ailments, and became popular in the village. By the time he left, he had made new friends and left his mark on the village. He later told me that it was the best holiday he'd ever had.

The day after he left, we too had need of his medical skills. I came out of the kitchen and stepped onto the porch, when I heard a faint whining sound. I looked onto the road outside and saw a small black puppy with a white-tipped tail sitting there, looking distressed. It was my favourite one of Korky's. Her front leg was twisted at a strange angle and was clearly broken.

We had not seen Korky or her puppies again since we left them in the care of Maria. They hadn't come back to visit since, and I assumed they had found another home. But somehow, this little puppy had remembered us and where we lived, and had crawled to us with a broken leg.

I called for Alex to bring a blanket. She ran down the steps with a large towel and sat on the road beside me. I tried to examine the broken leg, but the puppy was in so much pain she yelped at the slightest touch. Alex carefully wrapped her in the towel, and we took her inside the house.

As we closed the door, Maria arrived with Dimitri. He had a few plants for us, and Maria was keen to catch up on the gossip of Mike's visit. She had heard he had become popular in the village and wanted to ask his advice about her 'water problem'. They both looked at the puppy. Maria told us it wouldn't live with damage like that. Dimitri stroked her head and turned to me.

'I have my gun in the truck. I think it is best that I shoot her. It would be the kindest thing,' he assured me.

Maria looked at me with a sad expression.

'I think he's right,' she said. 'It would be the kindest thing to do.'

Alex disagreed, me too. I wanted to give this poor animal the best chance. There was no way we were going to let this dog be killed. We needed expert medical attention. Alex called the vet surgery in the next village but there was no answer, so she called the pharmacy near the surgery to ask if they knew where the vet was. We hadn't seen him since the nibbled tortoise episode but knew he rarely held surgery in the village; he spent most of his time in other areas of the island. The lady in the pharmacy confirmed that he wasn't expected for another week.

But Alex was not giving up. She called the local hospital.

'I have a dog with a broken leg. Will you see her?' she asked. They slammed the phone down.

Next, she tried the local doctor.

'Sorry, Alex, but I know nothing about animals so I really can't help you,' he said. 'But you could try Dr Lazarus. He is an orthopaedic surgeon with a practice in Edipsos. He has a surgery above the cake shop. I know he is an animal lover; he may help.'

He gave her the number, and Alex called.

'Yes, I know you only treat people ... Yes, I know that but ... Yes, and what about the Hippocratic oath? You took that, didn't you? ... No, it doesn't just include humans, it's all living things. ... Okay. Goodbye.'

As I had only heard one side of the conversation, I was still in the dark.

'So what happened?' I asked.

'He's agreed to see her today after his appointments. We must be there in one hour and he will look at the puppy.'

We arrived at Dr Lazarus's surgery. I waited outside in the hallway, holding the puppy wrapped up in a towel, while Alex went in to see him. She came out and told me to stay there. There was a waiting room full of patients wanting to see the doctor and he didn't want us sitting with them. I sat on the marble staircase, holding my wounded puppy, until the last patient brushed past me and the doctor called us in. We laid the little black dog on the examining table. Dr Lazarus lifted her leg and gently examined the break.

'It's a clean break,' he said, 'but I can't deal with it. If you want to fix it, you will have to go to Athens. I can do a temporary fix, but it will need to be properly set.'

He sent Alex to the pharmacy to get some bandages and plaster, then worked to form a tiny cast over the break. We took her back to the car, still wrapped in a towel, with a newly plastered white leg sticking in the air. We had to go to Athens quickly if we were to save this puppy. Alex called our vet in Glyfada and made an appointment for that afternoon.

As we drove home, I reflected on the destiny of this little dog. She was obviously born in the wild and had found us before. She had already died once in our garden and come back from the dead, then was nearly killed again by a shotgun before we stepped in to save her. If she had made her way to any other house in the village, it was likely that they would have destroyed her to save her from more suffering. She chose us, knowing her sanctuary awaited. And the doctor who had just plastered her leg, his name was Lazarus, the biblical character who rose from the dead. Fate was telling us something which we could not ignore. We had to save this puppy.

We put our dogs in the car, left cat food with Maria to feed our ever-growing population, and drove the four-hour journey to Athens with the little dog on Alex's lap, her stiff white leg waving in the air.

We arrived at our vet in Glyfada. He looked, X-rayed, and set to work. He put a metal pin inside her bone to join it and replaced the plaster cast. We decided to stay in Glyfada for the healing period, and spent some time with Debbie, who was pleased to see us and happy we would stay a while. We had already adopted this puppy and gave Debbie the honour of naming her. I was expecting a nice Greek name, but no, Debbie, being a practical person, named her after her colour. Our new member of our family would be called Blackie.

But we soon forgot this name as her true character revealed itself. Alex lost her temper one day when we came home and found Blackie had rifled through the bin and spread empty meat wrappers and old fish bones in every corner of the house. There was even a half-eaten fish head on my pillow.

'You little shitface,' Alex yelled. And the name stuck.

After that we would go for walks around the village. The locals would greet our dogs with a pat on the head or a small treat.

'Geia Jack, geia Bella, geia Shitface,' they would call.

We had to change her name back to Blackie whenever we travelled to England, but back in Greece, she was always known as Shitface.

The healing time for a broken leg in a puppy is relatively short (two to four weeks). Younger dogs have more bone-building cells and are growing anyway, so their bones are constantly remodelling. The plaster cast came off after two weeks, and she seemed fine.

The vet gave her all the vaccinations needed, then issued a pet passport to allow her to travel with us. Over the next few years, Blackie became a much-travelled and valued member of our family. We often took her to England, Glyfada and Pefki. From humble beginnings, she became a favourite of anyone who met her and continued to show us love and happiness every day for the rest of her life.

11

A LIFE ON THE OCEAN WAVE

With the sea being so close, I often jealously watched the speedboats in the bay bouncing over the waves and leaving trails of white wake in contrast to the blue Aegean. I often thought about the fun and adventure to be had speeding across the water, the wind in our hair, if we joined them. I had to buy a boat. But before I could own one, I needed a licence to drive it.

Although part of the European Union at the time, the law in the UK was vastly different to that in Greece. In England, anyone can purchase a boat up to twenty-four metres or eighty tonnes in weight and operate it in and around our coast and on most inland waterways, with no sort of training or boat licence or certification. Here, I needed to prove I could drive one and show a certificate. I would be let nowhere near the sea without the correct paperwork. But I found a loophole. As a member of the European Union, if I got a licence in the UK, it would be valid for Greece. I was still travelling and working intermittently in the UK, so booked in to take my Powerboat Level 2 qualification near to our home in England during my next trip.

On a cool Monday morning, I arrived at the harbour in Leigh-on-Sea in Essex. The teacher greeted me with a smile and introduced himself as Eric, and presented me to my four fellow students. He showed us to a small red inflatable with a silver engine, and asked us to jump on and hold tight as we sped out of the harbour and into the channel. It was exhilarating. The noise of the engine combined with the bumps over the waves and the feeling of speed had me hooked in the first few minutes. I loved it. After the initial rush, we returned to the harbour to practise steering in and out of spaces between moored boats and learn about safety procedure, including falling overboard and rescue techniques. We achieved this by throwing a life ring into the sea and fishing it out. It was too cold in the North Sea for anyone to jump in the water; we would likely have frozen to death before our rescue. At the end of the first day, we had all taken our turn at the helm and were feeling confident and comfortable with the controls.

The next day was classroom work. We spent two hours looking at flags and signs, descriptions of what they meant, and general maritime theory, which I tried to memorise for the upcoming exam.

At noon, Eric announced that the local pub was open and we should continue there. He went to the bar and ordered our drinks and joined us at the table.

'Questions?' he asked.

None of us had anything relevant to ask, so Eric opened his briefcase, took out a yellow folder, pulled out a stack of paper slips, and passed around our licences.

'I thought we would have an exam,' I suggested.

'Oh no, that's unnecessary. You all know what you're doing now. So good luck in the future and have fun.'

So, I was a fully qualified boat driver with a licence to prove it. I couldn't wait to get back to Greece and buy my boat.

On arrival in Greece, Alex met me at the airport. I proudly produced my new licence and told her to get ready for a seafaring life. She suspiciously eyed my document. Alex had come from a long line of sea captains. She suggested it wasn't much of a qualification if I passed in a day and a half.

'Okay, why don't you take the power boat course here? It's easy, and we would both be qualified by next week,' I proposed.

Alex readily agreed, so the next stop was the port police office in Glyfada. We enrolled her in a course starting in a few days. I had been unrealistically optimistic when I had told Alex how easy it was to gain a qualification. Eventually, after studying in a classroom part-time for six weeks with additional lessons in the harbour and the open sea which, unlike my lessons in the cold North Sea, did involve jumping in and being rescued, came the day of the examination. It was a three-hour written examination followed by a driving test in the sea, all overseen by uniformed officers with stern, unsmiling faces, holding clipboards. This was a million miles from my casual experience of gaining my boat licence over a beer in the local pub. She actually needed to become proficient and get a 'proper' qualification.

Little did I know Alex was destined to become the worst back-seat driver ever. She would have no interest in actually driving the boat, but would sit beside me and constantly criticise my driving.

'Look out for that oil tanker. No, don't go that way, go this way. Keep to the right, not the left, and stop sinking!'

All valuable advice, but it always made me nervous whenever we would go out to sea in our future boat together.

When I was alone on the boat, it was enjoyable. Because I wasn't getting advice thrown at me constantly, I thought I drove better and observed most of the rules. But I often forgot about the 'stop sinking' part.

But we were now both 'fully qualified', so we went on a boat hunt.

On the island, when looking to gain any type of motorised vehicle, tractor or car, everything is word of mouth. This includes boats. There are no local newspapers with a selection of vessels available, no handy websites containing an array of crafts to rely on. We have to ask around. After speaking to a few locals and being offered a couple of one hundred-year-old fishing boats, we finally found a local fisherman who had a cousin selling a 'nice' boat in a small seaside village south of Chalkida, the capital of Evia, about one hundred and thirty kilometres away.

So, we set out for the long drive south through the mountains to the capital. We arrived at the address given and saw it parked in the driveway: a beautiful, sleek white boat sitting proudly on its trailer, gleaming in the sunshine. It had a centre console with a steering wheel, a nice bench seat to the rear, and a gleaming fifty-five horsepower engine. It was perfect.

Alex knocked on the door and an old man appeared

wearing a tattered captain's hat and a blue T-shirt with a picture of an anchor printed on the front. He introduced himself as Costas and shook our hands. I pointed at the boat and complimented him on the sleek craft. He thanked me and said, 'That's not the one for sale. You came to look at the one around the back.'

That was disappointing. I already had my hand in my pocket to get the money out. I wasn't even going to haggle. He led us through a dark passageway into a garage filled with old lorry tyres and parts of outboard motors. Through the gloom was a mound covered with a green, oily tarpaulin. Costas pulled it and it slid to the ground, revealing our boat. It looked a little older and shabbier than the one gleaming in the driveway, but it looked sound and seaworthy. Costas took out 'the ears', a U-shaped device that slips over the water intake at the base of the engine, and connected a hose. We watched as water leaked from around the engine and slowly dribbled through another small hole further up. Costas seemed satisfied that the water was flowing through nicely, so turned the ignition key on the dash and the engine roared into life. Not knowing anything about boats, I assumed that if the engine worked, it must be fine. So, I agreed to pay the asking price, and took out the money and offered it to Costas, who held up his hands as if he was defending himself from an attack. I had expected to pay the money, hitch the boat up to the car and drive back to Pefki for a quick cruise around Skiathos. Unfortunately, I hadn't even thought about the bureaucracy needed to buy it.

We followed Costas to the harbour and entered an office with an official sign above the door announcing the port police. A young lady dressed in a naval uniform greeted us and showed us to her desk, where the fun began. I produced my passport, and Costas produced the boat papers. Alex sat steadfastly by my side and helped fill out the transfer forms in

Greek, translating any troublesome questions and continually reassuring me we had nearly finished. After three hours of sitting at this desk watching the young lady lick stamps and post them on the confetti of forms, I was delighted when she stood up and gave me a sheet of paper. We had finished at last.

No hope. The paper needed to be taken to the Chalkida tax office, where I needed to pay a 'small' tax to complete the deal, then bring back the receipt fully stamped in the right place with two photocopies. The tax office was about ten miles away. Morning had already become early afternoon, and the tax office was due to close for the day in thirty minutes. If we couldn't deal with it now, we would have to come back tomorrow. I drove like a true Greek and we arrived just as the office was closing. We rushed in, found the correct window, paid the tax, and armed with a still wet government stamp, we drove back to the port police office. The next two hours of more stamp licking went by at a slow pace until at last the process was nearly finished. Costas was still sitting there, totally unfazed, watching me fidget while the last forms were completed. The young lady stood up from her desk and gave me a piece of paper, which I assumed to be the end. No such luck. I now needed to go to the local photographer, get two passport photos, take them to the police station with my passport, and get them both officially stamped. I returned to the port office, handed the freshly stamped photos to the young lady, who stamped them again, handed me a pile of paperwork, and said goodbye. We had done it. We went back to Costas's house, paid him, hitched the boat to the car, and set off home.

As we drove through the mountains on our way to Pefki, I suggested to Alex that it would likely be a bit late for a boat trip today as it would be dark by the time we arrived. Alex looked at me and smiled knowingly. She hadn't the heart to speak to me before as I had been grumbling about the stupid Greek bureaucracy for the past hour of the trip.

'Sorry, my love. You can't use the boat yet. It has to be registered in Pefki before we can take it into the sea.'

All the bureaucratic systems suffered today had only been to take Costas's name off the boat and register it in mine. We would still need to go through more mind-bending bureaucracies in Pefki to licence it in our village. Until then, it would sit unused in our garden. That would be frustrating.

The next day we went to the harbour office, keen to register our boat. Based on yesterday's experience, it was doubtful that we would get time for a cruise before dark, but being a smaller office, and in our own village, maybe they would be more sympathetic and treat us kindly.

The bureaucratic grilling began. The first document requested was my boat licence. I proudly passed over my tatty piece of paper with my name written in biro and signed by my instructor. The police officer looked at the paper, then looked at me and asked, 'Where are the official stamps?'

In Greece, every official paper has a multitude of official stamps. They stamp some on top of other stamps, and sometimes there are so many that a second piece of paper needs to be added for yet more stamps. So this 'official' boat licence was extremely suspicious. He took my licence and disappeared into a back office. I heard mumbling, which soon rose to booming voices as an argument was clearly raging as to the efficacy of my licence. Finally, he returned after the squabble, sat at his desk and tapped at his computer and did a Google search of my licence. He compared mine to the image on the screen and reluctantly accepted it. Then he opened a drawer and took out a stack of forms that needed filling out, each promptly stamped several times before moving onto the next in the slowly shrinking pile of officialdom. Suddenly, he paused his stamping and announced they were closing for lunch and instructed us to come back later. I had no idea what we had accomplished this morning but I did not feel any closer to my Aegean cruise, so we crossed the road for lunch at the harbour taverna.

Still bleary-eyed from the morning of filling out forms, we returned to recommence the mind-numbing procedure. We had completed the last few papers when he asked for the boat insurance. That was something I had not considered, and we could not progress any further without it. We left the office and drove to the next village, paid for the insurance and returned with the policy certificate. He took a copy and added it to the pile, then gave us a typewritten form and told us all we needed now was a report by a ship surveyor.

'Where does he live?' I asked.

'We don't have one anywhere near here. Try Athens,' he replied, and closed the door.

If we were finally going to use our boat, we needed to get it surveyed. It was only really a rowing boat with an engine, so I felt a little confused that we needed to bring a professional from Athens to check it floated. But without that report, we were going nowhere. We sadly drove home, looked at the boat parked in our garden and went inside to start our research on boat surveyors. After a few phone calls to ship surveyors and being told to stop wasting their time, we finally struck lucky. We found a chap who agreed to write a report from a photograph, without visiting. I asked Alex if this was legal. It seemed a little like sending a photo to an MOT station rather than the car. Alex assured me it was common practice here and not to worry. I sent a WhatsApp message to the surveyor, paid his fee via a PayPal account, and within the hour, we had a PDF of a report on the condition of our boat.

Not wishing to look too guilty, we waited for a couple of days before returning to the harbour office. We used the time to wash and polish our vessel, buy new flares, check lifejackets and fill up the tank with petrol, so as soon as permission was granted, we could finally dip our boat in the water.

Early on the third day, we arrived at the harbour office clutching our precious boat report. We could always pretend he was a friend doing us a favour, as nothing happens quickly on the island so it looked deeply suspicious that we got it so fast. We need not have worried though. The police officers studied the report in detail while we sat on the chairs opposite, trying to look less nervous than we felt. If he asked us questions about the boat surveyor's visit, we would have been found out and perhaps sent away to do it again. The surveyor had assured us it was a valid document and not to worry, but we both still felt a little guilty that the survey was done by photographs. But we needn't have worried. He applied the last rubber stamp to our boat papers and handed us our permit, granting us a licence to travel twenty miles from land in any direction. As almost all Greek islands are well within twenty miles of each other, this was fine with us.

We were free to take our new boat out. Our enthusiasm was overwhelming and we couldn't wait to hitch the boat to the back of the car and tow it to the harbour. We located the slipway and reversed the boat down the ramp. With the trailer wheels in the water, we got out of the car, ready for the launch. I looked at our gleaming boat sitting proudly on the trailer, with the stern touching the sea, then realised I did not know how to get the boat off the trailer and into the sea. During my in-depth and detailed one and a half days of training, I never actually had to put a boat into the sea or recover it. It had always been bobbing in the harbour, waiting for me.

I looked at Alex. After all, she had undergone more vigorous training than I had, so surely she must know? She also looked blank. So, both of us had licences of various qualities, allowing us to drive a boat, but neither of us had the first idea of how to put one in the water. I looked at the ratchet arrangement on the trailer. It appeared to hold the boat in place via a strap attached to the boat and wound around a reel. I snapped the retaining clip back, and suddenly, now free of its restraint, the ratchet screamed as the boat slid backward and splashed into the sea, still attached to the long strap. I waded into the water and clambered onto the boat. It was floating nicely, so I pressed the button on the throttle to lower the engine and the propeller dipped into the sea. I turned the key, and it fired into life. I was about to call out to ask Alex to unclip the strap when I noticed I was ankle-deep in water. I looked down. The water was rising towards my knees. I was sinking.

I jumped out of the boat and waded to the slipway, and wound the handle to drag the boat back onto the trailer before it disappeared underneath the water. Being a heavy boat, and now heavier being half-full of water, I struggled to wind it back onto the trailer. Fortunately, water was running from the back during the lifting, so it became lighter with every turn of the handle.

Once it was back on the trailer, I looked at the stern of the boat. There were three perfectly round holes with water gushing out of each. I remembered seeing a few rubber bungs with brass butterfly screws when I was cleaning the boat. I wondered what they were at the time. Now I had a fair idea. I waited until the water had drained away and pushed one into each hole. They fitted snugly. I looked around the boat to see if I had missed any. This was another bit of essential information lacking from our training. I would have thought how not to sink would have been high on the list of dos and don'ts. Some boats have plugs to let the water out. But they had to be put in before you put the boat into the water, otherwise the only direction you are going is down.

Satisfied we were now leakproof, I released the ratchet and once again the boat splashed into the water. I left the strap attached while I reboarded. No leaks were visible, so I lowered the engine and turned the key. The engine started first time and gently ticked over. All seemed well now, so we were ready to sail. Alex unclipped the strap and drove the car and trailer away from the slipway, waded back through the shallow water and clambered over the side of the boat.

This was the first time either of us had been alone on a boat without supervision, and we both felt a little nervous about going too far out to sea. So, we decided on a trip to the next village around the coast, Ellinika. I reversed away from the shore, did a quick turn, and nuzzled the throttle forward. The boat responded smoothly as we left the harbour behind us, turned right to hug the coastline and set off.

We felt the exhilaration as the boat sped up and the front lifted above the waves as we reached our cruising speed. It was a magnificent experience as we rode the waves and watched the shore flash by. We reached the end of Pefki beach and rounded the rocky shore. In the distance, we could make out the church of St Nicholas proudly sitting on its own island, a few metres away from Ellinika beach. We headed towards the shore. As we passed the church, the engine coughed and spluttered. Then silence. Luckily, we still had a little momentum so we glided slowly towards the beach and heard a dull sound of the hull kissing the smooth sand beneath us.

I looked in the petrol tank. It was empty. I had filled it up before we left, and we had only travelled for around ten minutes, so where had it gone? I lifted the engine cover and saw petrol dribbling down the side of the motor. I didn't know at the time that the engine had been winterised. This is done when the boat is to be stored for the winter and fuel is drained, leaving all the petrol valves open to keep it clean.

This was another thing missing from our boat training courses. I had just left a slick of petrol from Pefki harbour to here, and had none left to get back. I tied the boat to a protruding rock on the beach and we called a taxi. The nearest petrol station was near Pefki. Although it had only taken a few minutes to get here by boat, it takes half an hour by road over the hills and through pine forests. After a further thirty minutes we were back at the boat with a full container of petrol and a toolkit.

Our taxi driver had a knowledge of boat engines, so helped to tighten up the valves and make sure we were safe to go back to sea. We spent the afternoon driving around the bay and getting used to the boat. We loved every moment of this new-found freedom. Instead of sitting on the beach admiring the view of the beautifully blue Aegean, we were out here admiring the view of the land. As the sun set, we headed back to the harbour, winched the boat onto the trailer and towed it towards home. Once past the deserted beach, I turned into our road. The boat unfortunately did not.

I watched as the boat and trailer continued along the beach road before swerving to the left and wedging itself between two trees. I manoeuvred the car back to the hitch and lowered the mechanism onto the ball on my tow bar. I pushed the handle down to secure it but it did not click into place. I pulled it off and investigated. A small stone had lodged itself in the mechanism and stopped it from locking properly. I had driven back from the harbour with the boat ready to come off at any time. Luckily it was away from the village so this time I did not destroy any shops or tavernas.

This was another thing lacking from our boat-licence training; how not to let the boat overtake the car would have been a valuable lesson. We went home to plan tomorrow's adventure.

The next day, after spending the previous afternoon getting

to know the boat and learning to drive it, we decided to motor all the way across the Straits of Artemision to visit a seaside village just below Trikeri, near Volos. We had often sat at a harbourfront taverna, looking across the open sea at the beautiful village perched on top of the mountain. Today, at last we had the chance to go there. We would travel away from the safety of the shore into open sea and across shipping lanes, so we carefully checked our fuel, flares and life jackets, and ensured that we tightly squeezed the rubber bungs into the holes this time before setting off. As we left the harbour for our ten-kilometre cruise to the other side, there was not even a ripple in the sea. No waves, just an oily surface reflecting the strong Greek sun. The sea was so smooth I felt confident enough to increase speed. The bow lifted, and we flew across the calm water with not even a bump. In a few moments, we had crossed the shipping lanes and were near our destination. As we rounded the point, small white houses with red-tiled roofs came into view surrounding a natural harbour. As we approached, we saw a delightful-looking taverna with octopus hanging on strings like curtains, drying in the sun. Blue tin tables welcomed us as I reduced power and we slowly glided into a parking spot. We tied up the boat and sat down to order lunch while admiring our little boat parked a few metres away. It was idyllic. We had cruised across the sea in our very own boat. The world was open to us now. We sat enjoying our meal, discussing our next destination.

'Perhaps we can visit Skiathos tomorrow,' I suggested.

Alex nodded her head enthusiastically as she took a bite of calamari.

I was sitting with my back to the sea and didn't see the change in the colour of the water. Alex was staring out to sea and asked, 'Was the sea that colour before?'

I turned around. No longer was the sea an inviting, smooth

azure. It had transformed into dark ink topped with white froth. The taverna tablecloth holders pinged off as the wind caught the plastic covering which flapped in the increasing breeze.

'Come on, let's go,' I told Alex.

We jumped onto the boat, untied, and headed for the open sea. This is when we found out the Aegean Sea is not always as portrayed on pretty postcards and in idyllic holiday brochures. Sometimes it can transform into a boiling cauldron of foam and lashing waves to rival a bad day in the North Sea. We were in big trouble.

The wind howled as the waves grew. Alex screamed above the gale, 'Turn back now or I'm coming to get you.'

This was not what I had in mind when I decided on a nice leisurely cruise that morning. I had imagined a quick boat ride and a nice lunch at a traditional harbourfront taverna while admiring my nice new boat. But instead, here we were, in the middle of the sea, trying to navigate through the perfect storm. This was challenging enough. But having your life threatened not only by the worst sea storm in living memory but also by an infuriated wife added slightly to my concern. I was not sure what frightened me more. But hope was on the horizon. I could see land approaching fast. And with it, an escape from both.

At last, we entered the harbour and the waves dropped to a light swell as we motored towards the small, protected beach. After Alex's near-death experience – and, by the look in her eyes, mine was not finished with yet – I was not ready to infuriate my wife even more by fiddling around and trying to tie the boat to a buoy. So, I ran the boat straight onto the sand with a satisfying sound of gravel scraping the hull. Without a word, Alex jumped off the front of the boat and marched towards the car. I had survived all the Aegean Sea could throw at me. Now the hardest part was to come. I had to go home with Alex.

The next day, Alex was speaking to me again, and we reflected on our boating mistakes. Launching without plugs and sinking the boat was one mistake. We had to remember that in the future. Crossing the Straits of Artemision during the perfect storm was another we needed to make a note of.

'It's a nice day. Shall we take the boat to Skiathos?' Alex suggested.

Alex is always braver than me. I was still wary of the open sea after our latest adventure and didn't feel up to the long cruise. It was only about twenty kilometres, and we could see the lush green island from our beach. But to get there, we would need to cross a large portion of open water, which scared me. By now, I knew how quickly the weather could change and needed to think carefully before venturing out again.

I went outside and checked the boat: life jackets, flares, plenty of fuel. But this time we packed an overnight bag and some extra cash; if we got to Skiathos and the weather turned bad, we could tie up and find a hotel. We left Maria in charge of the dogs and cats, warning her we may stay away overnight.

The sea was calm, leaving a white wake behind us in the blue sea. We kept close to our island and hugged the coast, avoiding the open sea until we were opposite Skiathos, then turned and headed straight across the open water towards the port. A ferry was just leaving the capital, so I reduced speed and carefully diverted to give it plenty of room before we entered the harbour.

Suddenly, the boat shook as an incredibly loud roar deafened us. We turned our heads just in time to see a jet airliner coming straight towards us at almost sea level. We were in its path. It was going to land on us. It was huge and only a few feet from our heads. We ducked as it narrowly missed our boat, and we watched smoke rise from its extended wheels as it dropped heavily onto the nearby tarmac. The surrounding water boiled with the pressure of jet exhaust, and the wind and fumes swept our hair back.

By avoiding the ferry, we had strayed to the end of the airport's runway. Skiathos is well known as a hair-raising place to land because of its short runway. The aircraft flies very low over the sea, wheels skimming the water, only to drop at the last possible moment. And we were in the way of that. We were just recovering from the shock when Alex screamed at me.

'There's another one coming,' she yelled over the noise.

I turned the wheel, pushed the throttle forward and sped up away towards the port.

Our welcome to Skiathos was not the best we could hope for, but the walk around the town wasn't much better.

After tying up our boat, we stepped up onto the harbour wall and walked into the town. The high-pitched whine of hundreds of mopeds had replaced the roar of the jet engines, buzzing around the town like a swarm of bees, all farting out smelly grey smoke into the already hot and uncomfortable air. We quickly looked for a cafe where we could get away from the unsocial insects and relax with a coffee. But they were everywhere. All the cafes obviously catered for English tourists and all had tables and chairs formed in rows directly fronting the speed track. Some had blackboards offering full English breakfast, others advertising *EastEnders* and *Coronation Street* live by satellite, most advertising happy hour: buy one beer and get another free. Although I was tempted by the free beer, I didn't like this noisy, smelly town. For me, this was not Greece, it was some sort of holiday camp. So, we went back to our boat and quickly left. We took a wide arc away from the airport and continued our cruise north, away from the town.

After our quick visit to the town and nearly getting run over by EasyJet, we were so far not very impressed with Skiathos. But this was to change as we continued our cruise around the perimeter of the small pine-covered island. As we passed each headland, beautiful beaches with white sand were revealed with small informal cafes and restaurants dotted along the coastline. We stopped at one restaurant for lunch. We didn't want to bring the boat near the beach because of people swimming nearby, so we dropped the anchor and swam to the beach. We enjoyed a wonderful lunch before swimming back to the boat for the short ride home.

The weather was perfect and the sea remained calm, such a contrast to our last boat trip. But we had learned a hard lesson. The sea is beautiful, but it's not always your friend. Being a captain himself, Alex's uncle Vasilis warned her when he heard about our plans to buy a boat.

'The sea loves heroes, my daughter. Be careful and never trust her.' We had already learned that valuable lesson and luckily survived our near shipwreck.

Now we had used our boat for a little pleasure cruising, I wanted to use it for the real action. I would become a fisherman.

Our boat was small, but we were getting used to it. Since our experience with the storm, we had been treading carefully and apart from our visit to Skiathos, hadn't gone too far out to sea. But much to the disappointment of the villagers, I hadn't sunk it yet. Well, not completely. I already had a reputation in the village as being slightly strange, but wonderful entertainment. Not much happens in our village, so anything out of the ordinary was interesting.

The local fishermen are a cagey bunch. For weeks, I had tried to get information on the best fishing spots, techniques, and the best bait to use. They always evaded my questions. No one wanted to give up their favourite fishing spot. They obviously realised that a complete amateur would likely splash around uselessly in their part of the sea and scare the fish away. They had a good point.

So, with no local knowledge, I had been fishing on my little boat but had caught nothing bigger than a sardine. I would watch the villagers arrive at the port in their small boats with strings of huge silver fish sparkling in the sunshine. I had even tried following them out to sea, hoping to watch where they went. But they were too wise for that and motored around in circles until I went away.

I would watch other boats in the distance, always with a cloud of seagulls circling above them. Some would swoop into the water to retrieve something discarded by the fishermen. When I first started going out fishing, sometime seagulls would follow me too. But they soon realised that if they hung around me, pickings would be very slim and they were liable to starve, so they flapped away looking for a more productive boat.

One day I was bobbing around, dangling my bait in the water. As usual, I had caught nothing, and I was considering lifting the anchor and trying somewhere else. Suddenly there was a splash as an enormous fish leapt out of the sea, did a somersault, landed on my boat, and flapped violently around my feet with its jaws snapping, trying to attack me.

It was huge, almost four kilos, with spines along its back and sharp teeth. I was terrified as I watched it slapping around the deck. I found myself hoping it would jump back into the sea. Here I was, having a lovely afternoon bobbing around in my little boat, hoping to catch a big fish but not really expecting to, when peace and boredom suddenly turned to terror. Something bigger must have chased it, or more likely it was chasing something else and took a wrong turn. Keeping my distance, I watched as the gnashing of teeth lessened and the fish became still. I looked at my fishing rod. The line was hanging limp in the water. If this fish hadn't committed suicide by jumping onto my boat, I would certainly have had yet another blank day. But today I was successful and had to show off.

I went back to the harbour, tied up the boat, and with my fishing rod over my shoulder, proudly carried my prize slowly past the old fishermen in the kafenio. Heads turned as they watched me take a seat under the shade of a tree and slap the silver monster on the table in front of me. As far as they were aware, I had caught fish and had to be taken seriously. One group of old men invited me to sit at their table and share a pot of Greek coffee while they questioned me on the location of my catch. What bait did I use? Was I bottom fishing, or drifting? It was my turn to be cagey. Not because I didn't want to give away my secret location – I didn't have one. It was because I didn't want them to know I didn't actually catch the fish that jumped onto my boat. That would certainly ruin my new-found credibility.

'Have you got your fishing licence?' one asked.

I didn't know I needed a licence. But because I had now actually caught a fish and had a small boat with an engine and a fishing rod, I had to make the application. This meant the dreaded Greek bureaucracy.

The next day, I visited the port police office, made my application, produced all of my boat papers, the licence to drive it, and insurances. I went to the next village for passport pictures. Finally, after three days, I had my fishing licence complete with stamps and everything.

I spent the next six weeks motoring around the bay, stopping, dropping the anchor, catching nothing, pulling it up again. As I was mostly fishing in water over fifty metres deep, my arms were looking like legs with the extra muscle and my naturally pink skin had changed to a deep red, leaving me looking like a flashing beacon. I suspected I was glowing in the dark.

Being a blond, pink person, I could never acquire a golden tan. Alex, being Greek with olive skin, only has to step out of the house to go three shades darker. I just go redder until it peels off and the process starts all over again. I live my life in the summer with a permanently peeling, blotchy red nose. If I'm not scratching mosquito bites, I'm clawing away at prickly heat, which gives me constant rashes up both arms. Before I leave the house, Alex makes me stand naked in the living room while she plasters me with factor 50 sun block, then adds nappy rash cream to my little creases to protect me even further. It is always embarrassing, but it's all worth it. Soon I would show them all that I am a fisherman to be reckoned with.

Apart from the big fish who jumped into my boat, in the past six weeks I had caught three sardines, an anchor, an old fishing net, and a strange, ugly striped fish which I couldn't identify, but it looked nothing like the beautiful silver specimens the other fishermen in the village were catching. To me, a fish is a fish, and being the biggest one that I had actually caught with a fishing rod, I was quite proud. But floating around day after day, catching almost nothing, was dispiriting.

This was strange. As a child, I had become quite proficient at catching fish in the local canal and rivers near my home. I knew what bait to use; I knew how to tie a hook, and which species of fish lurked below. I had even reached the point of knowing which technique was good for each species. As I grew up, I began deep-sea fishing from charter boats off the south coast of England. I pulled out cod, vicious-looking conger eels and a variety of flat fish. I was no novice. So why was fishing in Greece so different?

None of the local fishermen would help. All my questions

were met with blank stares, and the subject quickly changed. I needed expert help and local knowledge. I would ask Dimitri.

Our garden was looking green. The trees were growing. I even had a small orange hanging from a branch. This was incredible. As a child growing up in England, most of the local fruit trees were sour cooking apples, or hard pears. I would climb over garden fences to pick one of the bitter fruits and hesitantly bite into it, knowing the sourness would bite me back. Here, sweet, perfumed oranges grew wild alongside ripe purple figs and juicy pomegranates. But to me, growing an actual orange in my very own garden was a beautiful feeling.

As our garden was big, it still looked like a field. Alex suggested we divide it into two parts, keeping the back area near the river as grassland; after all, when the floods came, it was all likely to be washed away so there was no point in growing anything else. I would reserve the area of the garden near the house for seating areas and sunbeds. Alex loves the smell of roses, so we decided to plant a few to make a wall of colour to separate the back part of the land. But we needed something to support them. I suggested building a wooden rose arch. We could then train them to make a tunnel of flowers. Alex liked that idea but was thinking of something more elaborate. I said I could quickly build one, but Alex ignored me and was already calling Stamos the builder.

When she finished the call, I suggested that rather than pay Stamos to build one, we pop down to the village woodyard, buy some timber and nail it together. I assured Alex that I could make a marvellous job of it. Alex smiled at me knowingly.

'You look tired. You will only get hot in the sun and go even redder, and I'm running out of nappy rash cream. Let's have Stamos do it. He would appreciate the work,' she told me.

It was her way of telling me she actually wanted it done. She knew my history of DIY. I would sit and think about it for a few days, plan the construction, and likely saw my hand off and end up with bruised thumbs and splinters. After that, we would probably end up with something that swayed in the wind with nails sticking out in all directions, more like a stacking pallet. No, she wanted it to look nice.

So, it was agreed. I wouldn't try it; we would use a professional. What the heck, how much could a small rose arch cost? Unfortunately, I would soon find out my optimism was not well founded.

Stamos strolled around the garden, looking at the proposed site of the arch from all directions while shaking his head sadly. Finally he sat down and announced, 'A wood arch would be no good there. The wind would take it. We need more advice. I need to bring a specialist.'

He pulled out his phone, made a quick call, and sat down with us to drink his coffee. A few moments later, a truck pulled up and three burly chaps jumped out and came to join us. I went to make more coffee as Alex began the negotiations in rapid Greek. My limited understanding of Greek was no use here and I had to rely on Alex to translate. Even harder, these willing workers were not Greek, they were Bulgarian and speaking village Greek in a Bulgarian accent. I had no chance of understanding a word. After a while, hands were being shaken and the contract agreed. I was still trying to catch up on the situation, but Alex was being evasive and refusing to translate.

'So, what have you agreed to?' I asked.

'It's a surprise, and it's being done tomorrow,' she replied.

'It's going to be a perfect weatherproof arch. You are going to be so pleased.'

She always does this to me. Alex had originally agreed to buy the land we were standing on without telling me. She sneaks off and finds bulldozers without telling me. By now I was used to it, so there was no point in complaining. I would let her get on with it and help to pick up the pieces if it all went wrong.

The next day, a truck arrived and tipped a mountain of rocks into our garden. The three burly guys arrived and sat in a ring around the pile of rocks and chipped away at them with hammers.

Alex was still tight-lipped, but I realised what she was doing. She didn't fancy a wooden rose arch; she wanted one made from stone, and there was no way I would change her mind.

'It's going to cost a fortune,' I complained.

'No, the rocks were cheap, and the guys are working on day rates. I have agreed to cook lunches for them and supply regular soft drinks, so it's going to be quite inexpensive,' she told me.

The three chaps were hard workers, and they sat in the blistering sun all day with their knees around their ears, chipping and shaping the rocks into smaller sections. Once satisfied he had enough to start, one man took out his trowel, mixed a batch of cement and began to build.

Alex served lunch for them on the patio table. We left a good supply of cold drinks and a bucket of ice. We had to go to the nearby town for a little shopping, and while we were out, we went to see Niko at his taverna near the harbour and had lunch. When we returned home, we stepped into the garden to see the progress. Two beautifully built columns rose from our lawn. Their colours shone in the sun and looked lovely. The only problem was, they were in the wrong place. Alex had asked for the arch to be built centrally, so if we stood at the door, we could look straight through the arch, past the willow tree to the riverbank. They had built it off-centre, which looked odd. It wasn't just slightly off-centre, but about two metres to the left of where it should be.

'Stop!' Alex yelled. 'It's in the wrong place. Take it down and do it again.'

But it was too late. The stones had been concreted together. The only way of moving it would be to demolish it and start again.

'This is supposed to be the centrepiece of our garden. There is no way I am going to spend years looking at that, it will drive me nuts,' she said. 'Knock it down and start again.'

I didn't mind. To me, it looked good. Okay, a little off-centre, but Alex had other ideas. She wanted this to be right. The Bulgarian workers took a break and came to sit with me on the patio with worried looks on their faces while Alex yelled down the phone at Stamos.

He came immediately and joined Alex in a huddle with the Bulgarian workers, poking at the stonework with arms waving in the air. She was giving them all a hard time. I tried to enter the conversation, but not understanding a word of the hybrid Greek–Bulgarian village language, I went to sit on the patio, poured a beer and watched the squabbling from the shade. Finally, Alex seemed to calm down and nodded in agreement. Then she smiled, shook hands, and they left. Alex came to join me on the patio. I went to the fridge for another beer and poured Alex a Coke.

'So, what have you decided?' I asked.

'We have a brilliant plan.' She smiled. 'We are leaving the columns where they are and building another one on the other side, then putting an arch over the lot. The middle column will no longer be needed as it will be in the middle, but I can leave that half-built and put a pot on the top.'

'How much extra will that cost?' I asked. She had still not told me the cost of the original work, and I was worried about what the additional work would be. I could feel my bank balance draining.

'Well, we need a lot more rocks, and because of the bigger span, they need to have a steel frame made to support the top of the arch during the drying time. But they should finish it in two or three weeks. It shouldn't cost over three to four thousand euros,' she replied. 'I thought it was a fair price?'

The beer I was sipping suddenly developed a mind of its own, and instead of going the right way down to my stomach, took a diversion through my nose and onto the tablecloth.

'We can't afford that,' I protested. 'It's only meant to be a rose arch for a few plants to grow up. It's going to look like the entrance to a road tunnel. We will have trucks driving through it looking for a shortcut.'

'But it's a good price,' she retorted. 'We would have spent much more if we used all Greek workers, and it would take longer.' I was not convinced. But I thought back to our construction in Glyfada. I had recently built a Parthenon on our roof there, so in comparison, this was nothing.

Her mind was made up. We would have the biggest arch in the village. It didn't matter to Alex that along with the Great Wall of China and the pyramids of Gaza, you would be able to see our arch from outer space. What the hell, I thought. We would have a Parthenon in Pefki.

Work had to wait while the local metal shop made a steel frame to be used as a template for the rock construction, leaving a mountain of rocks on our lawn. We paid the guys for the work they had done so far. They would return.

12

REVENGE OF THE GIANT OCTOPUS

When I moved to Greece, being near the sea I had the perfect opportunity to practise my angling skills in a new place, without the British weather. I would take my boat, motor around the bay, stop frequently, drop the anchor, fish for an hour or two, catch nothing and go home. It was dispiriting, but I loved being in the boat out at sea and still had an enjoyable time. But I would have an even better time if I caught a fish once in a while.

Dimitri, being my gardener and general handyperson around the village, also had the reputation of being one of the best fishermen in the area. I was sure I could pump him for information. I had tried before, but he seemed to be as evasive as the other fishers in the village and always made an excuse to leave whenever the subject came up. Dimitri's favoured method of fishing was not with a rod and line, but with a trident. On a calm night, he would wait until the predators came from the open sea in search of small fish, and row out to his secret spot, with only a trident and a bucket containing a mixture of sand and olive oil. He would then shine a light on the water, take a handful of the sand and oil and throw it across the surface. This removed any glare, leaving the surface as clear as glass, revealing the fish below. He would then impale them on his trident. I had no wish to throw spears at fish; I wanted to catch them fairly. Fish against man in a struggle for supremacy. If I was going to catch fish, it would be with a rod and line. But first, I needed to find out where they were. I would force Dimitri to spill the beans.

I was tired of following him around the garden, begging for information. He always had something better to do than let me into the secret of nearby fishing spots.

'I just have to trim these roses. We will talk later,' he promised.

But we never would.

So, one day, Alex and I formed a plan. Dimitri arrived just after noon to do a little gardening. Alex called out of the window.

'Dimitri, we are going for lunch. Would you like to come with us?'

We had often had lunch together but had always chatted

about hunting, gardening, and making tsipouro. This time, we were determined to get some useful information on fishing.

We arrived at Niko's taverna and took a table by the sea under the shade of a straw canopy. Niko came to our table with a jug of wine and five glasses, filled ours and poured one for himself.

'What's good today?' Alex asked.

'We have lovely calamari that Dimitri caught last night.' He lifted his glass and nodded at Dimitri. 'We also have stifado (meat in a red sauce with pasta), and especially today we have aneípota (not talked about).'

I did vaguely wonder what 'aneípota, not talked about' was, but I was not really here for the food. I was here for information. Dimitri ordered the 'not talked about', I ordered the same, and Alex went with a Greek salad.

I topped up his wine glass and went straight in for the kill.

'Please tell me where I can catch fish,' I pleaded. 'I have tried everything. You have seen how hard I try. Just tell me one place. I promise not to tell anyone where the information came from.'

I hoped I would appeal to his better nature and he would feel sorry for me. After all, I would never be a threat to his fishing method. I didn't want to spear my fish, I just wanted to catch one or two on a fishing rod.

He opened his mouth to reply. I had him. He was at last going to tell me. I held my breath, then the food arrived. Niko put the plates on the table, sat down and poured himself a wine. He wanted to chat at the most crucial time. There was no way Dimitri was going to tell me in front of Niko, so we sipped our wine and chewed our food while I waited for him to go away. He sat there talking about how many bottles of oil he harvested last year, the beautiful figs he got from Yannis this morning. He told us about the new government regulation that insisted all olive oil bottles were to be served to clients in sealed bottles with labels. Of course, he was going to ignore that law. His olive oil was the best, and there was no way he was going to stick a label on his special olive oil just because the police told him to.

I listened patiently and continued to chew. I noticed Alex giggling beside me.

'What's so funny?' I asked.

'Do you know what you're eating?' she said.

I looked down at my plate. There were nicely fried fritters with slices of lemon, a few French fries and a salad on the side. I was so keen to get as much information on fishing spots, I hadn't even considered what I was currently chewing and had no idea what I had ordered.

'Chicken fritters?' I suggested.

'No, it's a large portion of lamb's testicles and fried brains, and you have nearly finished them all.'

I felt a gagging instinct at the back of my throat. Now I knew what 'not talked about' was, and why they were not talked about. But too late. I rolled the remaining testicle to the side of my plate, ate the last few fried potatoes and nibbled at the salad, leaving the rest while Niko and Dimitri finished their conversation.

Finally, Dimitri looked around to see if anyone was watching, took a paper napkin and drew a map.

'We are here.' He pointed at the map. 'You go along the coast until you come to the big arch, which is the camping site. Then you turn and head out to sea with the camping sign behind you. Keep going into the open sea until you pass the headland to the right and Turtle Island comes into view. Then keep going until you see the highest point. Stop, drop your anchor; the fish are there.'

I sat open-mouthed. I wondered how he could possibly

know. One piece of sea looks much like any other. I was expecting to be told about secret bays or small rocky islands. But I was being sent into the middle of the sea.

'Look.' He pointed to the hand-drawn map again. 'The sea is like a desert,' he told me. 'The fish are only in certain places.' He drew little rings here and there on the map. 'But go where I told you. You will catch fish. Tell no one it came from me.'

Armed with my new knowledge, I was ready to become a real fisherman. But fishing had to wait. First, I had agreed to take Alex and some friends on a boat trip.

I freely admit I am not the best sailor. When there are no other boats near me, I am fine driving. I keep to old-man speed and happily motor along, enjoying the Greek sunshine and transparent water. No, my problem is the other stuff. Launching, parking, dropping the anchor, recovering the anchor and trying to avoid sinking. I'm not good at any of that.

In our village, the small concrete slipway is next to the local kafenio, where local fishermen and boat owners relax, chat, and enjoy their morning coffees. From the time I leave my house to tow the boat the short distance to the harbour, word has already spread. Suddenly, the cafe has filled up. People have stopped what they were doing, eager to find a seat in the front row to watch the local xénos launch his boat.

Anyone who has ever tried to reverse a trailer or caravan will know that it makes little sense. Turn the steering wheel one way, and the trailer goes the other. The only way to deal with it is to turn the opposite way to where you want to go. Work that out!

The villagers were on their second coffee by the time I had straightened up and got the back of the boat in the water. I was fully aware that the eyes of the entire village were on me, so I was getting nervous.

I looked sideways at the old fishermen. I could see they were sniggering but trying to hide their amusement.

Undeterred, I opened the ratchet and let the boat slide off the trailer into the water with a splash. I clambered on board and lowered the outboard, turned the key and started the engine. Looking good. Then I could feel my feet were wet. I looked down to see the water on the deck rising past my ankles towards my knees as the boat slowly sank. Luckily, I still had the rope attached to the trailer, so I jumped out and slowly wound the handle until the waterlogged craft was back on the trailer, jets of water pouring out of the drain holes. I had forgotten to put the plugs in again.

The old fishermen in the cafe could no longer contain themselves and were in hysterics, tears of laughter running down their cheeks.

Finally, I emptied the boat of water. This time, I put the plugs in, and at last launched successfully. Alex and our friends jumped onto the boat and we set off.

I had heard about a lovely taverna opposite our village, near Volos. We decided to go there for lunch. It was only a twenty-minute cruise until we arrived at the beautiful, picturesque bay. The inviting taverna was on the small rocky beach, with blue tablecloths matching the colour of the sea and an aroma of cooking food wafting towards us. It was already quite crowded but we could see some free tables. It was charming, but being a rocky shore, there was nowhere to park.

A few boats were already in the small bay, secured to the shallow bottom by their anchors. I pulled up in the middle of these and let down my anchor. Alex and our friends slid off the side and swam the short distance to the beach. I wasn't feeling too comfortable leaving the boat with only one anchor securing us, so as an extra precaution I dropped the spare over the side. I was happy the boat was secure. It was time to join them in the taverna. I slid off the back of the boat towards the water for the short swim to the beach.

Dangling off the back of a boat with your legs waving in the air is not a dignified look, especially in front of a crowded beachside taverna.

I had tried to slip gently off the boat. But my shorts caught on the rope cleat. So, there I was, dangling by my bottom with my legs waving in the air and struggling to bring myself upright, when there was a ripping sound as my swimming shorts shredded and I plopped headfirst into the sea. Fully aware that I had entertained everyone sitting at the taverna, I was greeted with smiles and muffled laughter, especially as I walked past the tables showing my left buttock under the flapping, shredded shorts.

But I soon forgot my dangling experience as we tucked into our meal while admiring the view. The time came to leave. We swam together back to the boat and climbed aboard. It was Alex's job to pull up the anchor while I started the engine.

'The anchor is up,' she called over to me.

I pushed the throttle forward, and we started to move. The boat seemed a bit sluggish, so I pushed the throttle a little further. Suddenly I could hear screams and shouts from people at the taverna over the sound of the engine.

'Stop, stop!' they all yelled in unison.

I pulled the throttle back to neutral and looked behind me. I was towing five boats. I had forgotten to tell Alex that I had set the spare anchor to be extra safe, so she had only pulled up one. The other was being dragged behind us, collecting all the other boats' anchor lines along the way. A convoy of vessels was heading out to sea, but with only one driver.

With the other owners helping, we spent an hour untangling the boats. Luckily, the only damage was to my pride, but we all agreed to go back to the taverna for a round of drinks to apologise. Lucky for me, all the owners were Greek, and one was from my village. So, in the genuine spirit of Greek hospitality, I was soon forgiven. If I had done that in Portsmouth harbour, they would have drowned me. Here, they gave me a glass of ouzo.

By the time we arrived at Pefki harbour it was getting dark. We arrived under the cover of night, so the local villagers couldn't see me dragging the boat onto the trailer with my buttocks hanging out. That would have made them choke on their coffee.

Never mind. Tomorrow I was going fishing.

The next morning, I woke at 4.00 a.m. I was sure the old men wouldn't be in the cafe this early, and it was still dark, so I could sneak my boat into the water before they woke up. Without any eyes on me, it went smoothly. Trying to launch the boat with so many smiling faces watching and waiting for me to sink is always unnerving, and I always make mistakes, adding to my reputation of worst sailor on the island.

I motored out of the harbour. Under the dashboard light, I held the map Dimitri had drawn on a paper napkin. I cruised a few hundred metres level with the beach and found the camping site sign illuminated by a lamppost. Then, as per instructions, I turned left into the open sea. As I left the land behind, I realised I would not see the landmarks shown on the map because it was still dark. I would have to wait for sunrise. I was not used to waking up so early and still felt sleepy. The sea was flat calm, not even a ripple. I turned off the engine and waited.

A voice came into my ear. 'Kaliméra. Eísai kalá?'

I looked up and shaded my eyes from the sun. An old man was looking down at me. He was standing next to my boat, which was at a strange angle. I looked over the side. The left side of my boat was on the beach, the other side bobbing in the water. I looked around further and saw the kafenio with the usual villagers sat watching me. 'Good morning, captain!' they cried, before dissolving into fits of giggles. The current had pushed me back to the harbour after I fell asleep. I had been happily sleeping with my leg over the side, and my loud snoring had alerted the old man to my presence. I was back where I started. This was embarrassing. But I was fortunate. The current could have been going the other way and I could have drifted past Skiathos on my way to Turkey.

I pushed the boat off the beach, turned the stern towards the sea and pushed away. I started the engine and headed back towards the landmark to find my new fishing spot.

Following the hand-drawn map, I finally lined myself up with the highest point on Turtle Island and dropped the anchor. I felt my excitement rising as I put the bait on a small hook and let it go over the side.

After a few moments, the line went taut. I pulled my rod; the fish pulled back. This was a novel experience. Normally I would have to wait hours for a bite, only to pull out a sardine so small I didn't even realise I had hooked it. This was different. I could feel it wriggling. I finally managed to pull it the fifty metres from the bottom and over the side of the boat. It was small, only three to four inches, but it was an actual fish. An hour later, I had half a bucketful of small, various-coloured fish, none of which I recognised. Some looked like tiny versions of the ones I had seen at the local market, so I assumed they were edible.

Just before I packed up for the day, the line went tight again. This time, it was something bigger. I pulled. It pulled back. I eventually won the battle. On the end of my line was an ugly striped fish with lots of spikes protruding from its back and side near its fins. It looked horrible and seemed the same type I had caught before, but this one was about twelve inches long –

by far the biggest fish I had caught all day. I carefully unhooked it, trying to avoid the spines, and threw in it the bucket on top of the others.

I got back to the harbour, pulled the boat onto the trailer and drove towards home. Dimitri was standing by the períptero (kiosk) and flagged me down.

'How did you get on?' he asked.

'Really well,' I replied. 'Thank you for the information. I have half a bucketful.'

He put his finger to his lips and looked around to make sure nobody was listening.

'It's okay. But it's our secret. I will see you at your house. We can look at the fish.'

At home, I proudly displayed my catch to Alex. She looked in the bucket.

'Well done, but they're not very big, are they? Apart from that big, ugly one, they are all rather small.' She poked the big, ugly one with her finger, put her nail under the spike on its back and lifted. 'That looks nasty,' she said.

I didn't mind. I had proved to myself that I could catch fish in Greece. Now it was just a matter of time until I caught the bigger ones.

Dimitri arrived to inspect my bucket. He took one look at the contents and jumped back, holding his hands in front of himself defensively.

'That's a drakena. It's a deadly poisonous fish. If it had stung, you could have died. Don't go anywhere near it. It can still kill you even if it's dead. This is the biggest one I've ever seen. It is really dangerous.'

I felt a quick rush of pride to hear that I had caught the biggest one Dimitri had ever seen, even if it could have killed me. I was curious to find out what it was.

The Greeks call it drakena, and in the Adriatic it is called spiderfish, or dragon. It usually inhabits sand and mud. The fish is hard to notice since it is well camouflaged. Along its back and sticking out at its sides are black spines through which it releases poison into your body if you step on it, or in our case, try to eat it.

The main characteristic of the sting of this fish is a very strong pain that develops to its full extent up to half an hour after it stings you. The pain is so intense that it is barely tolerable. Symptoms of poisoning are usually only local, but sometimes general symptoms such as increased sweating, weakness, dizziness, nausea and vomiting occur.

Apart from swimmers who walk barefoot in the shallows, frequent victims are fishermen or cooks when preparing fish for meals. Therefore, in some countries, there is a legal obligation for fishermen to cut off the toxic poison immediately after the catch.

We let Dimitri take it out of the bucket and he skilfully prepared it by cutting away the poisonous spines and cleaning it, leaving two fillets.

'You can cook it now if you like. It's safe,' he told us.

I was wondering what else could be lurking down there under my boat that could cause me injury. Nobody had told me about this creature. All the fishermen knew about it, but it's likely they never expected me to catch any fish, so why go into detail about the dangerous ones that could kill me with a look?

But I was about to experience even more danger during my future fishing adventures.

After bobbing around on my little boat for a few weeks, I was at last catching fish. I had still not caught anything bigger than the palm of my hand, but 'mighty oaks from little acorns grow', so I felt confident I would soon be up there with the best fishermen in the village and joining their discussion on the best fishing grounds, baits and tactics.

I was happy. Every time I went out, I returned with half a bucketful of sparkling silver fish. One of our neighbours saw me returning one day and asked to look at my catch. Keti poked around in my bucket.

'They are not very big, are they?' she told me. She saw the look of disappointment on my face, then added, 'But the small ones are the sweetest.' She is such a kind lady.

After that, every time I went fishing, I would take my bucket to Keti. She would clean them, keep half for herself and bring the rest to us. It was a friendly arrangement. But I promised her that bigger ones were yet to come.

The local fishermen still evaded my questions and were aware that I had caught fish, but I suspected Dimitri had been instructed to share the secret fishing spot with me because he knew there would only be small fish there. It seemed to be a diversionary tactic to keep me away from the proper fish, and all the other fishermen were in on the deception to keep the xénos away from the real action. I had already become suspicious that I never saw any other boats nearby while I was fishing. If it was such a good spot, why didn't others join in the bounty? I confirmed my suspicions when one of the old fishermen asked me about my latest catch. I could see he was holding himself back from laughing as he was hiccupping and his eyes glinted. When I proudly revealed that I had caught almost a whole bucketful yesterday, a nearby group of other fishermen could not contain their laughter and spat tsipouro all over the table. I got up and left to the sound of gales of laughter behind me.

So, I changed tactics. For my next trip, I avoided my usual motor along the beach to the camping site then out to sea. I went the other way around the coast towards Asmini.

Regardless of the obvious derision in the village, I still dreamed of catching a whopper. I found a brightly coloured imitation fish in my bag and thought I would try it at the end of my line. It was about the size of the fish I had been catching, and the hook on the end was huge. No small fish would have a mouth big enough to bite on this. It was all or nothing.

This time, I didn't drop the anchor and instead turned off the engine and drifted with the current and light breeze. I had been bobbing around for about an hour and was considering starting the engine and moving to another spot, when suddenly my line went tight, and the reel screamed as it took the line down into the deep sea, half-emptying the spool of my reel.

I had a fish! I pulled hard. The fish pulled back harder. The rod slapped on the side of the boat as I fought to tighten the drag on the reel.

So is this what it feels like to catch a big fish in Greece? I thought.

I had caught big fish before during charter boat trips on the south coast of England. But there was always a skipper on hand to help with whatever you pulled over the side. They would grab my catch, remove the hook, and deal with whatever was flapping around the deck. They would even rebait my hook. Here, I was alone and unprepared for what was coming up to meet me.

Until now, apart from the monster that jumped into my boat, the largest fish I had caught in Greece was a green spiky thing that was more of a danger to me than I was to it. This was certainly not one of those. It was something big and even more scary.

Finally, I gained some line. The fish was coming up; I was winning. I wondered what it was. Would it be spiky? I asked myself. I hope it hasn't got big teeth.

As I had not actually expected to catch a fish when I left the beach in my little boat, all I had on board was a fishing rod, a hook, and a small tea towel to hold the slippery small fish if I was fortunate enough to catch one. I had abandoned my usual fishing grounds where I could fill a small bucket in a day. I was after bigger prey. This was it. As it rose towards me from the dark depths, I wondered what to do with it. I was getting a little scared. I gained some line; the fish pulled it back off my reel. This was a proper fight. As I gained, he would kick and take away all the gained line.

I had been fighting this fish for an hour when it seemed to give up, and I managed to pull the heavy weight towards the surface. I looked into the clear water, trying to get a glimpse of the monster at the end of my line. All I saw was a large shadow, which was getting rapidly bigger as it came towards me. I jumped back, pulling the rod as I fell, and a large octopus flew out of the sea and landed between my legs. It was huge and terrifying. This was the biggest octopus I had ever seen. Octopuses were a common sight in Greece, but they were usually hanging on a clothes line outside a seaside taverna, drying in the sun. These were tiny compared to this monster. From end to end, the tentacles were almost two metres across. When it first jumped on my boat, it had smooth orange skin, but as it became more irate, the colour changed from orange to red, then a frightening purple. Its skin developed lumps and peaks over its entire body. It was not a happy octopus. The more I shuffled away, the faster it came towards me until I had backed away as far as possible and had my back to the outboard motor. I could go no further without ending up in the sea. Perhaps this was what it wanted, to get me into his domain and finish me off. Just before it reached me, it reared up and shot at me with black ink, which hit my legs and dribbled over the floor of the boat. This was an angry octopus, and the hunter had suddenly become the prey. It was coming for me. But after spraying me with the nasty black liquid, it seemed satisfied and turned away from me, slithered to the front of the boat, and thankfully jumped off back into the sea.

I was so relieved. I didn't fancy the thought of this monster creeping around between my legs and attacking me. Those suckers looked scary, and I have heard they have a nasty beak somewhere under that lumpy purple flesh. Still covered in ink, I started the engine and headed back to port. I needed to go home and wash off the ink, and I really needed a stiff drink and a lie-down to recover. As I drove into the harbour, I thought that perhaps I really wasn't suited to fishing. The only large things I had caught in the past couple of months both wanted to kill me. What else was out there unseen, waiting for a go at me next? I decided not to go fishing tomorrow. The lawn needed mowing and I had lots of jobs to do.

As I pulled my inky boat onto the trailer, two uniformed officers, both holding clipboards, approached me. They were the port police and had come to inspect my boat and check my paperwork. The last thing I needed was an inspection by the port police. I just wanted to go home and get as far away from the sea as possible. But these chaps had decided to make my day even more stressful.

As you'll have realised by now, in Greece paperwork is everything. Even to dip the boat into the sea I needed a waterproof carrier bag full of documents, all bearing official stamps in triplicate and fully notarised. Other items you are legally required to carry include a first aid kit, several life jackets, and flares.

If you are inspected by the port police and found to have anything missing, they will levy a big fine. I was fairly sure I had everything in order. But with Greek bureaucracy, you can never be fully confident if they have applied a stamp in the right place and in the correct colour.

I got on well with everyone in our village. I knew I was

subject to jokes and ribbing, but it was all in good humour and I never took offence. Everyone would return my smiles and stop to chat. But these chaps were not smiling.

I was used to the casual dress of the village. Most of us would wander around in old T-shirts and trainers. We mostly wore elasticised jogging bottoms because of the vast amount of food eaten at lunch – we all needed a little expansion capacity. But these officials had smartly pressed uniforms with polished brass buttons and belt buckles, epaulettes on their shoulders and brass badges on their hats. I looked down and in their highly polished shoes saw a reflection of my inky legs from my recent encounter with the ferocious octopus. They were certainly here on business. They seemed to have ignored the other boats in the harbour, but it was likely all the other owners had been given warning and had run away, leaving me as the only one near a boat.

'Boat papers,' one demanded.

I opened the little door under the steering wheel and took out the waterproof wallet, and handed the contents to the officers. They studied these. They checked my insurance certificate, boat licence, and all the other forms and papers I had stuffed inside. Fortunately, they were all in order, and they wanted to see proof of the last engine service. But they hadn't finished yet.

'Fireworks,' the other demanded.

They were asking to inspect my flares. I opened the chamber under the seat where I stored them. They were floating around in a lake of seawater. I grabbed one; it dissolved in my hand. I was going to be in big trouble. My flares would never have gone off, even if I strapped them to a stick of dynamite. I wondered what my punishment would be. Would they revoke my fishing licence? Would I get a big fine? Surely they couldn't arrest me, I thought. I reached down into the cupboard again and found another. It was also wet and dripping, but this one stayed intact and didn't melt as I retrieved it from the pond. I handed the soggy paper tube to the officer. He inspected the wet cardboard container, checked the date on the side, handed it back, and spoke.

'That's fine. All in date.' And they left.

They were within the required date, so according to the port police, they were fine.

13

A NEW HOBBY

Because of my disastrous boating and fishing experience, some people have suggested I need a new hobby. I'm not much good at winemaking, and I only have one vine in my garden. The last time I looked, I only had three grapes (the next day, a bird flew off with two of them, so I ate the other). I considered joining George's boxing class held biweekly in his garage opposite, but wasn't really keen on hitting anyone, and was even less keen on being hit. So, I discounted that idea.

Greeks understand hobbies. After all, they invented the Olympics. From the times of ancient history, Greeks have been competing in competitions – running, horseback riding, chariot races, boxing, wrestling, and the pentathlon, a combination of five separate events: discus throwing, javelin, jumping, running and wrestling. They were all similar to modern-day events.

Today, pastimes include football, basketball, and even motor racing. But in the village, hobbies are more practical. Scuba diving is becoming popular, mostly because you can dive underwater with a spear gun in your hands to catch the bigger fish, who have become bigger fish by being clever enough to spot hidden hooks in tasty snacks offered to them dangling on thin lines from the boat shadows above.

Fishing has always been popular. Most of the villagers have always fished to supply food for the table, or for selling to local tavernas. But it has also caught on with others who just enjoy the experience with the potential of a meal at the end of the day. I have no idea what they would make of the English style of river fishing, which involves spending the whole day trying to catch them, and if successful, keeping the fish alive in a net, only to release them at the end of the day's fishing after looking at them and taking a few photos. As a kid fishing in the Grand Union boat canal, I never considered fried minnows or poached chub as a meal. I would always let them swim happily away.

Winemaking is a very popular hobby in our village. But it's only made from grapes. Greeks have never adopted the English habit of making wine from strange things like dandelions, elder-berries and potatoes. This is likely to be why the English wines are not very popular. But the Greeks have fine-tuned the art. Most taverna owners make their own wine: red, white, and sometimes resinated. They stumbled on the famous Greek retsina when pine resin was used as a stopper before corks became available. This mingled with the wine and gave it a taste which the Greeks found to their liking.

The villagers are very keen on the hobby of tsipouro making. In the autumn, jets of steam can be seen puffing from most houses as the distillation process gets underway. Then follows a long period of silence when nobody goes out because they had to taste the results of their labours and were nursing long hangovers. Many must wait until their eyesight comes back before venturing out again.

So yes, Greeks understand most hobbies, with some variations. But they don't understand planespotting.

A few years ago, Greece was the subject of world media attention. The arrest of twelve British tourists, one of whom was a woman, and two Dutch tourists by the Greek authorities caused an international storm. The holidaymakers were in Greece as part of an organised tour. They were not there for the nice beaches or quaint tavernas, or even to tour the ancient monuments of Athens. No, they had travelled all the way to Greece to stand near the fence of military airbases, writing numbers in their little books and taking photographs. They were promptly arrested in Kalamata and charged with spying and espionage for taking photographs of military aircraft at an off-limits military base. A crime in Greece that carries a twenty-year prison sentence.

The Greek authorities launched an urgent investigation which revealed notebooks and photographs detailing two other military bases and aircraft, including a Greek base in Megara and a NATO base at Araxos. So, thirteen men were carted off to a prison in Nafplio, while the woman was sent to the high-security Korydallos women's prison near Athens, where the fifty-one-year-old grandmother was strip-searched and held in solitary confinement for several days.

They were released on bail and returned for a trial where eight were convicted of espionage and sentenced to three years in jail. The other six were convicted of aiding and abetting and given one-year suspended sentences. Their anoraks were deemed to be of special interest and kept for further investigation.

Because of the press frenzy in England, the British government had to get involved.

They tried to explain to the Greek government that these were not spies, but spotters. They set up a meeting with high-ranking British diplomats to discuss the international incident.

'Don't you have such a thing as birdwatching in Greece?' asked one.

'What, with a gun?' said the official.

'No, binoculars,' replied the diplomat.

This wasn't getting anywhere. According to the Greeks, there was no point in just watching birds without shooting them, taking them home and eating them.

'How about trainspotting?' asked one hopeful diplomat. 'You have trains, don't you?'

'Yes, of course we have trains. But we don't sit and watch them, we ride in them. We certainly don't take photos of them unless there is some interesting graffiti on the side.'

They tried again.

'Stamp collecting?'

'No.'

'Tree worshipping?'

'No.'

'Rolling cheese downhill?'

'What? No.'

'Conkers, perhaps?'

'No.'

Finally, and with nothing to compare with hanging around

an airport beside a runway, writing aircraft numbers in a book for the sole purpose of collecting them, they left and returned to England for more consultation with the prime minister.

Meanwhile, the Greek press and media were also trying to understand this strange hobby. The Greek legal system had already decided they were spies and was sure they were going to sell the information written in their little books to the Turks, Russians, or even worse, the Americans. People in kafenios in Greece were discussing the situation and wondering why the British, who they looked upon as friends, were now spying on them. This was beginning to get out of hand.

Tony Blair raised their plight at a meeting with his Greek counterpart, Costas Simitis, who said he hoped the appeal would bring a 'positive development'. The meeting, where the two premiers also discussed bilateral issues including Britain's continued refusal to return the Elgin Marbles to Athens, sparked speculation that a deal had been brokered to return the sculptures in return for the spotters' freedom, although the rumour was denied by all involved.

At last, a Greek government official who had studied at a university in England revealed he had heard about these strange people who loved trains and aeroplanes. He managed to convince the other government ministers that they were not spies, but just stupid. Stupidity is not against the law in most countries. If it were, most of us would have criminal records.

They finally had their convictions overturned on appeal, except for one of the British men who did not return to contest his aiding and abetting charge. He was last seen at the end of a runway in Istanbul, running away from a pack of angry-looking policemen, trying to catch the midnight express with his anorak flapping in the breeze. He was never heard from again.

So, for me, planespotting was not an option. There were few of those in my village anyway. We were well off the flight corridors and the nearest airport was Skiathos, and there was nothing worth seeing there apart from the regular EasyJet flights trying to land on a runway shorter than my garden. But I would soon get bored with that. No, for me, the maritime life was the way to go. I hadn't sunk the boat for ages, and I had recovered from my confrontation with the giant octopus, so was raring to go again.

It was a scorching morning. We were already beginning to feel sluggish from the heat. The sea was flat calm, and Alex suggested we take the boat out.

'It's always a little cooler out to sea,' she said, 'and we can put the canopy up to shade you from the sun. If we catch lots of fish, we can light the barbecue later and cook them.'

I liked that idea. I had no interest in catching anything big. The octopus was more than enough excitement. No, today we would go to the spot Dimitri had told us about and cool off while pulling out tiddlers about the size of my index finger. If I caught twenty or more, it would be enough for a small meal.

I linked the boat to the car while Alex gathered the fishing rods, and we drove the short distance to the harbour. I looked out at the sea. It was still completely flat and reflecting the sun like a mirror. Not even a ripple.

As usual, the old men sat in the cafe near the harbour and watched. They pretty much had this kafenio to themselves. Tourists didn't really go for the strong, gritty Greek coffee made in a brika, and they had yet to discover the joys of tsipouro; they would rather go somewhere they could get a cappuccino or an English tea. But the old men were all there, and they hadn't seen my splashing around for a while and were no doubt hoping my seafaring skills hadn't improved. They needed a good laugh.

I went through my checklist.

Plugs securely fitted so I didn't sink. Check.

Engine up so it wouldn't scrape the bottom and tear off the propeller. Check.

Spare shorts just in case I caught my backside on the cleats again. Check

I backed the boat down the slipway, got out of the car and stood waiting as Alex released the holding strap and let the ratchet go. I stood with my feet in the sea as the boat slid off the trailer into the water, but I had forgotten to keep hold of the rope. I fumbled to grab it as the boat passed, towing the limp rope behind, and it drifted off into the harbour. Alex drove the car away from the slipway. The old men watched as I waded into the water and swam out to retrieve my drifting boat before it floated away into the open sea. I could hear howls of laughter from the cafe as I swam away. But I was used to that by now and was happy to make their day again.

I finally started the engine. Alex climbed onto the boat. We left the harbour and drove into the smooth open sea past the fishing boats all tied along the quay. Normally, on a calm day, there would be one or two boats tied to the harbour wall. But today there were so many that they had to be tied two deep. I had never seen so many in the village.

Once out at sea, I scanned the horizon. Not one boat was out. Usually, there would be random clusters as far as I could see. Today, not a single boat was to be seen. We were alone on the entire Aegean Sea.

We motored out to my normal spot, knowing we could get at least a few small fish. Alex speculated we may catch a bigger one today (I secretly hoped not). We dropped the anchor, then our fishing lines, and waited for the tug of a bite. After an hour, nothing, not even a nibble. After another hour, we were both feeling hot. With no sea breeze and the sun reflecting off the water, it was hotter than dry land, so we gave up and motored back to the harbour. The old men were still there, smiling and sniggering as we pulled the boat onto the trailer and left with an empty bucket to go home for a shower and cool off. We had caught no fish, but there was still the local taverna who would have some. So, we abandoned the idea of a barbecue and headed off for lunch. This new and healthy lifestyle suited me. But with health comes appetite. And with increased appetite comes increased waist size. I urgently needed a diet before I lost sight of my feet.

Living in this village, there are so many wonderful little restaurants and tavernas on our doorstep. The temptation is too great to resist. After all, the best food in the world is only a few minutes' walk or, more normally, a thirty-second drive from home. So, I decided to avoid fried food and bread in favour of barbecued fish and salad only. An instant way to lose weight. We drove to our favourite fish taverna near the harbour. Today we would eat barbecued sardines.

We took our normal table overlooking the harbour and ordered sardines.

'Sorry, no fish today. It's a full moon. We have nice fried meat,' the owner told us.

Was this some sort of anti-fish day? We may not eat fish during a full moon?

'What's the full moon got to do with it?' I asked.

He looked at me strangely, as if I were a little simple, and explained.

'We all know that during the full moon we do not find fish in the sea,' he told us, surprised that we didn't know this.

Apparently, during the time of the full moon, sardines, anchovies and all small fish go deep in the sea, away from predators who would see them too clearly on moonlit nights. The predators would follow the bait fish, leaving the sea empty. So the fishermen, knowing it would be pointless going out, spend these periods mending nets and maintaining their boats.

So that's why there were so many boats in the harbour today and we were the only boat fishing. Everyone knew this except me, and the old men of the cafe were certainly not going to miss their morning's entertainment by letting me in on the secret.

We realised it would be pointless fishing for the next few days. We needed something else to do.

We had spent most of our time locally, but we lived on a large island and hadn't really explored very much of it, so we decided to put that right and check out the island.

We drove through the nearby market town of Istiea and headed towards Edipsos, the main ferry port for North Evia. Most people prefer to take ferries from the mainland rather than negotiate the winding, mountainous roads from Chalkida. We had taken the ferry here many times but never stayed to look around; we usually headed straight home. But Alex was keen on exploring the famous thermal springs in this village.

This small, unknown town in northern Evia is a well-kept secret of the rich and powerful, visited by Winston Churchill, Aristotle Onassis, Maria Callas, Greta Garbo and Omar Sharif, together with some of the most prominent people in history; Emperors Hadrian, Septimius Severus and Marcus Aurelius heard of the healing powers and came.

A geological fault leading from the Pliocene volcano in nearby Lichades is thought to be responsible for the hot springs that bubble up all around the village. Hot, steamy water runs down the hills, creating waterfalls that splash into the sea and leaving the rocks a bright sunshine yellow from the sulphur emanating from the hot volcanic streams. Hotels have taken advantage of this bounty and constructed their buildings around the natural springs where you can bathe.

We found the most famous of these hotels and decided to try this for ourselves. It's a five-star hotel called the Thermae

Sylla Spa and Wellness Hotel. We had no intention of taking a room, we just wanted to try the volcanic pool. For a small fee, you can take a daily ticket to experience it for yourselves. The main pool is the centrepiece of the hotel. It is an irregular shape with a selection of shallow areas adapted to form Jacuzzis. There are jets on poles shooting hot water into the pool, with ladders and steps leading in and out. Palm trees surround the entire area, giving the look of a tropical oasis.

We took our towels and rubber hats from the spa reception and stepped down into the hot water. The first thing I noticed after the initial heat was the taste. It had a strong tang of salt and sulphur and a slight odour of eggs. This must have comprised highly concentrated mineral salt. When I took my feet off the floor, I at once floated. It felt like I was wearing a life jacket as I was naturally buoyant. We spent an hour floating around under the shade of the palms. It was an incredible feeling until we tried to leave the pool. My legs felt heavy, and I was having trouble climbing the small staircase to the pool surroundings. I looked back at Alex, who was suffering the same difficulty. We were both so relaxed and had been experiencing an incredible weightlessness. When we needed to use our muscles to exit the pool, they didn't work. It was a weird sensation, but we soon recovered to get dressed and continue our exploration of the island.

After our swim, we drove towards home via a small fishing village called Rovies. This was on the west side of the island overlooking the mainland and led to a road over the mountain. We found the village and set off up the mountain road. As we left the olive groves behind us, the pine forests began. The views were incredible. We were on top of the world. We stopped the car and walked around, admiring the view. Behind us was the mainland of Greece. The hills were lime green, and the mountains rising above were bare and sand-coloured, too high to support vegetation. Ahead of us was the bay of Volos, with its rolling hills going down to the blue Aegean Sea. In the distance was Skiathos, and a little further away, Skopelos. We stood and admired the scenery from the top of our mountain.

We were getting hungry so we drove back down the mountain and headed south along the coast towards Limni, which in Greek means lake. The small fishing town appears to be on the shore of a large lake thanks to a mountain which rises from the far end and wraps around the side and rear of the village. A narrow road leads up the hills to a large monastery which can just be seen high above the clouds. We navigated the narrow cobbled streets past the traditional red-roofed houses, each with tiny, well-cared-for small gardens and bougainvillea climbing the white walls.

We parked the car and walked along the seafront towards the small harbour. Tavernas and cafes were dotted along the street, all with tables and chairs arranged outside in the typical Greek fashion. Each had its ubiquitous resident cats and dogs snoozing under the tables and in the shade of green bushy trees with white-painted trunks. We were attracted to one restaurant in particular because of the fresh barbecue fish aroma emanating towards us. We followed the scent and found a table with a view of the harbour and the sea beyond. Two cats appeared as we ordered our lunch, and sat hopefully waiting for the food to arrive.

A friendly looking middle-aged lady came out and took our order. She welcomed us to her restaurant and introduced herself as Ella. Shortly afterwards, she returned with our food and a jug of wine. I noticed a few pigeons wandering around between the tables, which the cats ignored. One was standing on the next table eyeing our bread basket, waiting for an opportunity to make off with its contents. Suddenly, he flapped his wings and flew off to join a flock of these birds surrounding

Ella, who was throwing food onto the pavement. This was going down very well with the pigeons, who hungrily pecked away until it was all gone.

'Eláte edó poulákia. Sou écho kaló fagitó,' (Come here little birds, I have food for you) she called, opening another bucket, and continued to spread the contents to the hungry birds.

She must be an animal lover, I thought. There were several cats around the chairs and a couple of dogs, and there she was, feeding the local bird population.

Alex chewed a piece of bread and watched.

'Why is Ella feeding those birds blue food?' she asked.

I looked over. On the side of the bucket, in English in big red writing, were the words 'Rat Poison'. She wasn't feeding these poor unsuspecting birds. She was killing them.

Although pigeons are known as flying rats and spread diseases, we still didn't like the idea of watching this slaughter while enjoying a fried calamari lunch. I gave the cats under the table the last of the calamari and a piece of advice.

'Listen, cats. If Ella tries to feed you with a tasty piece of blue calamari, don't eat it.'

We paid the bill and hurried away from the taverna, hoping not to be hit by falling birds as Ella's toxic seed took effect.

The next day, we decided to do some more exploring. We had heard about a place called Lichadonisia, or the 'Seychelles of Greece'. It is close to the port of Edipsos on the north-western side of Evia, between the Maliacos and the North Evia Gulf. They comprise Monolia, Megali Strongyli, Mikri Strongyli, Steno, Voria, Limani and Vagia. These islands resulted from volcanic activity, and part of them was submerged during a great earthquake in 426 BC.

It was a beautiful view as we stood on the beach waiting for the glass-bottom boat to take us around the islands. The boat owner arrived and told us we were in luck today. A monk seal had been spotted this morning near one of the islands and we may get to see it.

I had already met the local wildlife in Pefki. Dolphins had become regular visitors to my boat while I was out fishing. The locals are not very keen on them because they scare away the fish. But I was never likely to catch fish anyway, so for me it was always a lovely experience.

Recently, we were enjoying lunch at our nearby fish taverna. Being a nice day, we sat outside looking across the road to the sea beyond. In the distance, I saw a head pop out of the sea. Hoping it was a dolphin, I ran across the road and stepped onto the beach as the head disappeared under the ripples then re-emerged a few metres away from its last position. This was no dolphin, it was a dog, and it was clearly in trouble as it kept disappearing under the water. I kicked off my shoes and ran fully clothed into the sea. I was on a mission to rescue this unfortunate creature.

I swam out to its last position, but it was nowhere to be seen. I splashed around, looking to see if it would pop up again, but it had gone. I sadly waded back to the beach, looking behind in case it had survived. Alex and George, the taverna owner, were standing on the beach waiting for me. I hadn't said a word to Alex when I ran to the beach. She had watched with surprise as I left her sitting at the table and ran into the sea for no obvious reason. I appeared, dripping, with a sad look. Alex was standing with her arms wide, waiting for an explanation of my erratic behaviour. I mumbled my explanation as we walked back to the restaurant, leaving a trail of water behind me. The taverna owner looked at me and smiled.

'That's no dog, it's a seal. It's been hanging around all day. I throw him a fish sometimes.'

He went back inside and returned a moment later with a towel. As he opened the door, I heard wails of laughter from inside. He obviously couldn't wait to spread the news of the local foreigner's latest exploits.

So now on this glass-bottomed boat, we might see another seal, but this time staying dry. The boat was full of tourists. Most had their phones on camera waiting to see the sights of the small tropical islands. Flashes came from below as we motored towards the first island. People were taking photographs through the glass bottom. I took a quick look, but saw little, just a shallow sandy seabed and a few shells. So I stayed on deck, hoping to get a glimpse of the seal. The first thing I noticed was the colour of the sea. It wasn't the normal Aegean blue; it was turquoise.

The water was shallow and crystal clear, giving the impression of a Caribbean Island rather than Greece. It was relaxing to be on the water with someone else in charge. No villagers sipping coffee waiting for me to shipwreck my boat, no howls of laughter while I tried to reverse the vessel onto the slipway. We had a real captain who knew the right way to drive without sinking it. I didn't have to worry about little things like putting the plugs in or scraping the propeller on the shallow rocks. It was a new experience knowing if we did sink, it wouldn't be my fault this time.

We followed the narrow passages between islands, looking at the nearby tiny clumps of land surrounded by warm sea. Some were rocky and barren, some had small cafeterias with a few sunbeds spread in small over the sandy beaches. A few people were swimming and looked as though they were floating on air, only betrayed by the occasional splash to confirm they were in the water. It was a beautiful and unexpected experience. As we emerged from a channel into more open water, the captain called over.

'Look,' he pointed, 'there it is, a seal.'

The entire population of the boat followed his finger and

rushed to one side. The boat suddenly tipped to a steep angle, the rail almost touching the water with the unequal distribution of weight.

I was getting ready to swim when it finally righted itself, but it was too late to see the seal. It had gone.

It was only about midday so we continued our adventures around our area of northern Evia; we still had a few places we wanted to visit. Next on the list was Ellinika. The church of Agios Nikolaos sits on its own island just over a hundred metres from the beach, and the only way to visit is to swim. We had already been here during our first boat adventure, but that was only to run out of petrol and leave an oil slick in our wake. At that time, we were too busy to take much notice of the beautiful beach and historic church. But today we had all the time in the world.

Waves were crashing onto the beach, being driven by the warm wind. It wasn't the usual calm water, so few people were swimming. It was a warm, sunny day though, so the beach was packed with sun worshippers topping up their tans before the winter finally arrived. Rows of sunbeds contained young bikini-clad girls with their bronzed muscular partners, all enjoying the sunshine.

I stripped to my swimming costume. Alex was content to sit and enjoy the sun and watch as I waded in. The sandy beach slopes slowly, so the journey starts with walking through shallow water, then a short swim through the waves to the rocky island. As I approached the small bay leading to the church steps, the water calmed and shallowed. Below me were black spiky sea urchins, gathered in groups under my body. I had already experienced the pain from these creatures when one day we took a boat trip to a nearby village for lunch. We tied up to a harbour wall near the taverna, and as we stepped off the boat onto the concrete wall, Alex's sunglasses dropped off and fell into the gap between the boat and the wall. We watched as they fluttered down in the sea and disappeared into the gloom.

'No problem,' I gallantly told Alex, 'I will save them.'

I jumped into the sea and followed them. The sea was only about four metres deep, so not a difficult dive. But it was dark down there, and I didn't have a mask so searched by feeling the bottom, digging my fingers between rocks into crevasses.

I saw a glint of glass and reached out to grab the sunglasses. Then an intense pain shot through my fingers and up my arm. By the time I reached the surface, my hand and arm were burning, but I had been successful and recovered the lost item. But at a cost. A sea urchin had attacked me.

My hand looked like a hedgehog. Sharp black needles were sticking out of my flesh, and some had found their way under my fingernails. The taverna owner gave me some olive oil and instructed me to pour it over the spikes while telling me how good these creatures taste. The only edible parts of these hermaphrodites are the ovaries or gonads, which are the orange bits inside the spiky shell.

The owner went into his kitchen and returned with a large black spiky urchin to show me. He laid it in a bowl and used scissors to cut the shell to reveal a multicoloured mess of slime. He took a spoon and scooped out a wobbly orange bit and held it under my chin.

I clamped my mouth shut. After seeing his appetising preparation of this delicacy, the only way I was going to open my mouth would be to vomit. They may be a supposedly tasty and desirable snack, but I was not convinced. Why would anybody risk this suffering to eat raw aquatic gonads? They can't be that good.

I spent most of the afternoon picking spines out of my hand and swearing. Apparently, these ferocious creatures are a protected species. Well, they are certainly safe from me. I'm not planning to eat one. The only upside is that they come with their own toothpick.

I had no desire to experience this again, so I found a channel through the prickly masses and crawled onto the beach. From there I climbed the stone staircase, entered the small building and stepped onto the cool white tiles, still dripping from the swim. Ahead was a table holding a candle burner and box of matches under an icon of Saint Nikolaos. I took a step towards the icon, intending to light a candle. Suddenly my feet were where my head used to be as I slipped on the wet tiles, bashing my scalp on something while flying through the air. I lay on the floor in a puddle of dark oil, looking up at a large lamp which was still swinging and dribbling oil onto my head. I tried to stand. One leg slipped away; the other had a mind of its own and went the other way. I performed the splits while trying to find purchase on the slippery floor. Slithering across the shiny tiles on my belly, I made it to the door and got a foothold on the rough concrete steps, then walked down towards the sea. Oil ran down my shoulders and dripped down my back as I entered the water. No problem, I thought. It would all wash off during my short swim. As I entered the water, I picked my way past the sea urchins until the water was deep enough to swim, then pushed off and floated away from the small island, leaving a rainbow-coloured slick behind me. The wind had suddenly picked up and the waves were increasing in height. But they were coming from the open sea behind me, so helped to carry me back to the crowded beach. The sea became angrier as I neared the sand. The sky darkened. A storm was coming.

I splashed around for a few minutes, rode the enormous waves, and tried to rub the remaining oil off my skin. My chest looked to be clean, but my legs still looked black and my hair was plastered to my head. I headed towards the beach. Alex was sitting about four rows back from the water. The front few rows of sunbeds were filled with young, tanned, attractive women stretched out in revealing bikinis watching me as I came towards the beach.

I was doing my James Bond impression, strutting out of the sea, holding my stomach in, when a giant wave came up behind me. I fell forward face first and somersaulted under the water. Suddenly my legs were in the air and going in different directions. As I tried to stand up, another wave hit me from behind. I tumbled over and tried to stand up again, only to find that I was facing the wrong way and was hit in the face by another breaking wave.

So there I was, lying on my back, head down in the sea, legs waving in the air, unsuccessfully trying to stand up while shooting seawater out of both nostrils. Then I suffered the ultimate indignity when two of the attractive girls leapt up to help me. As one touched my greasy skin, a disgusted look crept across her face as she pulled her hand away from my slippery, slimy flesh. I thanked them anyway and approached Alex sitting under a parasol. She almost didn't recognise this portly, dark sea monster covered in black oil. My hair was transformed from my normal blond to a dark-brown shiny wig, with sandy wellington boots covering both feet where most of the beach had become glued to the sticky skin. The short swim had almost done nothing to remove the oily mess, so the beach showers would likely be as useless. I needed detergent, so I followed Alex up the short path to the taverna overlooking the beach. I stood outside, dripping oily water onto the ground, while she went in and came back with a large bottle of washing-up liquid. As we went back down to the beach to shower, I looked back at the restaurant. All the staff and clients were hanging over the balcony, making the sign of the cross and smiling. This must be a regular occurrence here.

'We have baptised another tourist. More washing-up liquid needed.'

This will always hold fond memories for me, as this is where I accidentally baptised myself.

14

ACCIDENTAL MOUNTAIN CLIMBING

I t was another hot day. The novelty of the boat had slightly worn off when I realised how many creatures were lurking under the serene-looking Aegean, likely to attack me. I suspected I was probably the worst fisherman in our village, so rather than offer more entertainment to the old men waiting by the harbour in the kafenio, today we would disappoint them. Today I would do a little gardening.

I was poking around in the riverbed at the bottom of my garden. It had rained a week or two previously, and it had filled with water. But the hot sun had slowly dried it, and it was back to its normal state of a dusty base with a few rocks spread around. Weeds had taken advantage of the damp soil and were sprouting.

I often went to explore after rainfall. The river would reveal interesting bits and pieces left behind when the water subsided. It was a little like beachcombing after a storm, but in my case, on a much smaller scale. I often found interesting stones and pottery shards. Some looked to be ancient, and some would have remnants of colour from painted decoration. But today, I struck gold. I was kicking the rocks as I walked between the growing weeds when I saw a glint on the ground. I picked up the stone, turned it over, and it caught the sun's ray and gleamed. It was a small rock, dark green, but it had tiny flecks of gold shining through. I had heard that gold could be found in most parts of Greece but never imagined I would strike lucky, and in my own garden.

I remembered the legend of the Golden Fleece. Ancient villagers used sheepskins to line streambeds. Gold flakes became ingrained in the fleeces, which led to the rise of the myth surrounding the Golden Fleece. The adventures of Jason and his Argonauts may have been based on a real journey to get the secrets of this technique for extracting gold with the sheepskin that has built up in sand deposits.

Wow. I could be a modern-day Argonaut. I had the potential to find my very own Golden Fleece without the trouble of finding a crew being attacked by mythological monsters. I didn't need to go anywhere. The gold was right here.

I took my treasure into the house to show Alex.

'Yes. Very nice. But you promised we were going to explore the island today. The gold mine isn't going anywhere.'

'But you must see it. I think it's actual gold.'

Alex picked up my gold-laden rock and between her forefinger and thumb examined it.

'I can't see any gold,' she finally told me.

I took her by the hand outside into the sunlight.

'Look.' I pointed at the rock, which if held at a particular angle, you could just make out the flecks of gold about the size of a sand grain.

'It's not very big, is it?' she suggested. Alex was right. Perhaps I had overreacted and it wasn't really a gold mine. But one day I would have a better look; then she would know I was right all along.

Alex was used to my little habit of bringing interesting things to show her. She would patiently inspect the nice selection of pebbles I found on the beach. She would complain when I dragged an interesting chunk of driftwood home from the sea. She would take an interest in my collection of unfortunate creatures I had found.

By now, our home was filling with assorted bits and pieces I found on the beach or in the hills during my regular walks. I had bits of old pottery spread around the table. I had one corner dedicated to interesting creatures I had come across in the garden. One of my favourites was a tiny lizard. I found this little chap trying to commit suicide. He was sniffing around the cat's bowl, looking for some leftovers. If they had seen him, he would have been dessert.

Most of the village cats eventually turn up at our house. It's not uncommon to sit in the garden with over a dozen of these little predators lounging around, lying on cushions or sleeping in the trees. The local cricket population even cease their chatter when the cats are around. Commonly, these poor unsuspecting insects are pounced upon and eaten before they get a chance to add their music to the sweet sounds of Greek summer. Nothing gets past the cats. So, this tiny creature with a death wish must certainly have taken a wrong turn. Lizards are thought to be lucky in Greece. But this little guy would not be so fortunate if he ended up as a snack.

I grabbed a drinking glass and covered the lizard, slipped a piece of paper underneath, picked up the precious package and walked towards the end of the garden looking for a safe place to release it. As I walked past the first dozing cat, its ears pricked up as it watched me pass. Then another woke from his sleep and followed. In a few seconds, I was being pursued by ten of these feline hunters who had worked out that I was carrying something tasty, and they all wanted some.

This was no good. Wherever I released him, the cats were sure to snap him up in seconds. So I took him into the house and got busy making a home for him. I thought that if I could protect him for a while, he may grow big enough to survive the perils of my garden when it was safe to let him go.

I looked online to see what the best food was for lizards. Mosquitoes were their favourite food. I had plenty of those buzzing around. So, I found Alex's best salad bowl and put a small cup of water on the bottom with a few lettuce leaves. I took my little fishing net into the garden and caught some flying insects. Then I added the gecko and the bugs to the bowl, stretched clingfilm over the top and made a few breathing holes.

Now Gerald the gecko lives happily as part of the family. He never ventures out, so he stays safely away from the local cats. The salad bowl is no longer needed as he lives under the sofa. His favourite food is mosquito.

Another family member who moved in with us recently is Eric the cricket. He doesn't sing much as he only has one leg. Sometimes I watch as he waves his real leg around, trying to rub it against his phantom limb but without a sound. Eric is dumb. Shunned by other crickets, an outcast, he had nowhere to go, so he came to live with us.

Alex's Greek upbringing has taught her to keep a clean house. This is taken to extremes. She is forever dusting, mopping floors, cleaning the clean until the house is so perfect the floor could be licked. Even the dogs have a constant smell of bleach. I often ask her to sit down and relax, but her reply is always 'But what if someone comes to visit? They will think we live in a brothel'.

It's a little like the advice all mothers in England give their children. 'Always wear clean underwear. You may get run over, then where would you be?'

So, my infatuations with interesting objects found on the beach, together with my new pets, had begun to become a little annoying for Alex, who was struggling to keep up with my new habit of collecting stuff and keep the house tidy. One day, I dragged home a two-metre-long piece of a ship's mast, and left it in the garden while I went back to collect an interesting old rowing oar that had washed up. By the time I arrived home, the mast was poking out of the bins along the road where Alex had thrown it. We had begun to establish a pattern. I would bring the odd tangled fishing net, planning to nail it to the wall as a feature. Alex would wait for the first opportunity to throw it away. I was forever bringing home interesting stuff, bits of driftwood, old anchors that I caught while out fishing. Several large interestingly coloured rocks, a few buckets of coloured pebbles ... they would all last until I left the house and were all missing when I returned. Alex did not share my fascination with interesting items, but never commented or criticised me. She would just quietly throw everything away while I wasn't looking. In the end, I would make a diversion to pass by the local bins on the way home and throw them away myself to save Alex the trouble.

But like me, she has a soft spot for all living things. She enthusiastically supported me whenever I wanted to repair a damaged tortoise or adopt a lizard or two, and even allowed the one-legged cricket to live with us.

We had been busy over the past few months completing our build, sorting out the garden, building walls then demolishing them, getting arrested then released, upsetting the neighbours, and generally making a nuisance of ourselves. We had begun to explore the island and had already visited some lovely nearby places, and wondered what else northern Evia had to offer.

The house was comfortable and not much more work was needed. The garden was coming together and the trees growing. It was feeling like home. We still had a few finishing touches to add – the arch needed to be finished and a barbecue had to be built – but these would all come in time and there was no hurry. Today, we would explore the nearby waterfalls.

Alex knows I don't enjoy climbing. But it seems that every excursion around Greece includes climbing up mountains, rocky hills or thousands of steps. Perhaps it's my perception, but we always seem to go up, rarely down.

Alex had been told about the Drymonas waterfalls. They were only about thirty minutes from home up in the mountains between Istiea and Rovies. We arrived and parked the car near the entrance. Even with the windows closed, we could hear the roar of the water below us in the forest. The area comprised a series of waterfalls linked by a fast-flowing river which gurgled and spat as it flowed over the first rock ledge and down into the mist. As we followed the steep shale path, we held onto wooden handrails and walked carefully on the slippery timber decking until we arrived at the base of the first waterfall. There was a large circular pond formed by many years of water splashing from the rocks above. Alex wanted to walk behind the torrent of water, so we picked our way around the sloping earth and finally found a narrow path leading behind the fall. The cave smelled of damp and rotting vegetation, with trickles of water dripping through the ceiling. A mixture of light-green plants and lichen deprived of sunshine covered the walls, giving the impression of a Jurassic forest rather than a Greek mountain. We looked towards the back of the falls and saw a wall of water with the occasional flash of blurred sunshine. It was magnificent.

We left the cave and continued our walk. Following the path, we stood to admire the lesser waterfalls discharging into crystal-clear pools which looked inviting. I suggested to Alex we should strip off and jump in.

'No way,' she quickly replied. 'That is fresh water. There are bound to be snakes in there.'

I looked at the surface, which was calm and serene. It was as clear as tap water, and there were definitely no snakes there. I pointed to the pond, but she was still not convinced.

'Can you guarantee I can swim faster than a snake?' she asked. 'I thought not.'

We climbed the path back to the car. I got into the driver's seat and waited for Alex to get in beside me. In the mirror, I watched her cross the road and look at a large brown painted wooden finger pointing up through the woods along a path, which read 'Me aftó ton trópo pros to Xiro Oros: 3 km'.

'Let's go there,' Alex pointed.

'But it's a long way; the sign says three kilometres.'

'Don't worry, it will be a nice, simple walk through the woods,' Alex said.

Assuming it would be another waterfall, and with Alex's assurance that it would be a simple walk, I reluctantly agreed.

How did I know that Xiro Oros was the highest mountain in North Evia? I had unwittingly agreed to climb it.

Since I first arrived in Greece and married Alex, I realised that most places she wanted to visit were uphill. We have climbed the Acropolis in Athens, walked up the mountain of Leviticus and looked down on the Parthenon from above. She even made me climb a mountain while I was suffering from a bout of flu, with a temperature of one hundred and three. Alex had assured me that scaling up to the church halfway up a mountain would cure me. Surprisingly, it did.

Every time we encountered steps, Alex wanted to climb them. We have even been to Nafplio and climbed into the clouds. It was early in our relationship, and I was keen to impress my new wife. She decided it would be nice to visit the castle. I stood looking up at our destination and decided to talk her out of that idea.

'Look. It's a superb view of the castle from that taverna over there,' I tried.

'It's a better view from up there looking down,' she replied. 'And you will get a fantastic view of the sea from the castle.'

I tried again. I thought I would try chivalry this time.

'But it looks high. You may get afraid of the height,' I suggested. She looked at me and smiled ironically.

I thought about inventing a leg pain, or an old sporting injury received while playing rugby against the big boys. But I thought that may make me sound like a wimp, not the impression I wanted to give to my Greek goddess wife. I was trying to cultivate the image of an athletic, virile specimen of manhood. So, not being able to think of a good excuse which would also serve that purpose, I reluctantly agreed to climb the nine hundred and ninety-nine steps to the castle.

It was a hot day. After the first eighty-nine steps, I lost count. Sweat was pouring into my eyes, blurring my vision. Alex was ahead of me, bouncing up the steps two at a time, pointing at interesting flowers and stopping occasionally to admire the view and let me catch up. Halfway up, I was suffering. The water bottle was empty, and I was finding it difficult to lift my feet for another step. Just before expiring from exhaustion, I sat on a step and pretended to gaze in wonder at the panorama below. Alex bounded back down and sat beside me.

'Are you okay?' she asked. 'You look hot.'

'I'm fine,' I lied. 'Just admiring the view.'

I was fully dehydrated by the time we reached the castle. Alex was fine and looked fresh and cool. My hair was stuck to my forehead. The colour of my shirt had changed from white to a mucky sweat-stained brown. My face felt like I had stuck it in an oven. But I had made it. Unfortunately, I was not focusing on the beauty and the grandeur of the historic castle.

I was focusing on the car park next door.

So, here we were, in the middle of a forest on Evia, and I was unknowingly climbing a mountain.

I followed Alex through the forest up a steep path. She bounced over rocks and fallen logs like a mountain goat, showing no signs of the exhaustion I was feeling. I plodded up the hill with my head down, trying to keep from vomiting. After the first hour of walking uphill, I needed a rest. We didn't seem to be any closer to the elusive waterfall. I sat on a tree trunk and tried to get my breath. Alex came to sit with me.

'How much further is this waterfall?' I asked.

'It's not a waterfall, it's a mountain. We are nearly there,' she revealed. She knew full well that I was expecting to visit a waterfall, but true to form, she had not shared our true destination as she knew I would never have agreed.

This partially explained why I was so exhausted. We had climbed so high, there was less oxygen in the air. This was confirmed when an hour later we passed the treeline onto the rocky ground. It was far too high to support vegetation other than a little grass sporadically sprouting between boulders.

We had made it to the top of North Evia. The summit of the mountain is not a peak but a broad plateau with a sheer drop over the far end. I walked across and stared at the incredible view. My tiredness fell away as I looked at the tips of the mountains of central Evia to the south, and those across the water on the Greek mainland. I could see the city of Volos, and the distant Olympus and Athos mountains to the north. To the east were the beautiful green islands of Skiathos and Skopelos. I turned to Alex, expecting her to be standing beside me, admiring this panoramic vista. But she was nowhere to be seen.

I called out. 'Where are you?'

'Down here,' she replied. 'But I'm scared.'

I looked back along the path. Alex was there, hiding behind a rock. She had arrived on the plateau with me. She had taken one look at the vast emptiness, got frightened and run back off the plateau, back down the path, and was trembling from the safety of a large boulder.

I had seen this happen before with Alex. She loved to climb to dizzy heights, but for her it was the climbing she enjoyed, not the arrival.

We had a weekend in Arachova one year, just before the skiing season. We took a drive up to the Parnassos resort. The snow had yet to deepen enough for the ski runs to fully open. But the cable car was running, and the restaurant at the top was open, so we decided to go up for a coffee. We had no intention of skiing anyway. We had tried that before and although we had done no damage to ourselves, our pride suffered an almost terminal injury. Skiing wasn't for us, but we loved the view.

We sat on the balcony of the restaurant and looked at the mountain. It was cold but sunny. Patches of snow were dusted here and there on the slopes, but mostly it consisted of rocky lumps on beds of loose shingle. There were no plants or trees. It was far too high up here to support vegetation, just barren, virgin ground. I sat and sipped a coffee.

'I want to climb to the top of that mountain,' Alex announced.

It looked like a gentle climb, not a very steep gradient. But I didn't fancy walking all the way up there, so I suggested she go alone; I would watch from here.

I watched her become smaller as she ascended the hill, until she was just a dot on the horizon as she reached the summit. Then she froze and didn't move.

I waved. She waved back, but still didn't move. I waved again. This time, she waved furiously. There was something wrong. Perhaps she was injured, I thought. I left the cafe and ran towards the mountain. As I climbed, I could see she was not happy. She was still rooted to the spot and waving.

I was almost there and called out, 'Are you okay?'

'No, I can't get down,' she yelled back.

She had been quite happy to climb up the mountain, but when she arrived at the summit and looked back, she realised how high she had climbed, and panicked.

I took her by the hand and walked her down the mountain, step by step, with her hand clenching mine so tightly it was going blue.

Now we were on top of the highest mountain in North Evia with a trembling Alex refusing to go up or down. Once again I took her hand and gently led her down the rocky path until we eventually reached the forest. Soon Alex brightened and felt better being surrounded by trees rather than wide-open mountain tops. I released her hand and bounded through the woods, enjoying my favourite part of our Greek adventures: going downhill.

Back at the car, Alex had recovered from the scary Greek mountain and suggested we pass by the metal shop. We still had a pile of rocks in our garden and hadn't heard from any of the workers when they expected to finish our massive arch.

We arrived to see an enormous, curved metal frame sitting on the ground outside the blacksmith. It was painted in a dark shade of oxblood and they had filed the welded joints down. I had to admit, it was a beautiful structure.

It seemed a shame that we would use it only once as a support for rocks during the construction and I tried to think about what we could use it for when no longer needed. I considered the possibility of using it to form a bridge over our narrow river. It was certainly long enough and was the correct shape. I set this idea aside in my head for future retrieval. I would not share this brainwave with Alex. If I did, she would likely ask the arch builders to add another project to the list and it would end up costing another fortune. No, I would keep this to myself and hope she didn't get the same idea.

'I don't like the colour,' Alex complained.

'You don't need to like the colour,' I explained. 'It's only going to be there for a few days until the cement holding the rock dries, then it's going to be removed.'

'Okay,' she replied, 'but what are we going to do with it when the arch is built?'

'Just throw it away,' I suggested hopefully.

'I know, I have a great idea. Let's make a bridge over the river. We could have a stone bridge. That would look nice.'

I sprang to my defence.

'No, I don't think a stone bridge would be worth it. With the earth bank we would never see it, and if the flood water came, it could get knocked down by the force of the water. But using the metal may be a good idea. If the flood water took that away, we might solve the problem of the house built in the river.' That chunk of steel would certainly demolish it.

Alex was pleased I had agreed with her great idea, and in

doing so I had avoided the cost of the rock-built bridge. An excellent result.

It was time to call Stamos to finish the work. It would be nice to transform the untidy pile of rocks on our lawn into the biggest arch in the village. But this would have to wait. Tomorrow we were off to Glyfada.

15

THE BEAUTY OF DEBBIE

Although the house was finished and the garden was growing, Alex's parents had still not visited.

Debbie and Zissis were getting older. Debbie had always been a large woman, and for her whole life had been passionate about her food. Her appetite had not decreased as she grew older. Sometimes I would visit to find her devouring a large cream cake. She would look up at me with jam around her mouth, smile and assure me it was a special diet cake. But the years of enjoying her food had taken its toll. Walking was becoming more difficult, and she had developed a heart problem.

'What can I do, Peteraki?' she would ask when I suggested an entire cake was not good for her. 'I'm a big woman and need my food. I have to watch my waistline, if I could find it,' she would joke.

But Alex and I were worried. She had stopped taking exercise, refused to leave the house, and just sat in her favourite chair looking down at her neighbourhood from her small balcony. She would wave and smile as neighbours passed; many would come in to visit. After all, she was one of the last original residents in the street. Most of her old neighbours had either left to spend their autumn years in their villages or islands, others had passed away leaving their homes to family who sold them on. Now that Glyfada was one of the most desirable and expensive areas of Greece, the offers were far too tempting to refuse. Over the years, Glyfada had risen from a village with earth roads to a bustling metropolis.

Not only was Debbie a big eater, she made sure that everyone around her would also eat well. From the day I met Debbie, the biggest memory of her was 'large'; not just that she was a big woman, but everything she did was large. She was also loud. Debbie never spoke softly. It was always a few decibels above the volume of a pneumatic road breaker. Before her house was demolished and replaced by the apartment block where she now lived, on the land given to her by her father, Athens airport was nearby. The aircraft would take off over Glyfada. The sound of the engines would set off car alarms and rattle windows, and nothing could be heard above the screeching of jet engines, except the voice of Debbie. It always surprised me that she could have long conversations with a similarly loud neighbour, Stella, who lived diagonally across the road and on the fourth floor of an apartment block. Debbie would yell from her kitchen; Stella would reply from way up in the air. Others along the road would join the conversation with no need to pause when a jet flew low overhead. Everyone could hear Debbie.

When Debbie cooked, it was for an army. She had passed the war years and had experienced the famine of Athens. People died on the streets from hunger. If she had any say in the future, she would ensure that no one in her neighbourhood ever went hungry again. She would prepare the most remarkable food.

Before I lived in Greece, I was trim, sprightly. I could look down, see my feet. My belly was flat. When I breathed in, I could feel my navel flapping on my backbone. If I showered, I would need to keep moving to get wet. Those were the days.

Debbie began my transition. She would cook huge amounts of scrumptious food: glistening stuffed tomatoes covered in golden olive oil straight from the wood oven; giant tiropitas with rich, creamy feta cheese and crispy golden filo pastry; Greek salads served in washing-up bowls with litres of oil, slabs of feta, and oregano sprinkled over the top. This would be followed by a shoal of chargrilled red mullet, calamari fried to perfection, and a few buckets of fried potatoes.

She would watch me with a concerned look as I ate.

'You are not hungry?' she would ask after my third loaded plate. 'Eat something; you have eaten nothing,' she would complain as she loaded up another plate and put it in front of me.

I would feel my belt tightening. Sweat would appear on my top lip as I tried to please her and eat all that was offered. But I could never win. Debbie would always walk away, sadly shaking her head, disappointed that 'I had eaten nothing'. Then she'd return with a large cream cake with strawberries on top, a giant tray of baklava, and a bucket of yogurt covered with a kilo of honey to 'help me digest'.

Over the years, I became aware it was impossible to satisfy a Greek mother. I could have eaten the five offered plates, the entire baklava, consumed the table, legs and all. She would still walk away, sadly claiming I had eaten nothing. My waistline had increased so much, I gave up wearing trousers in favour of elasticised joggers. This was because every time I wore trousers, they had shrunk a little more and the belt needed a new hole. I was finding my shower needed more water, and every time I got into the bath, I would flood the floor with the resulting tidal wave. But this was a necessary part of my becoming Greek. It didn't matter where we went. There was always a Greek mother who would sit watching me with a disappointed look as I munched my way through the offerings in the vain hope I wouldn't offend her. It always ended with the immortal phrase used by all Greek mothers:

'Why have you eaten nothing? You don't like my food?'

But Debbie wrote the book. Others just followed her example. Every day, she would pass endless quantities of food out of her tiny subterranean kitchen window while she continued cooking, wearing only her knickers and bra while singing at the top of her voice. Everyone knew there was always a meal at Debbie's house.

Alex never got on with her father. She was three years old when Zissis finally came to live at the house in Glyfada, but this was only for a short time. His explosive temper had at last sealed his fate, and after a violent argument with his boss in Athens, he was sacked. With his sudden cessation of any income, he had to give up his small apartment and move in. Debbie was still working at the university in Athens, but her small wage was not enough to support the family. Zissis showed no interest in securing another job and spent his time in the house while Debbie's mother would cook, clean, and take care of the children. Alex was old enough to feel the tension and would cling to her mother whenever she was at home, but would ignore her father, as he would ignore her. After many arguments and pressure from the family, he finally took a job in a tourist office on the island of Corfu and left. He rarely visited the family home, but started sending money to subsidise the family. Alex saw her father on rare occasions during her younger years. Sometimes he would visit for a day or two if he had business in Athens, but he mostly stayed away. Alex was ten years old when he moved back.

Zissis had opened a restaurant in Corfu. He had never been a cook and had never lowered himself to manual labour, and certainly never waited on tables. He knew nothing about the restaurant trade. He had shouted at waiters before, complained about food to chefs, and generally made a nuisance of himself, but this hardly qualified him to run a restaurant. However, he saw a business opportunity and thought he could make some extra money.

He reasoned that every day he was escorting tourists on guided tours around the island. They would stop the bus at a traditional Greek taverna for lunch. Although he received a commission from the grateful taverna owner, he saw an opportunity to open his own restaurant and make even more money. Logically, it seemed to make sense. After all, he would supply his own customers.

At this time Debbie was becoming suspicious. Her telephone calls were not being returned and he was not calling home. So, Debbie packed young Alex and Christos in the car and set off on the journey to pay a surprise visit to Corfu. When the family arrived, they found him living with a Dutch tour rep and sharing her flat. Debbie was furious and chased his lover away before launching the long-overdue attack on her philandering husband. Alex remembers meeting the Dutch tour rep in the street.

'She had a beard,' Alex informed me, 'and she was ugly. My mum was beautiful. I had no idea what my father saw in this woman.'

After sorting out their differences, and Zissis promising everything was off with this woman, Debbie left Corfu and returned with her children to Glyfada while Zissis remained to start his restaurant business.

He employed a cook, a couple of servers and a manager, and left them to run the business. This did not end well. Although the restaurant was full every day, the profits were disappearing into the pockets of unsupervised employees, leaving Zissis to deal with the considerable loss. So, he gave up that money-making enterprise and returned to his family in Glyfada.

Soon, he secured another job, utilising his travel experience for another Greek company but this time in England, running a branch in London. He arranged to rent out the house in Glyfada and took his family to London. Debbie took a job in a small travel business in Swiss Cottage and they enrolled Alex and her brother Christos in an English school.

This was the hardest part of Alex's short life. Zissis and Debbie would leave their rented flat on Finchley Road at 7.00 a.m. Alex would dress herself and her younger brother, then hand in hand they would walk the long distance to school. Alex did not speak or understand English. So rather than persist and teach her the language, the school would sit her in a room to draw pictures, with no interaction from teachers or fellow pupils. Then at 3.00 p.m. she would collect Christos from his school, go back to the shabby flat, cook for her and her brother, and wait for Debbie to finish work. Her father didn't come home often. This lasted for only six months before Zissis lost his job again. It forced the family to return to Greece.

He found another job with a travel company in Piraeus while Alex and her brother recommenced their schooling in Greece. When Alex was thirteen years old, they were off to England again. This time, Zissis had secured a well-paid job in a London City travel company. He secured a house for the family in Northwood, in Middlesex, where I first met Alex.

I was just a butcher's boy. My job was to clean windows, mop floors, and help to make the prime minced steak to be sold from bulging trays displayed in the shop window. At first, this was a distressing experience. I was given large trays of unidentified animal parts with tubes, all floating around in deep-red congealed blood. It looked horrible, and in the early days I had to control my gagging instinct and look at the ceiling while stuffing handfuls of the grizzly offal into the hole at the top of the industrial mincer. However, what came out of the other end looked quite palatable. The meat and the tubes had been mashed and combined with the congealed blood, leaving what appeared to be a nice red tray of minced steak. I doubted whether this mincer had ever seen real beef, but the customers seemed to like it. When I left, I swore never to eat minced meat again unless I minced it myself using real, identifiable meat.

I will always remember an old lady who came to our shop once a week wearing a mink coat and carrying a small Pekinese called Truffles. She always asked for the same thing: a pound of prime fillet steak minced for Truffles. For us, that was steak day. If I had put a pound of prime fillet steak into the huge mincer, the monster would have eaten it. There was no way such a small amount of meat would pass all the way through a machine used to guzzling fifty-kilo trays of unidentified tubes and animal bits. So, they instructed me to weigh the fillet steak, take it to the back of the shop to the mincer, and turn the mincer on so the grinding could be heard. Then I would put the steak in the fridge, collect a handful of our prime minced steak made that day from unidentified animal bits, and serve it to Truffles. He loved it, and we enjoyed his fillet steak for lunch.

I was fifteen when I first saw the fourteen-year-old Alex walk past the shop window. She was the most beautiful creature I had ever seen. I had experienced crushes before, but never like this. Being only a youngster, I was probably going through puberty. But that was never talked about. So perhaps I didn't. In any case, I would never have had time for any mood swings or being rude to my parents and making their lives difficult. Their lives were already difficult, and I never saw them anyway. I would leave home in the morning to take the train at 5.00 a.m. and not return home until late evening. By that point, I was always too tired to give anyone a hard time. But seeing Alex for the first time, I was in love, and the rest is history.

Alex initially suffered at the Potter Street school. She didn't speak English and struggled to fit in. Other girls would wear make-up and shave their legs, whereas Alex, being olive-skinned and because of her Greek upbringing, would never be permitted to follow their example and shave or wear make-up, and was known as the hairy Greek with the yellow skin. But I knew she was the most beautiful of them all.

No sooner had I shared a few words with her, she was gone. Zissis had lost yet another job, and they had returned to Greece. The girl of my dreams had disappeared. But we would meet again in a few years.

When we demolished our family house in Glyfada and built the apartment block on the land, it marked the end of an era. Rather than the old house with fig trees in the garden, and damp, crumbling walls, we now owned beautiful modern apartments. We had the penthouse and our very own replica historical monument on the roof. Debbie occupied the first floor with Zissis. But it proved to be the last nail in the coffin of the old Glyfada. Gone were the days of screaming conversations with neighbours. Gone was the constant flow of coffee being shared with neighbours. Gone were the huge family meals on the old stone patio accompanied by the sound of Debbie's singing. The buzz of air conditioners and the hum of daytime TV had replaced it.

Debbie never seemed to recover from the loss of the old home. She was comfortable, she lived in a luxury apartment. But it had no soul. No more memories were likely to be created here. She had to rely on the old ones.

Some say that progress is a good thing. In most cases, it is. But sometimes when we move forward, we leave behind the most precious things that make our lives worth living.

I became part of the family when things had begun to progress in Glyfada. They had already demolished and replaced most of the houses in our street with towering apartment blocks. Our house was the last to surrender to the steamroller of progress. Over the next few years, the rest of Glyfada went the same way. More homes were disappearing and the noise of construction had replaced the jovial yelling from house to house. We were the last, but the street had already died. We would sit alone under the bougainvillea in the last remaining garden, overshadowed by the high-rise blocks around us which blotted out the sun. Instead of cheerful voices and the call of street vendors selling their ice, melons or local honey, we could only hear the distant hum of the traffic and aircraft engines from the soon-to-close Athens airport.

This is one of the main reasons we built on the island. Luckily, the village atmosphere is still there. The spectre of technology has yet to rear its head in Pefki.

In our village, we have a different outlook on life. We don't worry about the outside world. The important thing here is living our own lives. There is no need for a newspaper; a visit to the kafenio is all you need to catch up on the important stuff.

But what this does is to promote an incredible community spirit. Talking brings people together. Not only do you receive the relevant news of the village, but because everyone is talking to everyone, you build friendships and bind the community.

But instant gratification, fast food, and mobile phones have rapidly consumed Glyfada.

Recently, I was sitting outside a coffee bar in Glyfada. It was strangely quiet. The next table was full of several old men who would usually speak loudly over each other, arguing about their own political parties and which football team is superior. But this time, each of them were staring into their iPhones, stabbing the screen with their fingers. No talking, just absolute silence. Luckily, in our village we still talk.

We needed to get Debbie out of her apartment for a few days and reintroduce her to some real Greek culture; to feel the fresh, cool air of the island rather than spend her time looking out of the window. She needed to feel alive again and communicate with real Greeks in a good, open environment. She finally agreed to come with us to Pefki on the promise of the best seafood in Greece.

We left our Pefki home early for the drive to Athens to collect them. On Alex's advice, I had hidden the boat before we left. Debbie did not know that we had bought our own boat. She was from a long line of sea captains and grew up listening to stories of shipwrecks, dangerous voyages and maritime disasters. She would have been extremely worried if she knew that her only daughter had taken to floating around the Aegean Sea in a small boat. She would have been even more concerned if she knew my history of boating mishaps. So, we let her bask in ignorance. That would be best for all of us.

We arrived on our Glyfada street around noon. Before we collected the parents, we needed to pay a quick visit to Stella. Alex remembers her from her childhood when the street was populated by small, ramshackle houses and earth roads. We hadn't seen her for a long time. Our visits to Glyfada over the last few months had been brief because of the house construction in Pefki and the time taken to get it habitable. We had rather neglected our neighbours and local friends, and needed to do some catching up.

Stella lives on the top floor of her apartment block built on the land her old house used to stand on. She used to be the street's chicken and egg supplier. Now she lives alone with her cats and no one sees her any more. Gone is her loud foghorn voice yelling greetings up and down the street. Gone are the chickens that used to populate her front garden.

Alex pressed her bell. An incoherent crackle came from the intercom before the door buzzed and opened. We stepped into the small elevator and pressed the button for the top floor.

Stella opened her door, and a waft of cat smell assaulted us as she stood wearing an old nightgown reaching above her knobbly knees, with bare feet and a mop of unruly grey hair. But her smile was beautiful and her eyes were full of tears. I looked at Alex, who also had tears running down her cheeks. Stella was a remnant of her happy childhood, bringing precious memories flooding back.

We gave her some gifts brought from our last trip to England: some chocolate and tea bags.

'Did you bring any slippers?' she asked. 'I need slippers.'

'Yes,' Alex lied, feeling a little sorry for her bare-footed friend. 'But I left them at home. I will go and get them.'

Back in the lift, Alex and I were now on a mission. We needed to find some slippers before we collected the parents. We stepped onto the street for the short walk to the mall. Suddenly, there was a voice behind us.

'Geia sou Pétro, kai Alexándra.'

We turned to see another of our old neighbours hurrying to catch up. We stood and chatted for a few moments before bidding her goodbye. A few seconds later, we passed the local travel agent. Danos came running out of his shop, flung his arms around us both, and hugged us in welcome. More tears flowed as we exchanged memories before we continued on our quest. What would normally be a five-minute walk from our home to the shoe shop took over an hour. We met friends, best wishes were given and memories exchanged. We chose three pairs of slippers. Another hour later, we arrived back at Stella's house after meeting more old friends, drinking coffees, and feeling as though we had never left.

At last we were ready to collect Alex's parents. We loaded the suitcase into the car and went back for walking frame, wheelchair and sticks. We helped Debbie into the elevator and got her comfortable in the car. Alex sat in the back seat with her mother while Zissis sat beside me in the passenger seat. Zissis and I chatted for the duration of the trip and the drive passed quickly.

It was late afternoon when we arrived in Pefki, so instead of going straight home, we decided to visit the local taverna for a real village meal. We were all tired and hungry after our journey, so grateful to finally relax with the sound of waves lapping on the beach and soft Greek music emanating from the kitchen.

George, the taverna owner, came over to our table carrying

a large jug of wine, sat down and poured himself a glass. Debbie refused the offered wine by putting her hand over the glass.

'Just a little water for me,' she said.

George recited the menu.

'We have special stuffed calamari, fresh grilled octopus, a lovely red snapper my friend Costas caught today, and especially for you, we have giant grilled shrimps which have just arrived off my brother's boat.'

This all sounded wonderful. We'd had a long journey and my stomach was rumbling, and it would be the perfect meal for Debbie and Zissis to begin their stay in our island village.

Debbie listened without enthusiasm. This was rare. Debbie's favourite pastime was eating. She would normally question each dish in detail: how was it cooked, fried or grilled? What herbs are used? How big is the calamari? But this time, she gazed out to sea, seemingly lost in her own thoughts. and once he had finished, she looked at him.

'Do you have a little soup?' she asked.

This was worrying. I had never seen Debbie refuse a meal. This was new to me. I had noticed she was very subdued during the trip. Our attempts to engage her in conversation only resulted in a one-word answer or a smile. Normally, she would rattle the car windows with the pitch of her voice, but today it was too peaceful. Something was very wrong with Debbie.

I reached across the table and took her hand.

'What's wrong, Debbie?' I asked. 'Are you ill? Do you want to lie down?'

She reached into her bags and took out a crumpled paper and passed it to me. It was a telegram from Africa giving the sad news that her brother Vasilis had passed away. Zissis looked as curious as us. It was obviously news to him too.

Vasilis was the bear of the family. He was a rough, tough sea captain who lived most of his life sailing the oceans of the world. A few years ago, he had retired and settled down in Africa. He married his Kenyan wife Kathy and invested in a shrimp boat to pass his retirement.

We had seen little of him since he retired, but his rare visits were always full of fun and laughter. Like Debbie, he loved his food. He was the only man I ever saw who could eat a whole lamb at one sitting, even the head. His teeth had been extracted when he was a young man, mostly because of his love of gluey Greek sweets and desserts, and when not eating, he had a passion for the strong crystallised tree sap from the Greek island of Chios, mastika, which he used as chewing gum. This, combined with already weakened teeth, meant that slowly they began to break and fall out.

He was not a patient man, so during a visit to the dentist to deal with a troublesome molar, he demanded they were all pulled out then and there rather than suffer toothache ever again. He was fitted with dentures. According to Vasilis they were 'no bloody good, they didn't speak Greek', and they moved around when he tried to chew his food.

So, over the side of the ship they went, and they are still sitting somewhere on the bottom of the Aegean Sea.

I would watch as he chewed bones with his gums, which had hardened to clamps. He would even take bites from the hardest apples and still chewed mastika. His appetite for sweet things only increased as he grew older. Diabetes was one result of a long life of overindulgence, and in the end, he ate himself to death. On his last morning on earth, he asked Kathy for a bowl of sticky pudding covered in strawberry jam. As the last spoonful passed his lips, it was rapidly followed by his last breath. This would have been the way he wanted to go.

So, Vasilis was gone. But it was a life lived well and to the full. He was loud, brash, and looked fierce, but he had a heart of pure gold. He finally retired when he was ordered to carry a consignment of weapons to a war zone. Being a much-travelled sailor, he had seen the result of conflict and had no intention of further adding to the misery by helping to carry arms on his ship. He gave his ship over to another master and took the first flight back to Greece, vowing never to sail again.

We finished our meal and drove the short distance home. This was not the introduction to our new home we had dreamed about. After the news of Vasilis's passing, the atmosphere was subdued and sad. Debbie hobbled around the house and made the right noises, trying to look impressed, but her heart wasn't in it. We showed her to a bedroom and left her to sleep.

The next morning, she was a little brighter as we sat on our patio with coffee. We chatted together but could see her mind was not with us.

From the time we first met, Debbie had always been my second mother. She showed me nothing but love and kindness. But behind this, I always felt I was not fully trusted. A quick glance, an unguarded moment, sometimes revealed a look of suspicion combined with a slight fear.

Her own experience of marriage was not the best. Bouts of rage had always afflicted Zissis. He found it difficult to settle on any job and promoted a feeling of insecurity to the family. Debbie's father was a great man, but as a sea captain was absent from her life and she never knew when he would be there. He would sometimes come home after a six-month voyage and stay a day or two before disappearing to the other side of the world to collect another ship.

Her brother, who she loved, was also unreliable. He married several times, to various women all over the world, and never, as far as we were aware, divorced any of them. Even he was never there for his sister. So, Debbie lived a life of insecurity. Having no one to fully rely on, she had to be strong and shed blood for her family, becoming the ultimate matriarch. I had already accepted that she would probably always view me with a little suspicion. But her love for me was real, so I accepted that too. She needed to see Alex settled and comfortable, knowing her partner would give her the love and kindness she richly deserved.

I looked at Debbie's face and saw the age in her eyes and a darkness that occurs to some when they feel they are too tired to carry on. But behind that was a look of serenity. She cast her eyes around the house and looked towards the garden. Then she took my hand and, through tears of happiness, said:

'Bravo, my son.'

There was no longer the cloud of suspicion, no fear left in those beautiful eyes. I realised that I had broken down her last wall. She knew her work was done. Alex was safe with me. At that moment, I understood. She was passing the care of her only daughter to me. I would accept that honour and cherish Alex for the rest of my life.

Debbie was mother to two biological children: Christos, who will be my lifelong friend, and Alexandra, who I am honoured to call my wife. But Debbie was also a mother to hundreds of people she met. She changed lives for the better and will be remembered with love by all who met her.

Debbie's influence was never destined to be confined to her immediate family. She had too much love to give. Everyone who met her fell under her spell. She changed lives for the better by her shining example, and left this world a better place.

16

OUR ISLAND IS ON FIRE

T he next day, Debbie looked brighter and seemed more
like her old self. She enjoyed the constant stream of
comings and goings of our friends in the village. It reminded
her of old Glyfada. She was happy to sit at home and meet the

villagers who had all heard that Alex's mother was in residence and were keen to meet her. Baskets of fruit from their own trees were presented, eggs from their own chickens arrived packed in tissue paper. Some brought flowers from their gardens, and honey from their hives. When visiting anyone in Greece, you must take a small gift. A small bunch of flowers, a box of cookies, or a cake. Likewise, the host must do everything possible to make the visitor feel welcome. Traditionally guests are offered coffee, and spoon sweets. These are jars of preserved fruit in syrup. A small portion is served in a bowl and a teaspoon is placed beside it. It can consist of preserved oranges, lemons, pink quince or cherries, and is always home-made.

'You two go out. We are happy here. It's not as if we are going to get lonely. Anyway, it's far too hot. I would rather just stay in the shade,' she told us. 'You have lunch out today. I will cook something for us here. Just pretend we are not here and enjoy yourselves.'

It was mid-August, the height of the summer. The temperature was indeed oppressive. For the past couple of days, it had been rising steadily and had now reached forty degrees.

Tourists had arrived and the local hotels and guest houses were filled to capacity. The tavernas and bars were busy every day, and the beaches were brimming with people enjoying the sun in the shade of their umbrellas while being served iced drinks from a constant stream of servers criss-crossing the road, holding trays above their heads. I loved seeing the tourists in the village. It was such a boost to the economy, and it ensured the local business owners could put some profit away to help them through the rest of the year. Pefki is a small village, but in July and August its population swells by many times its usual number.

August is always a hot month in Greece. But this year, the heat was becoming unbearable. Being by the sea, the normal weather pattern was usually predictable. Early morning there would be a light breeze barely rippling the water. Then, as midday approached, the wind would pick up and the ripples would increase to small waves, sometimes with white tips, then calming again later in the afternoon.

But today, there was not even a breeze. The sea was like glass. Then at midday the wind began.

It was a hot, unpleasant breeze that burns your mouth as you breathe. The temperature was rapidly increasing and would only get hotter. Heat had been rising daily for a week now. The normally cool evenings of North Evia had become hot and stuffy. If Evia was uncomfortable, then our trip to Athens the next day would be unbearable. We would be taking Debbie and Zissis back to Glyfada and staying with them for a couple of days before flying to London for some business.

We had seen on the TV that some fires had begun in mid Evia, but this was normal for windy days in August. So rather than drive through the island, we took the ferry from Edipsos. As the ferry left the port, we looked south and watched the smoke rising from several small forest fires. We arrived at Arkitsa, left the ferry, and joined the national road towards Athens. The temperature reading on the dashboard had reached forty-three degrees as we got to the first toll station. The air smelled of smoke. Several fires had broken out on the mountains along our route, and one up ahead seemed danger-ously close to the road. As we passed, we could see the flick-ering flames consuming the upper branches of trees, being fed by the hot wind. By the time we reached the outskirts of Athens, it had reached forty-seven degrees. The air condi-tioning was struggling to cope as we drove the final few miles to Glyfada. We stood on our terrace and watched an enormous cloud of smoke filling the sky over Athens. The mountains were burning. Aircraft buzzed overhead on their route to the sea, where they dipped towards the surface, scooping up seawater, then rose into the air with their precious cargo to drop onto the fast-encroaching flames. Helicopters lowered yellow buckets into the sea and followed the planes to add their offering. But it was having little effect. The flames grew and the intensity of the smoke increased. Black ash was now falling from the sky, and the air tasted of smoke. As the sun set, the mountains glowed red in the darkness. The fires were out of control.

We left the terrace and went into the living room to catch up on the news on TV. Every station was reporting on the devastating fires. The firefighting aircraft had ceased their work for the night. It would be too dangerous trying to scoop up water from the sea and fly in darkness through the plumes of smoke.

The next morning, we went up to the terrace to continue watching the progress of the firefighting effort. The air comprised a mustard-yellow fog which enveloped the buildings and blotted out the sun, combined with the smell of burning which was overpowering and stinging our eyes. We checked the news. The fires were out of control. The mountains north of Athens were burning, another had started near Corinth. But more worrying was news of serious fires in northern Evia. Here in Glyfada we were largely protected. We were in a city and not close to the forests currently being devoured. But Evia was another matter. Being one of the greenest islands in Greece, with almost a thousand square kilometres of forest, everything we had worked for over the last three years was at risk. We had to get back.

I spoke to Debbie and Zissis, who understood our reasons for returning to the island.

'Please be careful,' Debbie told us.

We cancelled our flight tickets and headed back to Evia.

The ferry to Edipsos was empty. Nobody wanted to go to Evia now. The tourists were being advised to leave as the fires rapidly spread. As we approached the port, the green mountains were hidden by giant plumes of smoke. We drove the short distance home under a yellow sky. The stench of the smoke invaded the car – the air conditioning was doing little to filter it. I opened a window; the smell of burning became stronger. Soon we arrived in Pefki. The fires hadn't reached our village, but they were not far away judging from the colour of the sky and the malodorous burning in the air. As the day progressed, the smoke over the mountain increased in density. No longer was it a threatening sickly yellow; it had become darker, resembling a black thundercloud. It was heading our way. We had to protect ourselves and our property.

We took our hoses and started the sprinklers. We needed to dampen everything. The water sprayed around the garden while Alex and I set to work spraying the roof and walls of our home. Everywhere we looked around the village there were hoses spread across roads and gardens. Everyone had the same idea. We kept all the hoses running throughout the sleepless night. At dawn, with daytime approaching, the sun was invisible behind vast plumes of acrid smoke. The grass was squelching under our feet, and trickles of water were running down the walls from the hoses on the roof. The air was now stiff with the smell of burning, and looking towards the hill, we could see the distinct clouds; it was much nearer now.

The news came through that a serious fire had approached the village of Limni across the mountain. It had spread to Rovies, and residents and tourists were being evacuated. The fires had crossed the main road, cutting off their escape, leaving everyone trapped between the inferno and the sea. They redirected the ferries normally used to ship tourists and trucks to the mainland to aid in the evacuation. They approached the beaches like Second World War landing crafts and lowered the ramps, allowing coughing people with stinging eyes to run on board to safety. But this was just the beginning. As the fire raged, the forests surrounding the villages of North Evia were being consumed. Entire villages were being evacuated. Overhead power and telephone lines had melted, plunging most of the island into darkness, with no communication with the outside world. The fire was relentlessly coming our way. This differed from our experience in Athens. Here, there were no flashing lights of fire trucks, no firefighting aeroplanes in the sky, no helicopters buzzing above our heads carrying yellow buckets of water from the sea to douse the flames. No, we were alone.

Suddenly, we heard a siren in the village. A single police car had arrived and was driving around the streets with speakers telling us to evacuate at once. The roads out of the village had been closed and had become impassable. The only way to leave was by sea. Two ferries had arrived at Pefki beach and lowered their ramps. Tourists wheeled their suitcases onto the ships, leaving their hire cars outside hotels. Older residents were being pushed up the ramps in wheelchairs, and cars were arriving at the beach and discharging more people. Alex and I strapped our small inflatable dinghy to the car roof, drove it to the beach and tied it to a tree. We had no intention of leaving our precious home. If the worst came, we would run to the beach, take the small boat and escape into the sea.

As the daylight faded, one of the ferries left, carrying the tourists and the frailest villagers. The rest were going to stay. One ferry remained with its ramp lying on the sand. This would be the last means of escape if the fire consumed the village.

As the sky darkened into night, the red glow increased over the hill, then the flames appeared on the mountain ridge and unrelentingly crept towards us, leaving red smoke filling the sky. The villagers sprang into action. We could now see which direction the fire would attack us from and which homes were most at risk.

Dozens of villagers joined a fire engine with two uniformed firefighters as they sped towards the first home in its path. The fire had reached the garden and an outbuilding was burning. Jets of water were directed into the structure as the fire approached. Then there was a cry. The inferno had found another route to our village and was heading for the other end. The firefighters continued to douse the house, while other men left and rushed to the location of the new fire. It was at the entrance to Pefki.

Alex and I ran towards the new battlefront. We did not know what we were going to do. We had no hoses, we had no firefighting equipment, but these things don't enter your mind when you are desperately trying to protect your village. We stood by the harbour and looked up the hill. This landmark, well known to tourists and locals alike, was burning. It's the turn from the main road into Pefki. There is a welcome sign to the village, which was now on fire. The majestic Pefka trees, after which they named the village, would be the first welcome for visitors as they entered. But now they too were ablaze, with fire leaping into the air, raining hot ash and fiery twigs onto our heads. Someone in a nearby house had unrolled his hosepipe and was directing the water onto the huge fire. Another was filling a water bottle from a nearby tap in a pointless attempt to pour water onto the inferno. This was desperation.

There was nothing we could do here apart from try to protect our own property. By now, the hillside was fully alight. The flames had almost reached the main road, two hundred metres from our home. Two houses on the other side of the road were ablaze, their owners helplessly watching from the other side of the road, calling for anyone available to come to their aid. But having only one fire appliance in our village, it was a forlorn hope. The olive grove on the hill above our garden was burning, creating a deep-red smoke silhouette against the deeper red sky.

Alex and I took our hoses as far as they could reach and sprayed the road and the next-door land. We hoped the main road would act as a firebreak. The men of the village also realised this, and they lined the road, beating out any stray piece of flaming debris carried on the wind to the other side. The biggest risk was the strong wind carrying flaming debris, which would fly high into the air above our heads only to fall onto dry land and start other fires. We needed to ensure this didn't happen, at least not near our home.

In the small hours of the night, the fire was at its most furious. The entire mountain was alight, and the smoke was choking us as we relentlessly sprayed our hoses at anything remotely flammable. We soaked trees, grass, fences and gates. Our arms were aching and tiredness was taking its toll, but we couldn't stop.

Cars and pickup trucks screamed up and down the nearby main road, transporting buckets, some with large brooms hanging from the windows of cars. These would be used to beat the fire. It was pure desperation. There was no organisation, no help from official fire departments; only the one ancient fire engine, with two part-time firefighters who luckily happened to be here. All the firefighting planes were still flying around Athens, dealing with smaller fires there, leaving Evia to fend for itself. People did what they thought was best to protect our forgotten village. We had lost power when the overhead cables melted up on the hill. We were spraying our hoses by the light of the flames, which illuminated the village.

But at long last it became clear that the fire was lessening.

As dawn approached, we could see that the efforts of the people of Pefki had been successful. The fire had been held, and with nothing left to feed the inferno, it died into smoke and ash as the flames slowly disappeared. It was over. We had won without aid, without help from anyone. The brave people of our village stood proud and bravely saved us and our homes.

Alex and I stood beside the main road, and we looked up to the mountain. This was the beautiful green tree-covered mountain that we admired every day while sitting on our patio, sipping our coffee. Now it was just a black, charred, smoking hill devoid of greenery. I looked at Alex. She looked at me and giggled.

'Have you seen your face?' she asked.

'No,' I replied. 'Have you seen yours?' I giggled back.

We both had completely black faces with small white patches where we had rubbed our eyes. We were both covered in soot and sweat. Our clothes had changed colour to a dirty grey and our blackened hair was pasted to our sweaty scalps and faces. But we were happy. Our home was safe, and so were we.

After the past fearful few days, the next emotion would be anger. How could this ever have been allowed to happen? Where were the authorities when we really needed them? They were keen to charge us taxes, make our lives difficult with unnecessary bureaucracy; they would enforce punishing penalties for small planning irregularities and do their best to make things difficult. This could be forgiven, but only if we had our basic needs protected. This terrible night of the twenty-first of August, 2021, woke us up to the reality of living in a small Greek village. We had never felt more alone.

It took the next few days to clean up the village and take stock of the damage. They finally restored our electricity as they replaced cables on the mountains, and the telephones came back online. The mobile phone towers took a little longer, but when they were restored, our signal was better than before the fires. The village lost six houses on the other side of the main road, but none in the village. No injuries had been reported. Everyone in the village had survived unscathed. The road had done its job as a firebreak with the help of the exhausted villagers who stood their ground and ensured it didn't cross.

The government blamed global warming for these devastating fires that consumed almost all of North Evia. Over four hundred square kilometres of lush green forest were destroyed. Pine trees tapped for precious resin harvested over generations were no more. Countless olive groves burned which would lead to a national shortage of oil. Mature fruit trees were gone. It devastated the thriving industry of Evia honey production overnight with the loss of thousands of beehives, along with the precious insects who busily collected pollen from the lush pine forests and mountain oregano. The economy of the island was destroyed. People's livelihoods had been burned along with the land. The fires had also coincided with the height of the tourist season. They evacuated people from Evia, cutting short their holidays. Future bookings dried up, and the hotels who relied on the regular influx of visitors lost their livelihoods. Tourists had no interest in visiting a black, smoking island. The restaurants, tavernas and cafes who depended on the short tourist season to survive for the rest of the year had their season and income cut off. The aftermath of the disaster would be felt for years to come.

Global warming may have contributed, but in reality, the cause was incompetence and complacency from the government, who had other priorities. The twenty-first of August, 2021, would be a day Greece would never forget.

17

THE OLD OLIVE TREE

A few days later, the clean-up operation had finished. The fires near the village were a memory, and life needed to continue. The tourist season had ended abruptly this year, but we were fortunate that tourism isn't the main economy of the village. Although hundreds of square kilometres of forest had been burned to ash, thankfully most of the local agriculture had remained untouched. And even though thousands of olive trees were burned, most near our village had survived. Vineyards were mostly intact, and we still had the fishing industry.

People of the village walked more slowly. Laughter had vanished from the tavernas and cafes and had been replaced by a grim determination. A sombre feeling had descended over the village. Some establishments had closed, realising there would be no more tourists this year; others remained open, hoping to catch the last of the season, but their tables and chairs stood empty. But in Greece, hope dies last. Everyone had worked together to save the village from the inferno and were determined to work together to recover.

It could have been a lot worse for us. Compared to other villages, we were lucky.

Fortunately, our new home and garden had survived. Life was returning to normal. Stamos arrived with the Bulgarian workers. The blacksmith had delivered the steel frame, ready to complete our arch. The builders resumed their labours, cutting and chipping away at rocks, shaping them to fit the ever-growing structure.

Our home was almost finished. The last thing on the list to make it complete was to build the barbecue.

In Greece, barbecues are a serious business. There is no natural gas in Greece, so cooking relies on charcoal, electric stoves or bottled gas. We cooked most food over charcoal. We don't bother with the small tin barbecues found in most countries for cooking the odd hamburger or sausage. No, ours must be capable of roasting a whole lamb every year for the traditional Easter celebrations. So, we went to the builder's merchant to choose one, and it was delivered the next day.

It was beautiful. It was a concrete structure with a flatbed for the charcoal to be laid on. Either side was a metal frame that could hold the spits at differing levels. At one end a bicycle chain was wrapped around the metal in a zigzag effect and attached to a motor to drive the entire assembly. Attached to one side was a sink with taps that reflected the sunlight, and a small food preparation area with an elm chopping board. On the other side of the barbecue was a domed bread oven with a cast-iron door. This was a serious barbecue.

Stamos set to work and put a roof over the entire structure while our Bulgarian friends completed the last touches on our huge stone arch.

We had finished our home.

While Stamos and his workers did the final clean-up, Alex and I held hands and walked around the garden. From the day we first laid eyes on this weed-and-bamboo-covered piece of Greece, we had created something special as we slowly merged into village life.

The trees were growing beautifully. We had flowers in pots spread around the garden. The locals still think of us as a little strange because we grow things we can't eat: flowers, ornamental trees, a lawn. Maria has not given up on educating us about village life. She used all the space in our flowerpots to plant vegetables. We now have a strange mix of roses with cucumbers and peppers, tomatoes growing alongside carnations. The base of every tree has aubergines sprouting from the ground.

At the front of the house, a family of swallows have busily constructed a mud nest at the apex of the roof. We both considered this to be a good omen for the future. But we hoped these were useless birds and thereby ignored by Dimitri and his shotgun.

We continued our walk around our estate. We checked the earth bank in front of the river. We had created this to give at least partial protection from the raging torrent during the rainy season. It wouldn't help very much as the water would always find its way around it. A wall would have protected us better, but after our brush with the law, we preferred the occasional flooding to being locked up in a Greek jail. It had turned out to be quite a feature now as it was sporting a riot of colour from the flowers planted, with the additional benefit of the perfume exuding from the blooms, which mixed with the summer smell of oregano and sage from the nearby mountains.

Alex suggested we take a walk up the nearby hills to look at our home from above. We had only ever seen it close up, so it would be nice to get a bird's-eye view from the mountain looking down. We followed the winding lane up the side of the mountain and stopped under the giant olive tree, one of the oldest trees in Greece. It was an incredible view which took our breath away. A small information board on top of a stone pillar, in English and Greek, gave us the history of this incredible living thing.

This ancient olive tree above Artemision looks down on to the crumbling village. Long ago it was the fishing port over-looking the beautiful Straits of Artemision. Now the sea has receded, leaving a stretch of scrubland occupied by younger olive trees and brambles, a new road, and our new home far below, which appeared as a white and red dot surrounded by a small square of green. It looked like it had existed as long as the tree, but we knew better.

We sat in the warm Greek sunshine under her branches, with the perfumed air of wild oregano wafting from the mountains. The cicadas' persistent chatter emanated from the canopy, drowning the sound of the light breeze ruffling her leaves. She sees us, a glimpse of this human existence in time, but it means nothing to her.

The Battle of Artemision had raged in the sea below as she watched the smoke from Greek and Persian ships envelop kings, princes and slaves as they slipped below the white-tipped waves into the fathomless depths of Hades, where all are equal. Gazing across the water, she watched the million-strong army of King Xerxes. She heard the death cries of the Spartan king Leonidas in the Battle of Thermopylae as his three hundred warriors inevitably paid the ultimate price and laid down their lives as an example of freedom against tyranny.

She gently grew her olives as Jesus Christ was born in the manger far away, and saw new gods replace the old as priests arrived from faraway lands to build churches in the village below. She felt her branches flex when the Ottomans arrived to use her sturdy branches as gallows and send so many of her wards to the afterlife, leaving them hanging like overripe fruit alongside her fat black olives ready to be pressed into oil as they had been for countless centuries before.

There was only us and the tree. She is over three thousand years old; we mean nothing. We are just a fleeting shadow passing through a tiny period in her life, not even warranting a second glance.

She is Greece.

We left the tree to continue watching over her island, and hand in hand we walked down the mountain towards our home.

As we turned the corner, we were confronted by flashing blue lights and a police car outside our home. We hurried the short distance past the police car and entered the garden. Two police officers were waiting for us, each dangling a set of hand-cuffs. Maria and Stamos both looked worried. Next to Stamos stood the mayor, wearing a serious expression, and behind him, the three Bulgarian stone workers, all looking at the ground, refusing to make eye contact with us.

Alex squeezed my hand and whispered, 'I think we've done it this time.'

One of the police officers spoke.

'Do you have building permission for this giant arch and barbecue?' he asked.

Alex and I looked at each other. Again, we had no idea we needed permission for this. It could not possibly have caused problems with the river, and there was no way it could cause any issues with the neighbours. But we had to admit that we didn't have permission.

The officer approached me with the handcuffs, ready to snap them onto my wrists. I held out my hands to receive them. It was a fair cop. I should have learned my lesson from the wall which we had to demolish. Here we were again, in trouble and about to be arrested.

Just before the handcuffs were applied, I heard a snort coming from one of the Bulgarians. I looked up. He was trying to suppress a laugh. His shoulders were shaking as he tried to control himself while the others nudged him, but he could hold it no longer and emitted a throaty laugh. This set off his two friends who howled with laugher. Stamos joined in, and the mayor had tears running down his face.

I looked at the police officers holding the handcuffs, who were also laughing out loud.

'Got you!' Maria laughed.

We had been set up. This was the villagers' idea of a joke, and we had fallen for it. I felt immediate relief and smiled at Alex. She still had a stony expression. I could see she was conflicted. Would she laugh with the rest of us, or launch an all-out attack? Luckily, she chose the former and joined in the giggling.

'Lunch is on me,' shouted the mayor over the laughter.

Alex resisted the urge to use one of her usual expletives (malakas being her favourite) for fear of being arrested properly. 'You are all Mboufi xazoxarúmenoi,' (silly birds) Alex told them as we piled into the back of the police car for the short drive to the restaurant, blue lights still flashing, with Stamos and his workers following behind in the truck.

But unknown to them, Alex was already planning her revenge. When Alex smiles, she is at her most dangerous.

EPILOGUE

We took our car and drove from our village up into the mountains, leaving the greenery of Pefki behind. What were once green pine-covered hills were now devoid of any trees or vegetation. Only blackness surrounded us. Dark stumps protruded from the black ground like jagged dragons' teeth in a land of hell.

The ground was a dark ash as far as we could see. Mile after mile we drove with the same sight everywhere. It was a holocaust of nature. How could this beautiful land ever recover? We drove down into one blackened valley and up the next mountain road. Then deep in the burnt forest, we came across a church. Its snow-white walls sat proudly reflecting the sun on a surrounding green oasis. The fire had ravished the entire mountain, but this little church and garden had remained miraculously untouched, a tiny patch of sanctuary from the inferno.

We stopped the car and entered the unlocked church. The icon of Saint David of Evia shone in a sunbeam flowing through the window. The icon portrayed him dressed him in a blue robe, with a white beard and serene eyes. This was his church, high in the mountains, surrounded by ash and burnt stumps. He had watched over the church dedicated to him and saved this special place.

For us, this was a religious experience.

A year after the fire, we drove the same route. The mountains had erupted into a profusion of colour. Lime green and masses of multicoloured flowers had sprung up from the black earth, taking advantage of the new light the forest floor had been deprived of for centuries. Now the trees had gone, it was their turn to flourish. There was no longer dark, ashen earth. A new ecology had replaced it.

Mother Nature had laid her hand on Greece, and Greece had responded with new life.

We drove back towards Pefki. We were now part of this island. It was home, and we belonged to it, as some of it belonged to us.

We had built our home and were happy. We had become part of this wonderful village filled with beautiful people who wanted nothing but to live their lives the way they had done for centuries. Alex and I had known struggle and hardship in our lives, but no more so than all Greeks. Adversity is necessary in life. It promotes passion and determination to make things better. It certainly worked for us.

So will we just sit in our new home and let the remaining years of our life pass by in paradise? It's doubtful, but we will give it a go.

Until the next adventure, it's goodbye from Alex and me.

See you again soon.

A PARTHENON ON OUR ROOF RACK
AN EXCERPT

The next book in the series, *A Parthenon on our Roof Rack* explores Alex's introduction to British culture. Of course, much of the book is set in Greece, but my adapting to Greek culture can't compare with Alex's fiery temperament adapting to mine. But as an Anglo-Greek couple, it was necessary to introduce her to a different way of thinking.

With hilarious results.

Amazon Link to A Parthenon on our Roof Rack
https://bit.ly/Parthenon-3

A Quick Taster

Greeks are wonderful, open people. Formality is rare.

We often fly to Athens airport from the UK. As a Greek national, and holding a Greek passport, she just skipped through the automatic passport control. I was forced to join the hour-long snake of foreigners queuing for the one open booth, and to receive my stamp before being allowed onto the hallowed turf of Europe. I, too, was now a foreigner. Brexit has a lot to answer for.

After the first half hour, I had settled into dragging my feet, one brief step at a time, kicking my bag along the floor.

Breathing down the neck of the guy in front, in case anyone might sneak in front of me. It was almost silent in the hall. The only sound was from shuffling as the queue moved unbearably slowly, and the occasional click of stamps on passports.

Suddenly, there was an unfamiliar sound.

Tap, tap, tap.

It was Alex knocking on the passport booth window. The official was so shocked he missed the passport he was currently stamping and tattooed the desk instead. He left his desk, opened the door, and a whispered conversation ensued. Alex was talking quietly and pointing in my direction.

I'm saved, I thought to myself. Alex had felt sorry for me. My wait was over. I was going to receive VIP treatment. Soon I would be free. I was hot and bothered. My legs ached after a long flight. I dreamed of my first Greek coffee, which, thanks to Alex, would be at any moment. I stepped forward, waving my passport as Alex and the official approached me.

"Have you got one euro for the baggage trolley?" Alex asked.

Deflated, I reached into my pocket for a coin. Alex disappeared towards the baggage carousel. The official squeezed back into his booth to continue his work, leaving me in the line.

Thanks Alex, I muttered under my breath.

Usually, the customs hall does not include customs officers. But on this occasion an official stopped me and asked to open my bag. Alex stormed up behind me.

"Leave him alone, he's with me," she yelled in Greek.

The officer stood back and waved us through with a smile and a mumbled apology.

Sometimes I watch as Alex speaks to tax inspectors, police officers or the local mayor. She speaks using the same tone and Greek slang as she uses to her friends while enjoying a coffee. This is one thing I love about Greece.

But, to Alex's surprise, it is a little different at Heathrow. We approached passport control. Alex looked up and saw a union jack flag sticker pasted on a sign which read welcome to border control. Under this was a sour-looking, uniformed Home Office official ready to check our passports. Alex pulled her phone out of her bag to take a photograph.

"STOP," the official yelled and pointed to a No Photographs sign.

Alex was undeterred. She continued to fiddle with her phone.

"Madam. It is against the law to take photographs here. This is border control. You will be arrested."

Whereas in Greece, the immigration officer would probably join you in a nice selfie and likely ask for you to WhatsApp a copy to him. Here you are likely to be handcuffed and dragged away for integration, including intimate body search and large quantities of Vaseline.

This was Alex's first introduction to British culture, and so far, she was not impressed. I could feel the vibes of anger rising. She was getting ready for a fight she could not possibly win. I gripped her arm tightly.

Alex will follow rules, but only if they make sense. Not being allowed to drive though a red light makes sense. It could cause a tangled heap of wreckage with you as part of it. Not being allowed to stuff fifty kilos of olive oil into your aircraft baggage makes sense. It's never a good idea to take highly flammable liquid and add that to the other fifty thousand kilos of jet fuel already on board.

But not being permitted to take a simple photo of a flag made no sense at all.

"Please don't make a fuss," I pleaded. "Things are different here," I told her. "You may get away with this in Greece, but here you must follow the rules. No photographs."

Alex nodded and put her phone away but was still sulking as we went to collect our bags.

But formality in Greece is still strong in the family unit. Greeks have tremendous respect for the older members of their family. When speaking to older relatives, she will speak in plural to them as a mark of respect. It's a little like the royal 'we'. Instead of asking a direct question to them, which is considered rude, she will speak as if addressing more than one person. She will phrase it more like "how are you all today" This is how she addresses all her aunts, uncles, and father. It was different with her mother. They were close, more friends than mother and daughter, so she never spoke in plural to her, which suited them both.

Alex has a wonderful command of the English language. She is almost without an accent. Indeed, sometimes when she speaks on the phone, she sounds as though she was born in a castle from royal stock. Her cut crystal accent is perfect.

When she first came with me to our family home in England, she first met my father. She clicked out of accent mode, into BBC mode, and spoke in plural. My dear cockney father looked most confused. He was expecting to meet the daughter of Zorba the Greek, complete with hairy upper lip and an incomprehensible accent. There before him was a glamorous, immaculately presented beauty who used English words he had never heard of.

He whispered to me, "I thought you were bringing your Greek girlfriend to meet me. Who's this one?"

"Dad, meet Alex. She is Greek, from Athens. That's in Greece."

I had to emphasise he was talking to the right person. He had already decided she could not possibly be Greek, not with that appearance and accent. He had already convinced himself I had been dumped by the Greek one and found an upgrade.

"Who is she talking to? There's only me here," he said looking around the room in case someone else had entered.

"She's talking to you in plural as a mark of respect," I told him.

This made no sense to my dad who just nodded and smiled. But Alex charmed him. Like everyone who meets her for the first time, he was in love.

Next was the visit to my brother and sister. As we arrived, Alex's Greek accent was back. She laughed and joked with them as if they were lifelong friends. She even used the time to teach them a few useful Greek words, which I warned them not to use during their forthcoming holiday in Corfu.

Alex is no stranger to England. She studied at college, gained a degree. As a student, she had no English friends. Her life comprised hard study, and home with her Greek family with no socialising in between. Alex had little contact with real English people. She never had contact with a British family so missed any absorption into the culture. Although she was in England, she still lived the Greek life.

But this was about to change. She had agreed to marry me for better or worse. She would be British.

This was going to be fun.

A NOTE FROM THE AUTHOR

I write about Greece. It doesn't take too much imagination. I just look out of the window and see the beauty of my subject spread around me. The bright Greek sunshine in an unreal blue sky. Orange and lemon trees swaying gently in the cool breeze. The sound of crickets. The perfume of mountain herbs invading my senses, the distant tinkle of bells tied to the collars of goats grazing happily on the hills.

Writers are a strange bunch. We isolate ourselves in closed rooms with only a keyboard for company. We rip out our souls and spend months and years obsessively perfecting our art.

Few of us will ever become rich, but this is not why we do it. We write for love.

The most incredible compliment any writer can get is to hear from you. It's such a wonderful experience to look online to see someone who I have never met has enjoyed my book and taken some of their valuable time to tell me.

If you have enjoyed my book, please let me know by spending a few moments to leave a review for *A Parthenon in Pefki*.

Peter Barber, 2023

ABOUT THE AUTHOR

Peter Barber was born in Watford, in the UK, and flits between Bedfordshire and Athens with his Greek wife. He spends as much time as possible in Greece messing about in boats, enjoying both the weather and the company, but mostly the food and wine.

Having nothing to do on a Greek island is time-consuming. When not trying to sink his boat and amusing the locals, Peter writes books.

The Parthenon series is a trilogy based on Greek life.

Book 1: A Parthenon on our Roof
Book 2: A Parthenon in Pefki
Book 3: A Parthenon on our Roof Rack

CONTACTS AND LINKS

Email: peterbarberbooks@gmail.com
Website: https://peterbarberwriter.com/
Facebook: www.facebook.com/peter.barber.771/
Twitter: www.twitter.com/greekwriting

Writing About Greece

Join the Facebook community, Writing about Greece, a group founded by Peter Barber and his wife, Alex, dedicated to Greece and people who love Greece.

www.facebook.com/groups/369010324939088
or type
Writing About Greece in the Facebook search box.

We Love Memoirs

Join Peter Barber and other memoir authors and readers in the **We Love Memoirs Facebook group**, the friendliest group on Facebook.

www.facebook.com/groups/welovememoirs/

CREDITS

My thanks to **Theodora Litovoli**, who helped me so much with fact-checking for the relevant historical section in the book covering Alex's grandmother's experience in Anatolia prior to her journey to Greece.

Theodora graduated from Birkbeck University of London with an MA in European History. After graduation, she worked as a historical researcher in London, assisting with the 'Hidden History Heritage Project, 397–381 High Road, NW10' funded by the Heritage Lottery Fund. She is the author of the articles 'Understanding the hidden history of the premises at Nos. 379–381 High Road, Willesden' and 'The evolution of Church End and Willesden Green from 1823 to 1918', as well as 'Interview with an Asia Minor refugee who became a Communist rebel' and 'The Pontus Hellenism through a refugee's personal testimony'. Theodora currently works as a historical researcher investigating the Greek genocide 1914–1923. In 2019, she published her first book, *The Mentality of Refugees from the Vilayet of Aydin, 1922–1930*.

We aspiring authors have the ideas. We throw them at a page like mud onto a wall. But without the skill of a good editor, it would never go further than the writer's imagination. This book could never have been completed without the hard work, patience and determination of my long-suffering editor, **Nicky Taylor** (www.nickytayloreditorial.com). Nicky took my incoherent ramblings and with her magical touch, transformed my manuscript into a book I can now feel proud of. Nicky has made me a better writer, for which I will always be grateful.

I would also like to thank Ant Press and **Victoria Twead**, my publisher, who is a New York Times bestselling author in her own right, best known for *Chickens, Mules and Two Old Fools*. Victoria, through her wisdom and fabulous advice, has transformed my writing and ensured the best chance of success. Victoria manages very few authors; I am honoured she chose me.

I would like to thank my daughter and incredible illustrator, **Charly Alex Fuller**. She brings my words to life with her funny illustrations and cartoons. The expressions and humour in her drawings are an essential part of my books. It is said 'You can't judge a book by its cover', but Charly, you have proved them all wrong. Her time as a child spent sitting in my office scribbling her artwork while honing her talent has really paid off. Charly, I am proud of you. Her work has now been recognised by publishing houses worldwide. But I hope she still has time for the next book by her old dad.

And of course, my wife, **Alex,** without whom this book would never have been written. She introduced me to the most beautiful and ancient culture on earth, taking me below the surface to experience the real Greece. She steered me through my absorption into Greek culture with love and humour every day.

Alex will always be the love of my life.

MORE ANT PRESS BOOKS
AWESOME AUTHORS ~ AWESOME BOOKS

If you enjoyed this book, you may also enjoy these other Ant Press memoir authors. All titles are available in ebook, paperback, hardback and large print editions from **Amazon**.

These two booksellers offer FREE delivery worldwide.
Blackwells.co.uk and **Wordery.com**

More Stores
Waterstones (Europe delivery), **Booktopia** (Australia), **Barnes & Noble** (USA), and all good bookstores.

PETER BARBER
Award-winning bestselling author
The Parthenon series

1. A Parthenon on our Roof
2. A Parthenon in Pefki
3. A Parthenon on our Roof Rack

Musings from a Greek Village

VICTORIA TWEAD
New York Times bestselling author
The Old Fools series

1. Chickens, Mules and Two Old Fools
2. Two Old Fools ~ Olé!
3. Two Old Fools on a Camel
4. Two Old Fools in Spain Again
5. Two Old Fools in Turmoil
6. Two Old Fools Down Under
7. Two Old Fools Fair Dinkum
8. One Young Fool in Dorset (Prequel)
9. One Young Fool in South Africa (Prequel)

Dear Fran, Love Dulcie: Life and Death in the Hills and Hollows of Bygone Australia

BETH HASLAM
The Fat Dogs series

Fat Dogs and French Estates ~ Part I
Fat Dogs and French Estates ~ Part II
Fat Dogs and French Estates ~ Part III
Fat Dogs and French Estates ~ Part IV
Fat Dogs and French Estates ~ Part V
Fat Dogs and Welsh Estates ~ The Prequel

DIANE ELLIOTT
Lady Goatherder series

Butting Heads in Spain: Lady Goatherder 1
El Maestro: Lady Goatherder 2 (to follow)

EJ BAUER
The Someday Travels series

From Moulin Rouge to Gaudi's City
From Gaudi's City to Granada's Red Palace

NICK ALBERT
Fresh Eggs and Dog Beds series

Fresh Eggs and Dog Beds: Living the Dream in Rural Ireland

Fresh Eggs and Dog Beds 2: Still Living the Dream in Rural Ireland

Fresh Eggs and Dog Beds 3: More Living the Dream in Rural Ireland

Fresh Eggs and Dog Beds 4: More Living the Dream in Rural Ireland

For more information about stockists, Ant Press titles or how to publish with Ant Press, please visit our website or contact us by email.

WEBSITE: www.antpress.org

EMAIL: admin@antpress.org

FACEBOOK: https://www.facebook.com/AntPress/

INSTAGRAM: https://instagram.com/publishwithantpress

Printed in Great Britain
by Amazon

40094603R00175